I0021071

KALI LINUX CLI BOSS

NOVICE TO COMMAND LINE MAESTRO

4 BOOKS IN 1

BOOK 1
KALI LINUX CLI BOSS: MASTERING THE BASICS

BOOK 2
KALI LINUX CLI BOSS: ADVANCED TECHNIQUES AND TRICKS

BOOK 3
KALI LINUX CLI BOSS: EXPERT-LEVEL SCRIPTING AND AUTOMATION

BOOK 4
KALI LINUX CLI BOSS: NAVIGATING THE DEPTHS OF PENETRATION TESTING

ROB BOTWRIGHT

Published by Rob Botwright
Library of Congress Cataloging-in-Publication Data
ISBN 978-1-83938-617-6
Cover design by Rizzo

Disclaimer

The contents of this book are based on extensive research and the best available historical sources. However, the author and publisher make no claims, promises, or guarantees about the accuracy, completeness, or adequacy of the information contained herein. The information in this book is provided on an "as is" basis, and the author and publisher disclaim any and all liability for any errors, omissions, or inaccuracies in the information or for any actions taken in reliance on such information. The opinions and views expressed in this book are those of the author and do not necessarily reflect the official policy or position of any organization or individual mentioned in this book. Any reference to specific people, places, or events is intended only to provide historical context and is not intended to defame or malign any group, individual, or entity. The information in this book is intended for educational and entertainment purposes only. It is not intended to be a substitute for professional advice or judgment. Readers are encouraged to conduct their own research and to seek professional advice where appropriate. Every effort has been made to obtain necessary permissions and acknowledgments for all images and other copyrighted material used in this book. Any errors or omissions in this regard are unintentional, and the author and publisher will correct them in future editions.

BOOK 1 - KALI LINUX CLI BOSS: MASTERING THE BASICS

BOOK 2 - KALI LINUX CLI BOSS: ADVANCED TECHNIQUES AND TRICKS

BOOK 3 - KALI LINUX CLI BOSS: EXPERT-LEVEL SCRIPTING AND AUTOMATION

BOOK 4 - KALI LINUX CLI BOSS: NAVIGATING THE DEPTHS OF PENETRATION TESTING

Introduction

Welcome to the "Kali Linux CLI Boss" book bundle, where we embark on a transformative journey from novice to command line maestro in the realm of cybersecurity and penetration testing. Within these four comprehensive volumes, we will unravel the mysteries of Kali Linux's command line interface, equipping you with the knowledge and skills to become a true command line expert.

"Book 1 - Kali Linux CLI Boss: Mastering the Basics" lays the groundwork for your command line adventure. Here, we dive deep into the fundamental concepts of Kali Linux's command line, ensuring you have a rock-solid understanding of its core functionalities. You will master essential commands, explore file system navigation, delve into user and permission management, and become proficient in package management and troubleshooting.

As you progress to "Book 2 - Kali Linux CLI Boss: Advanced Techniques and Tricks," your command line prowess will reach new heights. We will explore advanced command line concepts and customization options, allowing you to manipulate files and directories with finesse, master networking commands, and elevate your shell experience through customizations and shortcuts.

"Book 3 - Kali Linux CLI Boss: Expert-Level Scripting and Automation" unveils the true power of scripting and automation. Here, you will learn to harness the capabilities of scripting languages like Bash and Python to automate complex tasks efficiently. Building upon your newfound scripting skills, you will tackle advanced automation projects, handle network and system tasks, perform web scraping, and bolster security through automation and incident response.

Finally, in "Book 4 - Kali Linux CLI Boss: Navigating the Depths of Penetration Testing," we embark on an exhilarating journey into the world of penetration testing. You will discover how to set up a comprehensive testing environment, conduct information gathering and reconnaissance, identify vulnerabilities, execute exploits, and secure networks and systems against potential threats.

Whether you are a cybersecurity enthusiast, a professional seeking to sharpen your skills, or someone entirely new to Kali Linux's command line interface, this book bundle is designed to cater to your needs. Each volume builds upon the previous, providing a well-rounded and progressively challenging exploration of the Kali Linux command line.

By the end of this journey, you will have transformed into a command line maestro, capable of wielding Kali Linux's CLI with confidence and expertise. The knowledge and skills acquired from these books will not only empower you to excel in the field of cybersecurity but also enable you to contribute to the ever-evolving landscape of ethical hacking and penetration testing.

So, let's embark on this transformative journey together, as we navigate the command line, explore scripting and automation, and venture into the depths of penetration testing with Kali Linux. Your adventure begins now.

BOOK 1
KALI LINUX CLI BOSS
MASTERING THE BASICS

ROB BOTWRIGHT

Chapter 1: Introduction to Kali Linux CLI

Kali Linux, often referred to as simply "Kali," stands as a powerful and renowned penetration testing and ethical hacking distribution, meticulously crafted to cater to the diverse needs of cybersecurity professionals, security enthusiasts, and ethical hackers alike. It has emerged as the go-to choice for those seeking a comprehensive and versatile toolkit that provides a wide array of tools and resources essential for conducting ethical hacking, vulnerability assessment, penetration testing, and other security-related tasks.

With its roots deeply embedded in Debian, Kali Linux has garnered a reputation for being a robust and highly customizable operating system specifically tailored for security practitioners. The development team behind Kali Linux consistently updates and maintains the distribution to ensure that it remains at the forefront of the rapidly evolving cybersecurity landscape.

One of the key distinctions of Kali Linux lies in its comprehensive collection of pre-installed security tools and utilities, which spans various categories, such as network analysis, web application assessment, wireless penetration testing, and digital forensics. These tools empower users to perform a wide range of tasks, from identifying vulnerabilities in target systems to simulating cyberattacks in controlled environments.

Kali Linux's user-friendly interface, coupled with its extensive documentation and a dedicated community of users and developers, makes it accessible and approachable even for those new to the world of ethical hacking and cybersecurity. Whether you are a beginner taking your first steps in the field or an experienced professional looking for a reliable and versatile toolkit, Kali Linux caters to all skill levels.

Furthermore, Kali Linux ensures that users have access to the latest security updates and tools through regular releases. The developers continually add new features and tools to the distribution while keeping existing ones up-to-date. This commitment to maintaining a cutting-edge environment allows security practitioners to stay ahead of emerging threats and vulnerabilities.

One of the most significant advantages of using Kali Linux is its ability to facilitate real-world simulation of security assessments and attacks in a controlled, ethical, and legal manner. This empowers professionals to test the security posture of networks, applications, and systems, thus enhancing their understanding of potential weaknesses and vulnerabilities that malicious actors might exploit.

In addition to its expansive toolkit, Kali Linux places strong emphasis on ethical and responsible hacking practices. Users are encouraged to adhere to legal and ethical guidelines when using the distribution to ensure that their actions are within the boundaries of the law. This focus on ethical conduct distinguishes Kali Linux as a valuable resource for professionals and organizations committed to protecting digital assets and maintaining ethical standards.

Kali Linux also excels in the area of versatility, supporting a wide range of hardware platforms and providing options for different installation methods, including live bootable USB drives, virtual machine environments, and traditional installations on physical hardware. This flexibility allows users to choose the setup that best suits their requirements, making Kali Linux adaptable to various scenarios and environments.

For those seeking an environment tailored to their specific needs, Kali Linux offers customization options that enable users to fine-tune their installations. Whether it's adding or removing tools, modifying configurations, or creating custom scripts, Kali Linux can be molded to align with the precise objectives of a security professional's workflow.

In summary, Kali Linux stands as a robust and indispensable resource in the realm of cybersecurity and ethical hacking. Its extensive toolset, commitment to ethical practices, regular updates, and user-friendly interface make it a valuable asset for individuals and organizations striving to safeguard their digital assets and proactively identify and address security vulnerabilities. Whether you are a beginner or an experienced practitioner, Kali Linux empowers you to navigate the complex landscape of cybersecurity with confidence and competence. The Command Line Interface (CLI) serves as a powerful and versatile means of interacting with a computer's operating system and executing various tasks through text-based commands. In the world of computing, the CLI has a long-standing history, dating back to the early days of mainframes and minicomputers, and it remains an integral part of modern computing environments. Understanding the fundamentals of the CLI is essential for anyone who seeks to navigate and manipulate computer systems efficiently. At its core, the CLI provides a textual interface for users to communicate with an operating system or software application by entering commands and receiving textual responses. This textual interaction contrasts with the graphical user interface (GUI), which relies on visual elements such as windows, icons, and menus for user interaction. The CLI's text-based nature enables users to perform a wide range of tasks, from file management and system configuration to software installation and network troubleshooting. To begin working with the CLI, users typically open a terminal or command prompt window, which provides them with a text-based interface to the underlying operating system. In a terminal, users can enter commands by typing them in, and the system responds with textual output, which often includes status information, error messages, or the results of the command's execution. Each command issued in the CLI consists of a command name followed by optional parameters or arguments that provide additional information or specify the operation's scope. For example, a simple command like "ls" in a Unix-based system lists the contents of the current directory, while "mkdir new_directory" creates a new directory named "new_directory" in the current location. Commands can vary significantly in complexity, with some requiring just a few characters and others involving longer and more intricate syntax. Understanding the structure and syntax of commands is crucial to using the CLI effectively. In many CLI environments, commands are case-sensitive, meaning that "ls" and "LS" may produce different results, so attention to detail is essential. To discover available commands and obtain information about them, users can often employ the "help" or "man" (manual) commands, followed by the name of the command they wish to learn more about. For instance, "help ls" or "man ls" would provide information about the "ls" command, including its usage, options, and a description of what it does. The CLI typically relies on a hierarchical file system structure to organize and manage data. In this structure, files and directories are organized into a tree-like hierarchy, with a root directory at the top and various subdirectories branching off from it. Users can navigate this hierarchy using commands like "cd" (change directory) to move between directories. For example, "cd /home/user" would change the current directory to "user" within the "/home" directory. Navigating directories is fundamental to working effectively within the CLI. In addition to basic navigation, the CLI allows users to create, copy, move, and delete files and directories using appropriate commands. These operations are essential for managing data and organizing information. Moreover, many CLI environments support the use of wildcards, such as the asterisk (*) and question mark (?), to perform operations on multiple files or directories simultaneously. For example, "rm *.txt" would delete all files with the ".txt" extension in the current directory. The CLI also provides robust text manipulation capabilities. Users can redirect the output of one command as input to another, enabling a chain of commands to perform complex tasks. Piping, a common technique in the CLI, involves using the vertical bar (|) to pass the output of one command as input to another. For example, "ls | grep keyword" would list files and then search for the keyword within that list. Text editors are often available within the CLI for creating and editing files. Popular text editors in Unix-based systems include "vi" and "nano," while Windows systems commonly use "Notepad" or "edit." These editors allow users to create and modify configuration files, scripts, and text documents directly from the terminal. Understanding the basic terminology associated with the CLI is essential for effective communication and problem-solving. Some common terms include "command," which refers to a textual instruction that the user enters to perform an action or request information. Arguments or parameters are additional inputs that users provide with commands to specify options or provide necessary information. For instance, "ls -l" uses the "-l" parameter to request a detailed long listing of files. The "directory" or "folder" is a container used to organize files, while a "file" is a named collection of data. "Path" denotes the location of a file or directory in the file system hierarchy, often described as an absolute path starting from the root directory or a relative path starting from the current directory. Errors or issues encountered when executing commands are referred to as "errors," "warnings," or "output," and they often include messages that provide information about the problem. In summary, the Command Line Interface (CLI) is a powerful tool for interacting with computer systems through text-based commands, offering flexibility, efficiency, and a wide range of capabilities for users and system administrators alike.

Chapter 2: Getting Started with Terminal Commands

To initiate your journey into the world of command-line interfaces, the first step is launching the terminal, which serves as your gateway to the powerful realm of text-based commands. The exact process of launching the terminal varies depending on your operating system, but once you have it up and running, you'll find yourself facing a blank screen, eagerly awaiting your commands. The terminal, sometimes referred to as a command prompt or console, provides you with a simple text-based interface through which you can communicate with your computer's operating system. It may appear as a black window with white text on Unix-based systems like Linux and macOS, or as a command prompt window on Windows. The terminal is where you will type your commands, and it's where you'll receive the responses and output generated by those commands. It's important to note that while the terminal may appear stark and intimidating to newcomers, it becomes an immensely powerful tool once you grasp its basics. The process of launching the terminal is typically straightforward, and the method varies depending on your operating system. On Linux systems, you can often find the terminal among your applications or access it through keyboard shortcuts like Ctrl+Alt+T. If you're using macOS, you can locate the terminal in the Utilities folder within the Applications folder. For Windows users, you can find the command prompt by searching for "cmd" in the Start menu or pressing Win+R, then typing "cmd" and pressing Enter. On some Windows systems, you may also have PowerShell, a more feature-rich command-line environment. Regardless of your operating system, once you've located and launched the terminal, you'll be greeted with a text-based interface that's ready to accept your commands. It's worth noting that the terminal's appearance can be customized to your liking through various themes and color schemes, but the core functionality remains the same. The terminal, at its essence, is a place for communication and interaction with your computer, offering you a level of control and precision that the graphical user interface (GUI) often cannot match. While the GUI provides a user-friendly and intuitive way to interact with your computer, it may not always offer the same depth of control and flexibility as the CLI. In the terminal, every action is initiated by typing commands, each consisting of a command name followed by optional arguments or parameters. The command name is like a magic word that tells your computer to perform a specific task or action. These tasks can range from simple file operations like copying and deleting to complex system configurations and software installations. The arguments or parameters provide additional information to the command, specifying what exactly you want it to do. For example, the "ls" command is used to list the contents of a directory, and you can add arguments like "-l" to request a detailed list with additional information. As you become more familiar with the CLI, you'll learn to use various commands and their associated arguments to accomplish specific tasks efficiently. Typing a command and pressing Enter is how you execute it in the terminal. The terminal then processes your command, performs the requested action, and provides you with feedback in the form of text-based output. This output may include a list of files, configuration information, error messages, or any relevant data related to your command. It's important to note that the terminal operates in a text-based environment, so your commands and their output are displayed as plain text. The simplicity of this text-based communication is one of the terminal's strengths, as it allows you to focus on the precise instructions you give to your computer. Throughout your journey with the terminal, you'll encounter various commands, each serving a specific purpose. Some commands are built into the operating system, while others may be third-party tools or applications that you've installed. These commands can perform a wide range of functions, from basic file management and text processing to system administration and network troubleshooting. As you gain experience, you'll become proficient in using the right commands to accomplish your goals efficiently. The terminal also supports various keyboard shortcuts and special keys that enhance your interaction with it. For instance, you can use the Tab key to auto-complete commands and file paths, making it easier to navigate the file system and minimize typing errors. The Up and Down arrow keys allow you to cycle through your command history, saving you from retyping frequently used commands. Additionally, you can use Ctrl+C to interrupt a running command and Ctrl+Z to pause it, among other keyboard shortcuts that streamline your workflow. Navigating the file system is a fundamental skill in the CLI, and you'll often find yourself using commands like "cd" (change directory) to move from one directory to another. For example, "cd Documents" would take you from your current location to the "Documents" directory, provided it exists within your current location. Understanding file paths is crucial when using the "cd" command, as it allows you to specify the location of the directory you want to navigate to. File paths can be either absolute or relative, with absolute paths starting from the root directory and relative paths starting from your current location. Another essential command is "ls," which lists the contents of a directory, providing you with an overview of the files and subdirectories it contains. You can customize the "ls" command by adding arguments like "-l" to display a detailed list, "-a" to show hidden files, or other options to tailor the output to your needs. File management commands like "mkdir" (make directory), "touch" (create empty files), "cp" (copy files), "mv" (move or rename files), and "rm" (remove files) allow you to organize and manipulate files and directories within the file system. Additionally, the terminal supports wildcards like "*" and "?" to perform operations on multiple files or directories simultaneously. These wildcards provide a convenient way to work with sets of files that share a common pattern in their names. The terminal's text-based nature also makes it an excellent environment for text processing tasks. You can use commands like "cat" (concatenate and display files), "grep" (search for patterns in text), "sed" (stream editor), and "awk" (text processing tool) to analyze, manipulate, and extract information from text files. Text editors are readily available in the terminal, allowing you to create and modify text files directly from the command line. Popular text editors include "vi," "nano," "emacs," and "vim," each offering its own set of features and keyboard shortcuts. These editors are essential tools for scripting, programming, and configuration tasks. As you delve deeper into the CLI, you'll discover that it provides an environment conducive to scripting and automation. Scripts are sequences of commands saved in a file, which you can execute as a single unit to perform repetitive tasks or complex operations. Scripting languages like Bash, Python, and Perl are commonly used for this purpose, allowing you to automate various processes and customize your computing environment. The terminal is also an invaluable tool for system administrators and network professionals, providing access to a wide range of tools for managing servers, networks, and services. Commands like "top" and "htop" offer real-time system monitoring, while "ifconfig" and "ip" allow you to configure network interfaces and troubleshoot connectivity issues. Security professionals and ethical hackers frequently use the terminal to assess the security of systems and networks. Penetration testing tools, vulnerability scanners, and network analyzers are readily available through the CLI, enabling professionals to identify vulnerabilities and weaknesses in target systems. Furthermore, the terminal's scripting capabilities allow security practitioners to automate tasks related to security assessments and incident response. In summary, the terminal is your portal to the powerful world of command-line interfaces, offering a text-based environment through which you can communicate with your computer's operating system. By typing commands, you can perform a wide range of tasks, from file management and text processing to system administration and network troubleshooting. As you embark on your journey with the CLI, you'll acquire essential skills, become proficient with various commands, and discover the immense flexibility and efficiency it offers. The terminal empowers you to control your computer with precision, automate repetitive tasks, and navigate the complexities of modern computing with confidence. In the realm of command-line interfaces (CLIs), mastering basic command syntax is fundamental to harnessing the power and versatility that the CLI offers. Understanding how to structure and execute commands is the cornerstone of effective interaction with the computer's operating system. Commands in the CLI consist of a command name followed by optional parameters or arguments that provide additional information or specify the operation's scope. The command name is the instruction you give to the computer, telling it what task or action you want it to perform. These tasks can range from basic file operations like copying and deleting to complex system configurations and software installations. Arguments or parameters are like modifiers that provide additional details to the command, enabling it to carry out specific actions or processes. They often follow the command name and are separated by spaces. For instance, consider the simple command "ls -l" used in Unix-based systems. Here, "ls" is the command name, and "-l" is an argument that tells the "ls" command to provide a detailed long listing of files. In the Windows Command Prompt, a similar command might look like "dir /w," with "dir" being the command name and "/w" being an argument to format the output in a wide list. Command syntax can vary significantly between different CLIs and operating systems, so understanding the conventions of the specific CLI you're working with is crucial. One common aspect of command syntax in most CLIs is that commands are typically case-sensitive. This means that the capitalization of command names and arguments matters. For example, "ls" and "LS" might produce different results in a Unix-based system. Additionally, spaces play a crucial role in separating the command name from its arguments. Spaces are used to delineate where the command name ends and the arguments begin. It's also essential to note that commands are executed by pressing the "Enter" key after typing them. Once you press "Enter," the CLI processes your command, carries out the requested action, and provides feedback in the form of text-based output. The terminal, or command prompt, displays this output for you to review, and it often includes information about the status of the command's execution, error messages, or the results of the command. The process of entering commands and receiving output forms the basis of your interaction with the CLI. It's a simple yet powerful way to communicate with the computer's operating system. A key concept in command syntax is the use of options or switches. Options are additional modifiers that can alter the behavior of a command. They are typically preceded by a hyphen (-) or a forward slash (/) and are often used to customize the command's output or specify particular actions. For example, the "ls" command in Unix-based systems can be enhanced with options like "-a" to show hidden files, "-R" to list subdirectories recursively, or "-t" to sort files by modification time. These options allow you to tailor the command's behavior to your specific needs. Sometimes, options can take arguments of their own. These arguments provide further details to the option. For instance, the "grep" command, used for searching text, allows you to specify a search pattern as an argument to the "-e" option. This enables you to search for specific patterns within a file or a set of files. Commands can also accept multiple arguments, and the order in which you specify them can affect the command's behavior. For instance, in the "cp" (copy) command, the first argument is typically the source file or directory, and the second argument is the destination location where the file or directory will be copied. Understanding the correct order and usage of arguments is essential to ensure that commands behave as expected. In some CLIs, command options and arguments can be combined into a single string. For example, in Unix-based systems, you can use the "-l" and "-a" options together as "-la" to display a detailed listing of all files, including hidden ones. This shorthand notation can save time when entering commands. The use of wildcards is another important aspect of command syntax. Wildcards are characters that represent patterns of filenames or directories, allowing you to operate on multiple files at once. A common wildcard character is the asterisk (*), which matches zero or more characters in a filename or directory name. For instance, the command "rm *.txt" would delete all files in the current directory with the ".txt" extension. Another wildcard character is the question mark (?), which matches a single character. For example, "ls file?.txt" would list files like "file1.txt" and "file2.txt" but not "file10.txt." Wildcards are particularly useful when you need to perform actions on multiple files that share a common pattern. As you become more proficient with command syntax, you'll learn to use options, arguments, and wildcards effectively to streamline your tasks in the CLI. Each CLI and operating system has its own conventions and syntax rules, so it's essential to consult the documentation or built-in help for specific commands to understand their available options and proper usage. By mastering the basics of command syntax, you'll be well-equipped to interact with the CLI efficiently and confidently, opening up a world of possibilities for managing your computer and performing various tasks from the command line.

Chapter 3: File System Navigation and Management

In the command-line interface (CLI), navigating directories is a fundamental skill that enables you to move between different locations within the file system. Directories, sometimes referred to as folders, serve as containers for organizing files and subdirectories. Understanding how to change your current directory and explore the file system hierarchy is essential for efficient CLI usage. The "cd" command, short for "change directory," is the primary tool for navigation. By using "cd," you can move from your current location to another directory. The basic syntax of the "cd" command is straightforward; you simply type "cd" followed by the path of the directory you want to change to. For example, to change to a directory named "Documents" in your current location, you would enter the command "cd Documents." It's important to note that paths can be either absolute or relative. An absolute path specifies the exact location of a directory or file in the file system, starting from the root directory. For instance, "/home/user/Documents" is an absolute path that points directly to the "Documents" directory, regardless of your current location. In contrast, a relative path is specified in relation to your current location. For example, if you are already in the "/home/user" directory, you can use a relative path like "cd Documents" to move into the "Documents" directory without specifying the full path. Using relative paths is often more convenient when navigating the file system because it allows you to move around without typing long absolute paths. The "cd" command with no arguments or with the tilde (~) symbol typically takes you back to your home directory. For example, "cd" or "cd ~" would return you to your home directory, regardless of your current location. This is a convenient way to quickly return to your home base in the file system. Another useful feature of the "cd" command is the ability to use double dots (..) to move up one directory level. For instance, if you are in the "/home/user/Documents" directory and you enter the command "cd ..," you will move up to the "/home/user" directory. This feature simplifies navigation when you want to move back to a parent directory without specifying the full path. Navigating to directories with spaces or special characters in their names requires special handling in the CLI. To work with such directories, you can enclose the directory name in quotation marks or use backslashes to escape spaces and special characters. For example, if you have a directory named "My Documents," you can navigate to it using commands like "cd 'My Documents'" or "cd My\ Documents." The use of tab completion is a helpful technique to expedite directory navigation. When you start typing a directory or file name and then press the "Tab" key, the CLI will attempt to auto-complete the name for you. If there is only one possible match, the CLI will complete it automatically. If there are multiple matches, the CLI will display a list of options for you to choose from. This feature reduces typing errors and saves time when working with long or complex directory names. Sometimes, it's useful to navigate to directories by specifying a relative path based on your current location. For example, if you are in the "/home/user" directory and want to navigate to a subdirectory named "Pictures," you can use the relative path "cd Pictures" instead of the full path. Relative paths are particularly handy when you are moving within a specific branch of the file system hierarchy. When you encounter a directory name with spaces or special characters while using relative paths, you can still enclose the name in quotation marks or use backslashes to navigate effectively. Understanding the file system hierarchy is essential for efficient navigation. In most operating systems, the file system is organized as a hierarchical tree structure, with a root directory at the top. The root directory is represented by a single forward slash (/) in Unix-based systems like Linux and macOS, while it is represented by a drive letter (e.g., C:) in Windows. Beneath the root directory are various subdirectories, and each subdirectory may contain further subdirectories and files. By using the "cd" command and specifying directory paths, you can traverse this hierarchy to access different parts of the file system. To view the contents of the current directory, you can use the "ls" command (or "dir" in Windows), which lists the files and subdirectories present. Navigating directories efficiently becomes increasingly important as you work on more complex tasks. Whether you are organizing files, writing scripts, or configuring system settings, being able to move quickly and confidently within the file system is a valuable skill. By mastering directory navigation commands like "cd," understanding path types, and using tab completion, you can explore the file system with ease and precision. In summary, navigating directories is a fundamental aspect of working with the command-line interface. The "cd" command, combined with an understanding of absolute and relative paths, allows you to move efficiently within the file system hierarchy. With practice, you'll become adept at exploring directories, managing files, and accessing the resources you need to accomplish your tasks in the CLI. In the world of command-line interfaces (CLIs), efficient file and directory management is a fundamental skill that empowers users to organize, manipulate, and interact with their computer's file system. Understanding how to create, copy, move, rename, and delete files and directories, as well as managing their permissions, is essential for effectively working with data and resources in the CLI. Creating a new directory is a straightforward operation accomplished with the "mkdir" (make directory) command, followed by the name of the directory you want to create. For example, to create a directory named "projects," you would enter the command "mkdir projects." Directories are essential for organizing files and structuring your file system to suit your needs. Once a directory is created, you can navigate into it using the "cd" (change directory) command. Files, on the other hand, can be created using a variety of methods, including text editors, scripting languages, or even the "touch" command, which creates an empty file. For instance, "touch newfile.txt" would create a new text file named "newfile.txt" in your current directory. Copying files is a common operation for creating duplicates or backups. The "cp" (copy) command allows you to copy files from one location to another. The basic syntax of "cp" is "cp source destination," where "source" is the file you want to copy, and "destination" is the location where you want to copy it. For example, to copy a file named "report.txt" to a directory named "backup," you would use the command "cp report.txt backup." You can also use the "cp" command to copy multiple files simultaneously by specifying multiple source files and a destination directory. For example, "cp file1.txt file2.txt backup/" would copy "file1.txt" and "file2.txt" into the "backup" directory. Moving files, sometimes referred to as renaming files, is achieved with the "mv" (move) command. The "mv" command allows you to change a file's name or move it to a different directory. To rename a file, you simply specify the current name as the "source" and the new name as the "destination." For instance, to rename a file from "oldfile.txt" to "newfile.txt," you would execute the command "mv oldfile.txt newfile.txt." To move a file to a different directory, you provide the current file location as the "source" and the destination directory as the "destination." For example, to move a file named "document.pdf" to a directory called "archive," you would use the command "mv document.pdf archive/." When moving or renaming files, keep in mind that the destination directory should exist, or you can specify an absolute path to create a new directory during the move. Deleting files and directories is a task that should be approached with caution, as it permanently removes data. The "rm" (remove) command is used to delete files, while the "rmdir" command is used to delete empty directories. To delete a file, you simply specify the file's name as an argument to the "rm" command. For example, "rm unwanted.txt" would delete a file named "unwanted.txt" from the current directory. To remove a directory, you would use "rmdir" followed by the directory name. However, "rmdir" can only delete empty directories; if a directory contains files or subdirectories, it will not be deleted. To remove a directory and its contents, including files and subdirectories, you would use the "rm" command with the "-r" or "-rf" (recursive force) option. For instance, "rm -r mydirectory" would remove the directory "mydirectory" and all its contents. This recursive deletion is a powerful but potentially dangerous operation, so it should be used with caution. When working with files and directories, it's essential to understand the concept of file permissions. File permissions dictate who can read, write, and execute a file or directory. In Unix-based systems like Linux and macOS, file permissions are represented by a set of three permissions for the file owner, group, and others. The three basic permissions are read (r), write (w), and execute (x). To view and modify file permissions, you can use the "ls" command with the "-l" option to display a detailed listing that includes permission information. For example, "ls -l myfile.txt" would show the permissions for "myfile.txt." To change file permissions, the "chmod" (change mode) command is used. You specify the desired permission changes using a numeric code or symbolic notation. Numeric codes represent permission settings using octal values (e.g., 755 or 644), while symbolic notation uses letters to indicate permission changes. For example, "chmod 755 myfile.txt" would grant read, write, and execute permissions to the file owner and read and execute permissions to the group and others. Symbolic notation can be more intuitive, allowing you to use letters like "u" for the user (owner), "g" for the group, and "o" for others. To add or remove permissions, you use the symbols "+" and "-" along with the permission letters. For example, "chmod u+w myfile.txt" would add write permission for the file owner, while "chmod go-r myfile.txt" would remove read permission for the group and others. Managing file and directory permissions is essential for maintaining data security and ensuring that only authorized users can access or modify files. File and directory ownership is another critical aspect of managing files and directories. Each file and directory is associated with an owner and a group, which determine who has control over them. The "chown" (change owner) and "chgrp" (change group) commands allow you to modify ownership and group associations. For instance, "chown newowner myfile.txt" would change the owner of "myfile.txt" to "newowner," and "chgrp newgroup myfile.txt" would change the group of "myfile.txt" to "newgroup." Managing files and directories in the CLI provides you with fine-grained control over your computer's file system, enabling you to organize data, create backups, and secure sensitive information. Understanding how to create, copy, move, rename, and delete files and directories, as well as manage their permissions and ownership, is essential for efficient file system management. By mastering these file and directory management commands and concepts, you can maintain a well-organized and secure file system that supports your computing needs.

Chapter 4: Essential Networking Commands

Configuring and managing network settings is a crucial aspect of working with computers, whether you are setting up a home network, connecting to the internet, or configuring network services on a server. In the command-line interface (CLI), you can control various network-related aspects, such as configuring network interfaces, setting IP addresses, managing network services, and troubleshooting network issues. This chapter explores network configuration tasks and commands that allow you to effectively manage network connections and services.

Viewing Network Information

Before making any changes to your network configuration, it's essential to gather information about your current network setup. The "ifconfig" command (or "ip" command in modern systems) displays detailed information about your network interfaces, including their current configuration, such as IP addresses, netmasks, and MAC (Media Access Control) addresses. Running "ifconfig" or "ip a" in the terminal will list all available network interfaces along with their respective information. You can also use the "netstat" command to view network-related statistics and active network connections. For example, "netstat -nr" displays the routing table, which shows how network traffic is routed.

Configuring Network Interfaces

The primary task when setting up a network is configuring network interfaces, such as Ethernet or Wi-Fi connections. The "ifconfig" command (or "ip" command) can be used to configure network interfaces manually. For instance, to set the IP address of an interface, you can use the following command:
Copy code

sudo ifconfig eth0 192.168.1.2 netmask 255.255.255.0

This command assigns the IP address "192.168.1.2" and the netmask "255.255.255.0" to the "eth0" interface. To configure a default gateway (the router your computer uses to reach other networks), you can use the "route" command:

csharpCopy code

```
sudo route add default gw 192.168.1.1
```

This command sets the default gateway to "192.168.1.1." To make these changes persistent across reboots, you'll need to edit your network configuration files. On many Linux distributions, the "interfaces" file contains network interface configuration settings.

Network Services

Network services are essential for communication and functionality on a network. Commands like "service" or "systemctl" allow you to manage these services, start or stop them, and enable or disable them at system boot. For example, to restart the Apache web server, you can use the following command:

Copy code

```
sudo systemctl restart apache2
```

Similarly, to enable the SSH service to start automatically at boot, you can run:

bashCopy code

```
sudo systemctl enable ssh
```

By controlling network services, you can customize your system to serve various network-related purposes, such as web hosting, file sharing, or remote access.

Firewall Configuration

Firewalls play a vital role in network security by controlling incoming and outgoing network traffic. The "iptables" command is a powerful tool for configuring firewall rules in Linux systems. You can use it to define rules that allow or block specific traffic based on source and destination IP addresses, ports, and protocols. For example, the following command blocks all incoming traffic on port 80 (HTTP):

cssCopy code

```
sudo iptables -A INPUT -p tcp --dport 80 -j DROP
```

To save your firewall rules and ensure they are loaded at system startup, you can use the "iptables-persistent" package on Debian-based systems or the "firewalld" service on Red Hat-based systems.

Network Troubleshooting

Network issues can be complex, and the CLI provides various tools to diagnose and troubleshoot problems. The "ping" command is a valuable tool for testing network connectivity between your computer and another host on the network. For instance, to check if you can reach a web server at "example.com," you can use:

Copy code

```
ping example.com
```

The "traceroute" command helps you trace the route that packets take through the network to reach a destination, showing each hop and its response time.

Copy code

```
traceroute example.com
```

For more advanced troubleshooting, the "tcpdump" command allows you to capture and analyze network packets in real-time, helping you identify network anomalies and issues.

cssCopy code

```
sudo tcpdump -i eth0 -n -vvv -X tcp port 80
```

By examining packet contents and headers, you can pinpoint network problems and security concerns.

DHCP and DNS Configuration

Dynamic Host Configuration Protocol (DHCP) and Domain Name System (DNS) play pivotal roles in network configuration. DHCP automatically assigns IP addresses and other network parameters to devices on a network, while DNS translates domain names into IP addresses. You can configure DHCP client settings using the "dhclient" command or configure a DHCP

server using tools like "dhcpd" or "dnsmasq." DNS configuration often involves editing the "/etc/resolv.conf" file to specify DNS server addresses. For example, to set your DNS server to "8.8.8.8" (Google's public DNS), you can edit the "resolv.conf" file and add:
Copy code
nameserver 8.8.8.8

Network File Transfer

Transferring files between computers over a network is a common task, and the CLI provides tools for this purpose. The "scp" (secure copy) command allows you to securely copy files between hosts using SSH. For example, to copy a file named "file.txt" from your local system to a remote server, you can use:

typescriptCopy code

```
scp file.txt user@remote-server:/path/to/destination/
```

Similarly, the "rsync" command is useful for synchronizing files and directories between systems over a network, preserving permissions and minimizing data transfer.

Network configuration and management are essential skills in the world of command-line interfaces. By understanding how to view network information, configure network interfaces, manage network services, set up firewalls, troubleshoot network issues, configure DHCP and DNS, and perform network file transfers, you can effectively control and optimize your network environment. These skills are valuable for system administrators, network engineers, and anyone working with computers in a networked environment, enabling you to maintain secure and efficient network operations.

In the world of computer networks, issues and disruptions can arise for various reasons, disrupting communication and productivity. To effectively diagnose network problems and get your systems back on track, you need a systematic approach and the right tools at your disposal. This chapter explores strategies, techniques, and command-line tools for diagnosing network issues and resolving them promptly.

Step 1: Identify the Problem

The first step in diagnosing a network issue is to identify the problem accurately. This may involve gathering information from affected users, understanding the nature of the issue, and defining its scope. A network problem can manifest in many ways, such as slow internet connectivity, intermittent outages, or the inability to access specific services. Gathering as much detail as possible about the problem is crucial for effective troubleshooting.

Step 2: Check Physical Connections

Physical connectivity issues are common culprits of network problems. Inspect the physical connections of network cables, ensuring they are securely plugged into their respective ports. If you are using wireless connections, check for any signal interference or obstructions that may affect the signal strength. Physical problems can lead to unstable or disrupted network connections.

Step 3: Verify Network Device Status

Check the status of network devices such as routers, switches, and access points. Ensure that these devices are powered on and functioning correctly. Look for any indicator lights that may indicate hardware or power issues. Sometimes, simply power cycling these devices can resolve network problems.

Step 4: Examine Network Configuration

Review the configuration settings of your network devices, including routers and firewalls. Ensure that IP addresses, subnet masks, gateways, and DNS settings are correctly configured. Incorrect configuration settings can lead to network communication problems. Use the "ifconfig" or "ip" command to check the network interface settings on your computer.

Step 5: Test Connectivity

Test network connectivity by pinging other devices or internet resources. The "ping" command is a valuable tool for this purpose. For example, you can use "ping google.com" to check if you can reach Google's servers. If the ping fails, it may indicate a connectivity issue or DNS problem.

Step 6: Check Firewall and Security Settings

Firewalls and security software can sometimes block network traffic. Review your firewall settings to ensure that they are not blocking legitimate network traffic. Temporarily disabling the firewall can help identify if it is the cause of the issue.

Step 7: Monitor Network Traffic

Monitoring network traffic can provide valuable insights into network behavior. Tools like "tcpdump" or "Wireshark" allow you to capture and analyze network packets. By examining packet contents and headers, you can identify unusual or problematic network activity.

Step 8: Investigate DNS Issues

Domain Name System (DNS) problems can lead to network connectivity issues. Use the "nslookup" or "dig" command to troubleshoot DNS resolution problems. Check if the DNS server settings are correct and try resolving domain names to IP addresses.

Step 9: Look for Software Conflicts

Software conflicts or misconfigurations on your computer can impact network connectivity. Check for any recently installed software that may be causing conflicts or network disruptions. Review network-related configuration files, such as "/etc/network/interfaces" on Linux systems.

Step 10: Test from Multiple Devices

If the network problem affects multiple devices, it is likely a network-wide issue. Testing from multiple devices can help determine if the problem is localized to a single device or if it is a broader network problem.

Step 11: Contact Your Internet Service Provider (ISP)

If you have ruled out issues with your local network but still experience connectivity problems, contact your internet service provider (ISP). They can perform remote diagnostics and determine if there are any problems with your internet connection.

Step 12: Review Logs and Error Messages

Logs and error messages can provide valuable clues about network issues. Check system logs and network-related logs for any error messages or warnings that may indicate the source of the problem. Use commands like "dmesg" and "journalctl" on Linux systems.

Step 13: Check for Bandwidth Saturation

Excessive network traffic can saturate your internet connection, causing slow or disrupted connectivity. Review network traffic patterns and consider implementing Quality of Service (QoS) policies to prioritize critical traffic.

Step 14: Update or Roll Back Drivers

Outdated or incompatible network drivers can lead to network issues. Ensure that your network drivers are up to date. If recent driver updates are causing problems, consider rolling back to a previous version.

Step 15: Seek Professional Help

If you have exhausted all troubleshooting steps and are still unable to resolve the network issue, it may be time to seek professional help. Network experts or IT professionals can perform in-depth diagnostics and resolve complex network problems.

Diagnosing network issues can be a challenging but necessary task to maintain reliable and efficient network operations. By following a systematic approach, checking physical connections, verifying network device status, examining network configurations, testing connectivity, and considering various troubleshooting steps, you can identify and resolve network problems effectively. Remember that network issues can vary in complexity, and some may require the expertise of professionals. Continuously monitoring and maintaining your network can help prevent issues from arising and ensure smooth network operations.

Chapter 5: User and Permission Management

In the realm of computer systems, user accounts and groups play a fundamental role in managing access, security, and permissions. User accounts allow individuals to interact with a computer, while groups provide a way to organize users and define their collective access rights. This chapter delves into the concepts of user accounts and groups, detailing how to create, manage, and administer them effectively using command-line tools.

User Accounts

User accounts are a cornerstone of user management in computer systems. Each user account represents an individual who can log in, access resources, and perform tasks on a computer or network. User accounts are associated with unique usernames and passwords, which serve as credentials for authentication. To create a new user account from the command line, you can use the "useradd" command. For example, to create a user named "johndoe," you would execute:

Copy code

```
sudo useradd johndoe
```

This command creates a new user account with the default settings, including a home directory and group of the same name as the username. To specify additional options during user creation, you can use flags with the "useradd" command. For instance, the "-m" flag creates the user's home directory, and the "-G" flag adds the user to specified supplementary groups. Managing user account passwords is crucial for security. The "passwd" command allows users to change their own passwords. To change your password, simply run "passwd" without any arguments and follow the prompts. Administrators can also change other users' passwords by specifying the username:

Copy code

```
sudo passwd johndoe
```

To lock or unlock user accounts, the "passwd" command can be used with the "-l" (lock) or "-u" (unlock) option. Locking an account prevents the user from logging in until it is unlocked.

Groups

Groups are a means of organizing and managing user accounts efficiently. They provide a way to assign common access permissions and privileges to multiple users simultaneously. In Unix-based systems, there are two types of groups: primary and supplementary. Every user belongs to a primary group, which shares the same name as the user. Supplementary groups allow users to belong to multiple groups. To create a new group, you can use the "groupadd" command. For example, to create a group named "developers," you would run:

Copy code

```
sudo groupadd developers
```

Once the group is created, you can add users to it using the "usermod" command with the "-aG" option:

Copy code

```
sudo usermod -aG developers johndoe
```

This command adds the user "johndoe" to the "developers" group. To view the groups to which a user belongs, you can use the "groups" command followed by the username:

bashCopy code

```
groups johndoe
```

Managing group memberships is vital for controlling access to resources. You can remove a user from a group using the "gpasswd" command with the "-d" option:

Copy code

```
sudo gpasswd -d johndoe developers
```

This command removes the user "johndoe" from the "developers" group. Groups often have associated group permissions on files and directories. These permissions determine what actions members of the group can perform on those resources. The "chown" and "chmod" commands are used to change file ownership and permissions. For example, to change the group ownership of a file named "file.txt" to the "developers" group, you can use the following command:

bashCopy code

```
sudo chown :developers file.txt
```

To grant read and write permissions to the group on the same file, you can execute:

bashCopy code

```
sudo chmod g+rw file.txt
```

By managing groups and their associated permissions, administrators can control who can access and modify specific resources.

User Account Management

User accounts require ongoing management to maintain security and access control. To delete a user account, you can use the "userdel" command:

Copy code

```
sudo userdel johndoe
```

This command removes the user account "johndoe," but it leaves the user's home directory and files intact. To delete the user's home directory as well, you can use the "-r" option:

Copy code

```
sudo userdel -r johndoe
```

Managing user accounts also involves disabling or locking accounts. The "passwd" command can be used with the "-l" (lock) option to disable an account:

Copy code

```
sudo passwd -l johndoe
```

Locking an account prevents the user from logging in while keeping the account itself intact. To unlock the account, you can use the "-u" (unlock) option:

Copy code

```
sudo passwd -u johndoe
```

For security and auditing purposes, administrators can set password expiration policies for user accounts. The "chage" command allows you to configure password expiration settings:

Copy code

```
sudo chage -M 90 johndoe
```

This command sets the maximum number of days between password changes to 90 for the user "johndoe." Regularly reviewing and auditing user accounts is essential to ensure that they align with organizational policies and access requirements. The "getent" command can be used to list all user accounts on the system:

Copy code

```
getent passwd
```

By examining user account information, administrators can identify and address any discrepancies or issues.

Group Management

Effective group management is crucial for organizing users and controlling resource access. To delete a group, you can use the "groupdel" command:

Copy code

```
sudo groupdel developers
```

This command removes the "developers" group. Before deleting a group, ensure that no users remain members of the group to prevent orphaned files or access issues. To rename a group, you can use the "groupmod" command:

Copy code

```
sudo groupmod -n newdevelopers olddevelopers
```

This command changes the group name from "olddevelopers" to "newdevelopers." Group management also includes modifying group permissions on resources. The "chown" and "chmod" commands allow you to change group ownership and permissions, as mentioned earlier. Regularly reviewing and updating group memberships and permissions ensures that users have the appropriate access levels to perform their tasks. Auditing groups and their permissions is essential for maintaining a secure and organized environment.

User accounts and groups are integral components of managing access, security, and permissions in computer systems. Effective user and group management involves creating, configuring, and maintaining user accounts and groups to meet organizational needs. By utilizing command-line tools and following best practices for user and group management, administrators can ensure that their systems are secure, organized, and accessible to authorized users.

In the world of operating systems and file systems, file permissions and ownership are critical aspects of security and access control. These mechanisms determine who can read, write, execute, and manipulate files and directories on a computer or server. This chapter explores the concepts of file permissions and ownership and how to manage them effectively using command-line tools.

File Permissions

File permissions define what actions a user or system process can perform on a file or directory. There are three basic file permissions: read, write, and execute. The read permission allows a user to view the contents of a file or list the contents of a directory. The write permission allows a user to modify the contents of a file or create, delete, and rename files within a directory. The execute permission allows a user to execute a file if it is a program or script. File permissions are represented using a combination of letters and symbols. For example, the permission "rw-r--r--" means that the file owner can read and write the file, while others can only read it. To view file permissions in the command line, you can use the "ls" command with the "-l" option:

bashCopy code

ls -l myfile.txt

This command displays detailed information about "myfile.txt," including its permissions.

Changing File Permissions

To change file permissions, you can use the "chmod" (change mode) command. The "chmod" command allows you to add or remove permissions for the file owner, group, and others. You can specify permissions using symbolic notation, such as "u" for the user (owner), "g" for the group, and "o" for others. To add or remove permissions, use the symbols "+" or "-" along with the permission letters. For example, to add write permission for the group to a file, you can execute:

bashCopy code

chmod g+w myfile.txt

To remove execute permission for others, you can run:

bashCopy code

chmod o-x myfile.txt

You can also use numeric codes to represent permissions. Each permission is assigned a value: read (4), write (2), and execute (1). By summing these values, you can create a three-digit code that represents the permissions. For example, the code "644" signifies read and write permission for the owner and read-only permission for the group and others. To change permissions using numeric codes, use the following syntax:

bashCopy code

chmod 644 myfile.txt

File Ownership

File ownership dictates who has control over a file or directory. Each file is associated with an owner and a group. The owner is the user who created the file, and the group is a set of users who share certain permissions. To view file ownership in the command line, you can use the "ls" command with the "-l" option, as shown earlier. The "chown" (change owner) and "chgrp" (change group) commands allow you to modify file

ownership and group associations. For example, to change the owner of a file to a user named "newowner," you can execute:
bashCopy code

```
sudo chown newowner myfile.txt
```

To change the group of a file to a group named "newgroup," you can run:
bashCopy code

```
sudo chgrp newgroup myfile.txt
```

Changing file ownership or group membership typically requires administrative privileges.

Managing Permissions and Ownership

Effective file permissions and ownership management are essential for maintaining data security and access control. Administrators often use these mechanisms to ensure that only authorized users can access, modify, or execute files and directories. When dealing with multiple users and groups, it's crucial to strike a balance between access control and usability. Regularly reviewing and auditing file permissions and ownership can help identify security risks and ensure that access remains appropriate. The "find" command is a powerful tool for searching and managing files based on criteria such as permissions and ownership. For instance, to find all files in a directory that are writable by anyone, you can use the following command:
luaCopy code

```
find /path/to/directory -type f -perm -o=w
```

This command searches for regular files ("-type f") with permissions that include write access for others ("-perm -o=w"). To change permissions or ownership for multiple files at once, you can use the "chmod" and "chown" commands with the "find" command. For example, to change the owner of all "txt" files in a directory to "newowner," you can run:
bashCopy code

```
find /path/to/directory -type f -name "*.txt" -exec chown
newowner {} \;
```
This command searches for files with the ".txt" extension and executes the "chown" command for each matching file. Effective file permissions and ownership management is not only about security but also about ensuring that users can perform their tasks efficiently. Balancing security and usability is crucial for maintaining a functional and secure file system.

File permissions and ownership are fundamental concepts in computer systems, determining who can access, modify, and execute files and directories. Effective management of these mechanisms is essential for maintaining data security and access control. By understanding how to view and change file permissions, modify ownership and group associations, and manage permissions and ownership across multiple files, administrators can ensure that their file systems are both secure and accessible to authorized users. Regularly reviewing and auditing these settings is crucial for maintaining a secure and well-organized file system that meets the needs of users and organizations.

Chapter 6: Package Management with APT

The ability to install and remove software is a fundamental skill for any computer user or system administrator. Software is the lifeblood of modern computing, enabling a wide range of functionality from productivity applications to system utilities and games. Next, we will explore the process of installing and removing software on various operating systems using command-line tools.

Package Management

Package management is the cornerstone of software installation and removal in many Linux distributions and Unix-based systems. It provides a unified and organized way to package, distribute, and manage software. Each Linux distribution typically has its own package manager, such as "apt" for Debian-based systems, "yum" or "dnf" for Red Hat-based systems, and "pacman" for Arch Linux. The package manager handles software installation, dependencies, updates, and removal. To install software using a package manager, you can use commands like "apt-get," "yum," or "pacman," followed by the name of the package you want to install. For example, to install the "curl" package on a Debian-based system, you can run:

arduinoCopy code

```
sudo apt-get install curl
```

To remove software, you can use the package manager's uninstall or remove command, followed by the name of the package you want to remove. For example, to remove the "curl" package, you can execute:

arduinoCopy code

```
sudo apt-get remove curl
```

Compiling from Source

In some cases, you may need to compile and install software from its source code. This process involves downloading the source code, configuring the build options, compiling the code into executable binaries, and installing the resulting software. Before you can compile software from source, you will need to ensure that you have the necessary development tools and libraries installed on your system. You can use the package manager to install these development tools, which typically include a compiler (e.g., GCC) and build essentials (e.g., make). To compile software from source, you will typically follow these steps:

Download the source code, usually in a compressed archive format like tar.gz or zip.

Extract the source code from the archive using commands like "tar" or "unzip."

Navigate to the source code directory.

Configure the build process by running a configuration script or command.

Compile the software using the "make" command.

Install the compiled software using the "make install" command.

The exact steps and commands may vary depending on the software package and its build system. Compiling from source allows for greater flexibility and customization but may require more effort and manual management of dependencies.

Windows Software Installation

On Windows operating systems, software installation is typically done using executable installer files. These files have the extension ".exe" or ".msi" and often come with graphical user interfaces (GUIs) for a user-friendly installation experience. To install software on Windows, you can double-click the installer file and follow the on-screen instructions provided by the installer. Alternatively, you can use the command prompt to install software silently or without a GUI. The "msiexec" command is commonly used for installing Windows Installer packages (MSI files) from the command line.

For example, to install an MSI package named "example.msi," you can run:

bashCopy code

msiexec /i example.msi

To uninstall software on Windows from the command line, you can use the "wmic" command with the "product" alias. First, open a command prompt with administrative privileges. Then, to list installed software, you can run:

arduinoCopy code

wmic product get name

To uninstall a specific software package, you can use the following command, replacing "SoftwareName" with the actual name of the software you want to remove:

bashCopy code

wmic product where "name='SoftwareName'" uninstall

macOS Software Installation

On macOS, software installation is typically done through the App Store, package managers, or direct downloads from websites. Homebrew is a popular package manager for macOS that provides a convenient way to install and manage software packages from the command line. To install Homebrew, you can run the following command:

bashCopy code

/bin/bash -c "$(curl -fsSL https://raw.githubusercontent.com/Homebrew/install/HEAD/install.sh)"

Once Homebrew is installed, you can use it to install software packages. For example, to install the "curl" package, you can run:

Copy code

brew install curl

To uninstall a package, you can use the "brew uninstall" command:

Copy code

brew uninstall curl

Alternatively, some macOS applications come in the form of disk image files (DMG) or package installer files (PKG). To install a software package from a DMG file, you can mount the DMG, drag the application to the Applications folder, and then unmount the DMG. To install a PKG file, you can use the "installer" command, providing the path to the PKG file:

luaCopy code

sudo installer -pkg / path /to/ package .pkg -target /

To uninstall software installed via a PKG file, you can often use the "pkgutil" command.

Software Removal

Removing software is as important as installing it, as it helps free up disk space and keeps your system tidy. Properly uninstalling software ensures that all associated files and configurations are removed. When using package managers like "apt" or "yum" on Linux, you can use the package manager's uninstall or remove command, as mentioned earlier. For example, on a Red Hat-based system, you can use "yum" to remove a package:

arduinoCopy code

sudo yum remove package_name

On Windows, you can uninstall software using the "Add or Remove Programs" (Windows 7) or "Programs and Features" (Windows 10) control panel. You can also use the "wmic" command, as explained earlier, to uninstall software from the command line. On macOS, you can use package managers like Homebrew to uninstall software packages. Additionally, you can manually delete application files from the Applications folder to uninstall software installed via DMG files.

Installing and removing software is a fundamental skill for computer users and administrators across various operating systems. Understanding package management on Linux and Unix-based systems, software installation on Windows, and package management and direct downloads on macOS provides the tools and knowledge needed to manage software effectively. Regularly uninstalling software you no longer need helps maintain system performance and disk space. By following best practices for software installation and removal, you can keep your computer or server organized, efficient, and up to date with the software you require.

Keeping software packages up to date is a crucial aspect of maintaining a secure and reliable computing environment. Outdated software can have security vulnerabilities, bugs, and missing features, making it essential to regularly update and upgrade packages. Next, we will explore the process of updating and upgrading packages on various operating systems using command-line tools.

Package Update vs. Package Upgrade

Before diving into the update and upgrade process, it's important to understand the difference between the two terms. Package update refers to the process of updating individual software packages to their latest available versions. This ensures that each package receives the latest bug fixes, security patches, and feature enhancements. Package upgrade, on the other hand, involves upgrading the entire operating system or distribution to a new version or release. This may include a significant change in features, system libraries, and kernel updates. The methods for updating and upgrading packages differ, and it's crucial to perform both regularly to maintain a secure and functional system.

Updating Packages on Linux

Linux distributions often provide package managers to facilitate package updates. These package managers include tools like "apt," "yum," "dnf," "pacman," and others, depending on the distribution. To update packages using "apt" on Debian-based systems like Ubuntu, you can run:

sqlCopy code

```
sudo apt update sudo apt upgrade
```

The "apt update" command refreshes the package database, while "apt upgrade" installs the latest versions of all packages on your system. On Red Hat-based systems like Fedora, you can use "dnf" to update packages:

Copy code

```
sudo dnf upgrade
```

On Arch Linux, the "pacman" package manager is used to update packages:

Copy code

```
sudo pacman -Syu
```

These commands ensure that all installed packages are updated to their latest versions, including security updates. Regularly updating packages helps maintain a secure and stable system.

Upgrading the Operating System

Upgrading the entire operating system or distribution is a more involved process. It involves transitioning to a new version or release, which may include changes to the system's core components. To upgrade the operating system on Debian-based systems, you can use the "dist-upgrade" option with "apt":

sqlCopy code

```
sudo apt update sudo apt dist-upgrade
```

This command not only upgrades packages but also handles changes in dependencies and system libraries that may be required for the new release. On Red Hat-based systems like CentOS or Fedora, you can use "dnf" to perform system upgrades:

sqlCopy code

```
sudo dnf system-upgrade download --releasever=34 sudo dnf system-upgrade reboot
```

These commands download the new release and perform the system upgrade. The specific release version (e.g., "34") should be adjusted based on the target release. Arch Linux users can upgrade the distribution by using the "pacman" package manager:

Copy code

sudo pacman -Syu

In all cases, it is crucial to back up important data before performing a system upgrade. System upgrades can introduce significant changes and potential compatibility issues, so caution and thorough preparation are necessary.

Updating Packages on Windows

On Windows operating systems, updating software packages is typically handled through automatic updates from software vendors. Applications like web browsers, antivirus software, and system utilities often include automatic update mechanisms to keep the software current. For example, web browsers like Google Chrome and Mozilla Firefox automatically download and install updates. In cases where automatic updates are not enabled, users can manually check for updates within the software application's settings or preferences. Windows itself receives updates through the Windows Update feature, which is usually configured to run automatically. To manually check for Windows updates, you can go to "Settings" > "Update & Security" > "Windows Update" and click "Check for updates."

Updating Packages on macOS

macOS provides a software update mechanism that allows users to keep the operating system and Apple software up to date. This mechanism can be accessed through the "App Store" application, where users can view and install available updates. To check for updates on macOS, you can follow these steps:

Click the Apple menu (⌘) in the top-left corner of the screen.

Select "App Store."

In the "Updates" tab, you can view available updates and click "Update" next to each item.

Additionally, some third-party software installed on macOS may offer automatic updates or in-app update checks. Users should enable these features to ensure that their software is kept current.

Package Management Best Practices

Maintaining a system with up-to-date packages is essential for security and stability. To ensure the smooth operation of your computing environment, consider the following best practices:

Regularly update individual software packages to stay current with security patches and bug fixes.

Check for operating system updates or upgrades as recommended by the distribution or vendor. Create backups of important data before performing system upgrades to safeguard against potential data loss. Enable automatic updates for critical software applications whenever possible. Review release notes and changelogs for updates and upgrades to understand what changes are being introduced.

By following these best practices, you can ensure that your system remains secure, stable, and capable of running the latest software features and improvements.

Updating and upgrading packages are essential tasks for maintaining a secure and functional computing environment. On Linux and Unix-based systems, package managers like "apt," "yum," "dnf," and "pacman" provide straightforward ways to update packages. For upgrading the entire operating system, specific commands and procedures vary by distribution. On Windows and macOS, software updates are typically managed through automatic updates from software vendors and operating system updates. Regularly updating and upgrading software packages and operating systems helps protect against security vulnerabilities and ensures that you have access to the latest features and improvements. By following best practices and staying informed about updates, you can keep your computing environment up to date and secure.

Chapter 7: Process Control and Monitoring

Processes are the heart of any operating system, serving as the building blocks of system functionality and user applications. Understanding how to manage processes effectively is crucial for system administrators and power users. This chapter explores the concepts of managing processes on various operating systems using command-line tools and utilities.

What Are Processes?

Processes are instances of running programs on a computer or server. Every action, from launching a text editor to running a web server, is carried out by one or more processes. Each process has its own unique identifier called a Process ID (PID), which distinguishes it from other processes. Processes can run in the foreground or background, allowing users to interact with applications and the system simultaneously. Understanding the life cycle of processes, how to start and terminate them, and how to manage their resources is essential for efficient system operation.

Viewing Processes

To view the list of processes running on a system, you can use commands like "ps" on Unix-like systems or "Task Manager" on Windows. The "ps" command with options like "-e" or "-aux" provides detailed information about running processes. For example, to list all processes running on a Unix-like system, you can run:

Copy code

```
ps -e
```

On Windows, you can press "Ctrl+Shift+Esc" or "Ctrl+Alt+Delete" and select "Task Manager" to view a list of running processes. This interface displays process names, status, CPU and memory usage, and more.

Starting Processes

To start a new process from the command line, you can use the appropriate command or utility for the desired application. For example, to launch a text editor like "nano" on Unix-like systems, you can open a terminal and type:
Copy code

nano

This command starts the "nano" text editor, allowing you to create or edit files. Similarly, to open a web browser like "Google Chrome" on Windows, you can open the Command Prompt and type:
sqlCopy code

start chrome

This command launches the Chrome browser. Many applications have specific command-line utilities or options for starting them, allowing for automation and scripting.

Foreground and Background Processes

When you start a process, it typically runs in the foreground, which means it interacts with your terminal or console. You can interact with the process directly, and it may display output and accept input in the terminal. To run a process in the background, you can append an ampersand ("&") to the command when starting it. For example, to run a process called "background_process" in the background, you can execute:
Copy code

background_process &

This allows you to continue using the terminal while the process runs independently. To bring a background process to the foreground, you can use the "fg" command followed by the job number. Job numbers are assigned to background processes, and you can list them using the "jobs" command. For instance, to bring the first background process to the foreground, you can run:
bashCopy code

fg %1

Terminating Processes

Terminating processes is essential for managing system resources and ensuring the stability of the system. To terminate a running process, you can use commands like "kill" on Unix-like systems or "Task Manager" on Windows. The "kill" command allows you to send signals to processes, instructing them to terminate gracefully. For example, to terminate a process with a specific PID, you can run:

bashCopy code

```
kill PID
```

By default, the "kill" command sends a "SIGTERM" signal, which asks the process to exit gracefully. To forcefully terminate a process, you can use the "SIGKILL" signal by adding the "-9" option:

bashCopy code

```
kill -9 PID
```

On Windows, you can open "Task Manager," select the process you want to terminate, and click the "End Task" button. Alternatively, you can use the "taskkill" command from the Command Prompt to terminate a process by name or PID:

rCopy code

```
taskkill /F /IM process_name.exe
```

Processes can also be terminated by their own code if they encounter an error or reach their natural end.

Process Prioritization and Resource Management

Managing processes often involves prioritizing and allocating system resources efficiently. The "nice" command on Unix-like systems allows you to adjust the priority of a process. Processes with a higher "nice" value are less likely to consume CPU resources, while those with a lower "nice" value have higher priority. For example, to start a process with a lower priority, you can run:

bashCopy code

```
nice -n 10 my_process
```

This command starts "my_process" with a higher "nice" value, giving other processes higher priority.

On Windows, you can use the "Priority" setting in "Task Manager" to adjust process priority. Be cautious when changing process priorities, as lowering the priority of critical system processes can impact system performance.

Monitoring and Resource Usage

Monitoring processes and their resource usage is essential for system administrators. Tools like "top" on Unix-like systems or "Resource Monitor" on Windows provide real-time information about CPU, memory, disk, and network usage. To view a dynamic list of running processes and their resource usage on Unix-like systems, you can run:

cssCopy code

top

On Windows, you can press "Ctrl+Shift+Esc" to open "Task Manager," which provides similar information in different tabs.

Resource monitoring tools help identify resource-intensive processes, allowing administrators to take appropriate action to optimize system performance. Terminating or adjusting the priority of resource-hogging processes can prevent system slowdowns and crashes.

Process Control Signals

Processes can communicate with each other and with the operating system using signals. Signals are notifications sent to processes to inform them of events or requests. Common signals include "SIGTERM" for graceful termination, "SIGKILL" for forceful termination, and "SIGHUP" for hang-up. Signals can be sent using commands like "kill" on Unix-like systems. For example, to send the "SIGHUP" signal to a process with PID 1234, you can run:

bashCopy code

kill -SIGHUP 1234

Processes can handle signals to perform specific actions, such as saving data or reinitializing. Understanding signals and how processes respond to them is important for effective process management.

Managing processes is a fundamental skill for system administrators and power users. Processes are the core components of system functionality and user applications, and understanding how to start, terminate, prioritize, and monitor them is essential for maintaining system stability and performance. By using commands and utilities specific to the operating system, you can efficiently manage processes, allocate system resources, and ensure that your computing environment operates smoothly.

Monitoring System Performance
Monitoring system performance is a critical task for system administrators and IT professionals responsible for the health and reliability of computer systems. A well-monitored system can detect issues early, prevent downtime, and optimize resource utilization. Next, we will explore the importance of monitoring system performance and various tools and techniques to achieve it effectively.

Why Monitor System Performance?
Monitoring system performance is essential because it provides valuable insights into the health and efficiency of a computer system. By continually assessing key metrics, administrators can identify and address performance bottlenecks, security vulnerabilities, and hardware failures. Proactive monitoring helps prevent system downtime, improves user experience, and ensures that resources are used optimally. Key reasons to monitor system performance include:

Early Issue Detection: Performance monitoring allows early detection of issues such as high resource usage, disk space depletion, and network congestion before they lead to system failures or outages.

Resource Optimization: Monitoring helps administrators identify underutilized resources that can be reallocated to improve system efficiency and reduce costs.

Capacity Planning: Monitoring assists in capacity planning by providing data on resource trends, helping organizations make informed decisions about resource upgrades or scaling.

Security: Performance monitoring can reveal signs of suspicious or unauthorized activity, aiding in the early detection of security breaches and vulnerabilities.

Compliance: Many industries and organizations require compliance with specific performance and availability standards. Monitoring ensures compliance and helps demonstrate adherence to these standards.

Key Performance Metrics

To effectively monitor system performance, administrators must track key performance metrics that reflect the system's health and behavior. Common performance metrics include:

CPU Usage: Measures the percentage of CPU utilization by processes and tasks. High CPU usage can indicate resource contention or inefficient applications.

Memory Usage: Tracks memory consumption by processes and the system. High memory usage can lead to performance degradation and system instability.

Disk I/O: Monitors read and write operations on disk drives. Elevated disk I/O can slow down application responsiveness and lead to data loss.

Network Throughput: Measures data transfer rates on network interfaces. Monitoring network throughput helps identify network congestion and bottlenecks.

Load Average: Indicates the number of processes waiting in the system's run queue. A high load average can suggest resource saturation and performance issues.

Disk Space: Monitors available disk space on storage devices. Running out of disk space can lead to application crashes and data loss.

Latency: Measures the delay in response times for system components and network services. High latency can impact user experience and application performance.

Monitoring Tools and Techniques

Several tools and techniques are available for monitoring system performance on different operating systems and platforms. Here are some commonly used tools and techniques:

Command-Line Tools: Many operating systems provide built-in command-line tools for monitoring system performance. Examples include "top" and "htop" on Unix-like systems and "Task Manager" on Windows.

Performance Monitoring Software: Dedicated performance monitoring software, such as Nagios, Zabbix, and Prometheus, offers comprehensive monitoring capabilities and customizable dashboards.

Log Analysis: Analyzing system logs, including system logs, application logs, and security logs, can provide insights into system behavior and performance.

Resource Utilization Metrics: Collecting resource utilization metrics using tools like SAR (System Activity Reporter) on Unix-like systems helps track CPU, memory, and disk usage over time.

Network Monitoring Tools: Network monitoring tools like Wireshark and tcpdump capture and analyze network traffic, helping detect network-related issues and performance bottlenecks.

Web Performance Monitoring: Web performance monitoring tools like Google PageSpeed Insights and GTmetrix assess web application performance and provide recommendations for improvement.

Application Performance Monitoring (APM): APM tools like New Relic and AppDynamics specialize in monitoring the performance of web applications and services.

Custom Scripts: Administrators can create custom scripts and scripts using programming languages like Python and PowerShell to collect and analyze specific performance metrics.

Alerting and Notifications

Effective performance monitoring includes setting up alerts and notifications to inform administrators of critical events and thresholds. Alerts can be configured to trigger when predefined conditions are met or exceeded. Common alerting scenarios include:

CPU or memory usage exceeding a certain threshold

Disk space reaching a critical level

Network latency or packet loss exceeding acceptable limits

Application-specific errors or anomalies

Security breaches or suspicious activity

Alerts can be delivered via email, SMS, or integrated with messaging platforms like Slack or Microsoft Teams. Immediate notifications enable administrators to respond promptly to critical issues and minimize downtime.

Historical Data and Trend Analysis

Collecting historical performance data is essential for trend analysis and capacity planning. By analyzing historical data, administrators can identify long-term patterns, resource trends, and seasonal variations. This information is valuable for predicting future resource needs and making informed decisions about hardware upgrades or scaling efforts.

Performance data can be stored in databases or time-series databases and visualized using tools like Grafana and Kibana. Historical data can also be used for generating reports and compliance documentation, demonstrating system performance over time.

Security and Privacy Considerations

When monitoring system performance, administrators must consider security and privacy concerns. Collecting and storing performance data may include sensitive information about users, applications, and network traffic. To address these concerns, administrators should:

Implement access controls and encryption to protect performance data from unauthorized access.

Anonymize or pseudonymize data to remove personally identifiable information (PII) before storage and analysis.

Comply with data protection and privacy regulations, such as GDPR, HIPAA, and CCPA, when handling performance data.

Chapter 8: Working with Text Files and Streams

Text File Editing

Text file editing is a fundamental skill for computer users and professionals alike, allowing for the creation, modification, and management of textual data. Text files serve as the backbone of configuration files, scripts, code, documentation, and various other types of information. Next, we will explore the importance of text file editing and the tools and techniques used to perform these tasks effectively.

The Role of Text Files

Text files are a versatile and universally recognized format for storing and sharing data. They consist of plain text characters and are human-readable, making them accessible to both users and software applications. Text files come in various forms, including configuration files (e.g., YAML, JSON), scripts (e.g., shell scripts, Python scripts), markup languages (e.g., HTML, XML), log files, and documentation files (e.g., README files). Their simplicity and compatibility make text files a preferred choice for many purposes.

Common Text Editors

Text editors are software applications designed for creating, editing, and saving text files. There is a wide range of text editors available, catering to different user preferences and requirements. Some of the most common text editors include:

Notepad: A basic text editor included with Microsoft Windows, suitable for simple text editing tasks.

TextEdit: The default text editor on macOS, capable of handling plain text and rich text formats.

nano: A simple, terminal-based text editor available on many Unix-like systems, known for its ease of use.

vim: A powerful, terminal-based text editor with a steep learning curve but extensive capabilities once mastered.

Emacs: Another feature-rich, terminal-based text editor known for its extensibility and customization options.

Visual Studio Code: A popular, cross-platform code editor developed by Microsoft, widely used for coding and text editing tasks.

Sublime Text: A versatile code and text editor known for its speed and extensive plugin ecosystem.

Atom: An open-source code and text editor developed by GitHub, designed to be highly customizable.

gedit: The default text editor on many Linux distributions, offering a balance between simplicity and functionality.

Each text editor has its own set of features, keyboard shortcuts, and interface designs, making it essential to choose one that suits your needs and preferences.

Basic Text Editing Techniques

Regardless of the text editor chosen, there are common text editing techniques and commands that apply across most editors. These include:

Opening a File: To open an existing text file, use the "File" menu or a command like "open filename" in the text editor.

Creating a New File: To create a new text file, select "New" or use the "touch" command (e.g., "touch newfile.txt" in a terminal).

Editing Text: Click on the desired location in the text, or use arrow keys, to position the cursor for text input.

Inserting Text: To insert new text, type directly on the keyboard, and the text will appear at the cursor position.

Deleting Text: Use the backspace or delete key to remove characters to the left or right of the cursor, respectively.

Cut, Copy, and Paste: These actions are performed using keyboard shortcuts or menu options, such as Ctrl+X (cut), Ctrl+C (copy), and Ctrl+V (paste) in Windows or Command+X, Command+C, and Command+V on macOS.

Saving Changes: To save changes made to a file, use the "Save" or "Save As" option in the text editor's menu or the "Ctrl+S" (Windows) or "Command+S" (macOS) keyboard shortcut.

Undo and Redo: Text editors often provide "Undo" and "Redo" options to reverse or redo recent actions (e.g., Ctrl+Z for undo and Ctrl+Y or Ctrl+Shift+Z for redo).

Search and Replace: Text editors allow you to find specific text strings within a file and replace them with new text.

Navigation: You can navigate within a file using keyboard shortcuts, such as arrow keys, or by scrolling with the mouse or touchpad.

Line Numbers: Many text editors display line numbers, aiding in code debugging and document referencing.

Syntax Highlighting: Code editors often provide syntax highlighting, which color-codes different elements of the code for improved readability and error detection.

Auto-Indentation: Code editors may automatically indent code blocks for improved code structure.

Advanced Text Editing Techniques

Advanced text editing techniques depend on the specific capabilities of the text editor being used. Some advanced features include:

Multiple Cursors: Editors like Visual Studio Code and Sublime Text allow you to place multiple cursors in different locations, enabling simultaneous editing of multiple lines.

Search and Replace with Regular Expressions: Some text editors support regular expressions in their search and replace functionality, allowing for complex text manipulations.

Code Folding: Code editors often support code folding, which hides and collapses sections of code for easier navigation in large files.

Snippets and Macros: Editors may provide functionality for creating and using code snippets or macros to automate repetitive tasks.

Customization and Extensions: Many modern text editors can be customized and extended using plugins or extensions to add new features or integrate with other tools.

Version Control Integration: Text editors may include or support version control integrations, allowing you to manage code changes with tools like Git.

Text File Formats and Encoding

Text files can use different formats and character encodings, which dictate how the textual data is stored and interpreted. Common text file formats include plain text, UTF-8, UTF-16, ASCII, and more. It's important to choose the appropriate format and encoding to ensure compatibility and proper display of text data across different systems and applications.

Text file editing is a fundamental skill for working with textual data in computing. Understanding the role of text files, choosing the right text editor, and mastering basic and advanced text editing techniques are essential for efficient and productive text file manipulation. Whether you are writing code, configuring settings, documenting procedures, or managing data, text file editing is a core skill that serves as a foundation for various computing tasks.

Redirection and Piping

Redirection and piping are powerful concepts in the world of command-line interfaces, enabling users to manipulate the flow of data between commands and files. These techniques enhance the flexibility and efficiency of working with the command line and are essential skills for both beginners and experienced users. Next, we will explore the concepts of redirection and piping, along with practical examples to illustrate their usage.

Understanding Standard Input, Output, and Error

Before diving into redirection and piping, it's crucial to understand three fundamental data streams used in command-line operations:

Standard Input (stdin): This stream represents the source of input data for a command. By default, it is connected to the keyboard, allowing users to provide input interactively.

Standard Output (stdout): This stream represents the destination for normal output data from a command. By default, it is connected to the terminal, where the command's output is displayed.

Standard Error (stderr): This stream is similar to stdout but is specifically used for error messages and diagnostic information.

Redirection: Changing Input and Output

Redirection allows users to change the source of input or the destination of output for a command. It involves using special characters and symbols to specify the desired input or output location. Here are some common redirection operators:

>: Redirects stdout to a file, overwriting the file's contents if it already exists. For example, **command > output.txt** will redirect the output of **command** to a file named **output.txt**.

>>: Redirects stdout to a file, appending the output to the file if it already exists. For example, **command >> output.txt** will append the output of **command** to the end of the **output.txt** file.

<: Redirects stdin from a file, allowing a command to read input from that file instead of the keyboard. For example, **command < input.txt** will use the contents of **input.txt** as input for **command**.

2>: Redirects stderr to a file. Similar to stdout redirection, this sends error messages to a specified file. For example, **command 2> error.txt** will redirect error messages to the **error.txt** file.

2>>: Appends stderr to a file, similar to **2>** but with appending behavior.

&> or 2>&1: Redirects both stdout and stderr to a file or another command. For example, **command &> output.txt** or **command 2>&1** will capture both normal output and error messages in the **output.txt** file or pipe them to another command.

Examples of Redirection

Let's look at some practical examples of redirection:

Output to a File: Suppose you have a command that generates a list of files in a directory. You can redirect the output to a file like this:

bashCopy code

ls > filelist.txt

This will create a file named **filelist.txt** containing the list of files.

Input from a File: If you have a command that accepts input from a file, you can redirect input from a file like this:

luaCopy code

sort < input.txt

This will sort the contents of **input.txt** and display the sorted result on the terminal.

Combining stdout and stderr: When running a command that produces both regular output and error messages, you can capture both streams in a single file:

luaCopy code

mycommand &> output.txt

Appending to a Log File: If you want to keep a log of commands and their outputs, you can use append redirection to add entries to an existing log file:

Copy code

somecommand >> logfile.txt

Piping: Passing Data Between Commands

Piping, represented by the **|** symbol, allows users to send the output of one command as input to another command. This enables the chaining of multiple commands to perform complex operations efficiently. Piping is a fundamental concept in Unix-like systems and is widely used to process data on the command line.

Examples of Piping

Let's explore some examples of piping:

Filtering with grep: The **grep** command is used to search for patterns in text.

bashCopy code

```
cat log.txt | grep "error"
```

This command reads the **log.txt** file, pipes its contents to **grep**, and filters lines containing the word "error."

Counting with wc: The **wc** (word count) command is used to count lines, words, and characters in text.

bashCopy code

```
cat data.txt | wc -l
```

This command counts the number of lines in **data.txt** by piping the file's contents to **wc -l**.

Sorting: Sorting lines of text is a common operation.

bashCopy code

```
cat unsorted.txt | sort
```

This command reads **unsorted.txt**, sorts its lines alphabetically, and displays the sorted result.

Combining Commands: Piping allows you to combine multiple commands to perform complex operations. For example:

bashCopy code

```
ls -l | grep "file" | sort
```

This command lists files in a directory, filters for lines containing the word "file," and then sorts the filtered list.

Using Redirection and Piping Together

Redirection and piping can be used together to create sophisticated data processing pipelines. For example, you can capture the output of a complex command sequence in a file or send the combined output of multiple commands to another process.

Consider the following example:

luaCopy code

```
grep "error" log.txt | sort > errorlog.txt
```

In this command, the **grep** command searches for lines containing "error" in **log.txt**, the result is piped to **sort**, and finally, the sorted output is redirected to **errorlog.txt**.

Common Use Cases

Here are some common use cases for redirection and piping:

Log Analysis: Redirecting log files to grep and other tools for error analysis and troubleshooting.

Data Transformation: Piping data through text processing commands like **awk**, **sed**, and **tr** to reformat or transform it.

Text Search: Using **grep** to search for specific text patterns in files or command output.

Data Extraction: Extracting specific information from structured data using text-processing tools.

File Operations: Performing complex file operations involving copying, moving, and deleting files.

Redirection and piping are fundamental concepts in command-line interfaces, offering powerful capabilities for manipulating data streams and optimizing command execution. By understanding these concepts and practicing their usage, users can harness the full potential of the command line to efficiently process and manage data.

Chapter 9: Basic Scripting and Automation

Introduction to Shell Scripting

Shell scripting is a valuable skill that allows users to automate tasks, execute commands in sequence, and perform complex operations using a command-line interface. Next, we will explore the fundamentals of shell scripting, its significance, and how it can be used to enhance productivity in various computing environments.

What Is Shell Scripting?

At its core, shell scripting is the practice of creating and running scripts, which are sets of commands written in a shell scripting language. A shell script is a text file that contains a series of commands and instructions that can be executed in a shell environment. Shell scripting languages, such as Bash, PowerShell, and Python, provide powerful features for automating tasks and performing system administration tasks.

The Role of the Shell

The shell, also known as a command-line interpreter, is a program that allows users to interact with an operating system through text-based commands. Shells act as a bridge between the user and the operating system, interpreting user input and executing commands on the user's behalf. Shell scripting leverages the capabilities of the shell to automate tasks and streamline workflows.

Why Use Shell Scripting?

Shell scripting offers several advantages:

Automation: Shell scripts automate repetitive tasks, reducing the need for manual intervention and saving time.

Consistency: Scripts ensure consistent execution of commands and tasks, reducing the likelihood of errors.

Efficiency: Complex operations can be performed with a single script, improving efficiency and productivity.

Customization: Users can create custom scripts tailored to their specific needs and requirements.

Script Portability: Shell scripts can often be run on different systems and platforms with minimal modification.

Script Sharing: Users can share and distribute scripts to colleagues or the community to promote collaboration and knowledge sharing.

Shell Scripting Languages

Various shell scripting languages are available, each with its own syntax and features. Some of the commonly used scripting languages include:

Bash: The Bourne-Again Shell, often referred to as Bash, is a popular Unix shell that is widely used for shell scripting on Unix-based systems like Linux and macOS.

PowerShell: Developed by Microsoft, PowerShell is a shell and scripting language designed for Windows systems, providing extensive automation capabilities.

Python: While not a traditional shell language, Python is a versatile scripting language that can be used for shell scripting on various platforms.

Perl: Perl is known for its text-processing capabilities and is often used for system administration and scripting tasks.

Ruby: Ruby is a dynamic, object-oriented scripting language that is used for various purposes, including shell scripting.

The choice of scripting language depends on the specific requirements of the task and the environment in which the script will be executed.

Basic Shell Script Structure

A shell script typically follows a structured format, consisting of the following elements:

Shebang: The shebang line, often the first line of a script, specifies the path to the shell interpreter that should be used to execute the script. For example:

```
bashCopy code
#!/bin/bash
```

Comments: Comments in a script provide explanations and documentation. They are preceded by a # symbol. For example:
bashCopy code
This is a comment

Commands: The core of the script contains a series of commands that are executed in sequence. For example:
bashCopy code
echo "Hello, World!"

Variables: Variables are used to store and manipulate data within a script. They are typically assigned values using the = operator. For example:
makefileCopy code
name="John"

Control Structures: Shell scripts can include control structures like conditional statements (if, else, elif) and loops (for, while) to control the flow of execution.

Functions: Functions allow you to encapsulate a set of commands for reuse throughout the script.

Sample Shell Script

Here's a simple example of a Bash shell script that prints a message:
bashCopy code
#!/bin/bash # This is a comment name="Alice" echo "Hello, $name!"

In this script, the shebang line specifies that Bash should be used as the interpreter. A comment provides information about the script, and a variable (**name**) is defined to store a name. The **echo** command is used to display a message on the screen, including the value of the **name** variable.

Executing Shell Scripts

To run a shell script, follow these steps:

Save the script to a file with a **.sh** extension (e.g., **myscript.sh**).

Make the script executable using the **chmod** command:
bashCopy code

```
chmod +x myscript.sh
```
Execute the script by running:

bashCopy code
```
./myscript.sh
```
The **chmod +x** command grants execute permissions to the script, allowing it to be run as an executable.

Practical Use Cases

Shell scripting can be applied to a wide range of tasks and scenarios, including:

File Management: Automating file backups, renaming files, and organizing directories.

System Administration: Managing users, configuring system settings, and performing routine maintenance tasks.

Text Processing: Parsing and manipulating text data, such as log file analysis or data extraction.

Automation: Automating software installations, updates, and system configurations.

Monitoring and Reporting: Creating scripts to monitor system resources, generate reports, and send notifications.

Web Scraping: Writing scripts to extract data from websites and APIs.

Task Scheduling: Using scripts with cron jobs or task scheduler to automate repetitive tasks on a schedule.

Data Transformation: Converting data from one format to another, such as CSV to JSON.

Shell scripting is a valuable skill that empowers users to automate tasks, improve efficiency, and harness the full potential of the command-line interface. Understanding the fundamentals of shell scripting, choosing the appropriate scripting language, and practicing scripting techniques are essential for mastering this versatile tool. In the following chapters, we will delve deeper into shell scripting concepts and explore practical examples to enhance your scripting skills.

Automating Simple Tasks

Automation is a powerful concept that allows users to simplify their daily routines, increase productivity, and reduce the risk of errors. Next, we will explore the fundamentals of automating simple tasks through scripting, demonstrating how scripting languages can streamline repetitive processes and save time.

The Need for Automation

In our increasingly digital world, individuals and organizations are faced with a growing number of routine tasks that can be time-consuming and error-prone. Automation offers a solution to these challenges by allowing tasks to be performed automatically and consistently. By automating simple tasks, individuals and businesses can free up valuable time and resources for more complex and strategic activities.

Automation with Scripting

Scripting is a key tool for automating simple tasks. A script is a set of instructions written in a scripting language, such as Bash, Python, or PowerShell, that can be executed by a computer. These scripts can be used to perform a wide range of tasks, from file management to data processing and system administration.

Advantages of Automation

The advantages of automation through scripting are manifold. First and foremost, it saves time by eliminating the need for manual intervention in repetitive tasks. This time-saving benefit can lead to increased efficiency and productivity. Additionally, automation reduces the risk of human errors, which can be costly and time-consuming to rectify.

Simple Task Automation Examples

Let's explore some examples of simple tasks that can be automated through scripting:

File Backup: Creating a script to automatically back up important files to an external drive or cloud storage.

Data Cleaning: Using a script to clean and format data in spreadsheets, removing duplicates and inconsistencies.

Log Analysis: Automating the analysis of log files to identify patterns or errors.

Report Generation: Generating regular reports by automatically extracting data from databases or other sources.

File Renaming: Renaming a batch of files with a specific naming convention.

Software Updates: Automating the process of checking for and installing software updates.

System Monitoring: Using scripts to monitor system resources and send alerts when predefined thresholds are exceeded.

Selecting a Scripting Language

The choice of scripting language depends on the task at hand and the user's familiarity with the language. Some scripting languages are more suitable for certain tasks than others. For example, Bash scripting is well-suited for system administration tasks on Unix-like systems, while Python is a versatile language for general-purpose scripting.

Scripting Basics

Scripting languages provide a set of basic constructs for writing scripts. These constructs include variables, conditionals, loops, functions, and file operations. Understanding these basics is essential for writing effective scripts.

Variables: Variables are used to store data. In a script, you can assign values to variables and use those values in calculations or operations.

Conditionals: Conditionals, such as if statements, allow you to make decisions in your script based on certain conditions.

Loops: Loops, like for and while loops, enable you to repeat a set of instructions multiple times.

Functions: Functions are blocks of reusable code that can be called from within your script. They help modularize your code.

File Operations: File operations allow you to read from and write to files, making it possible to manipulate data stored in files.

Sample Automation Script

Here's a simple example of a Bash script that automates the backup of a directory:

bashCopy code

```bash
#!/bin/bash
# Source directory to be backed up
source_dir="/path/to/source"
# Destination directory where backups will be stored
backup_dir="/path/to/backup"
# Create a timestamp for the backup folder
timestamp=$(date +"%Y%m%d%H%M%S")
# Create a backup folder with the current timestamp
backup_folder="$backup_dir/backup_$timestamp"
mkdir -p "$backup_folder"
# Copy files from source directory to backup folder
cp -r "$source_dir"/* "$backup_folder"
# Print a message indicating the backup is complete
echo "Backup of $source_dir completed to $backup_folder"
```

In this script, comments provide explanations for each step. Variables are used to define the source and destination directories, and a timestamp is generated for the backup folder. The **cp** command is used to copy files from the source directory to the backup folder, and a message is printed to indicate the completion of the backup.

Running Automation Scripts

To run the automation script, follow these steps:

Save the script to a file (e.g., **backup.sh**).

Make the script executable using the **chmod** command:

bashCopy code

```bash
chmod +x backup.sh
```

Execute the script:

bashCopy code

```bash
./backup.sh
```

The script will create a backup of the specified directory, and the user doesn't need to manually copy files or create backup folders.

Automation Considerations

While automation offers numerous benefits, it's important to consider a few key factors:

Testing: Test scripts in a safe environment to ensure they work as expected and don't have unintended consequences.

Error Handling: Implement error handling to gracefully handle unexpected situations and failures.

Security: Be cautious when automating tasks that involve sensitive data or system-level operations, and ensure proper security measures are in place.

Documentation: Document your scripts, including comments and explanations, to make them understandable and maintainable.

Automation through scripting is a valuable skill that can simplify daily tasks, improve efficiency, and reduce errors. By understanding the fundamentals of scripting languages and practicing automation techniques, users can harness the power of automation to their advantage. In the next chapters, we will delve deeper into scripting concepts and explore more advanced automation scenarios.

Chapter 10: Troubleshooting and Tips for Beginners

Common Errors and Solutions

In the journey of learning and mastering shell scripting, encountering errors is an inevitable part of the process. Errors can be frustrating, but they also provide valuable learning opportunities. Next, we will explore some common errors that scriptwriters encounter and provide solutions to address them, helping you become a more proficient script developer.

Syntax Errors

Syntax errors are among the most common issues faced by scriptwriters. These errors occur when the script does not conform to the syntax rules of the scripting language being used. They can prevent the script from running or produce unexpected results.

Example: Syntax Error in Bash Script

bashCopy code

```
#!/bin/bash echo "Hello, World!" if [ 1 -eq 1 then echo "1 equals 1" fi
```

In the above Bash script, there is a missing closing square bracket (**]**) in the **if** statement, resulting in a syntax error.

Solution:

The syntax error can be fixed by adding the missing closing square bracket:

bashCopy code

```
#!/bin/bash echo "Hello, World!" if [ 1 -eq 1 ] then echo "1 equals 1" fi
```

Quoting Issues

Quoting issues can lead to unexpected behavior in scripts. These issues typically involve problems with single quotes, double quotes, or backslashes.

Example: Quoting Issue in Python Script

pythonCopy code

```python
#!/usr/bin/env python message = "Hello, World!" print("The
message is: " + message) print('The message is: ' + message)
```

In the Python script above, there are both single and double quotes used to enclose the strings, which can cause confusion and potential errors.

Solution:

Consistency in quoting style can resolve the issue. Choose either single quotes or double quotes and stick with the chosen style:

pythonCopy code

```python
#!/usr/bin/env python message = "Hello, World!" print("The
message is: " + message)
```

Variable Scope Errors

Variable scope errors occur when a variable is used in a context where it is not defined or accessible. Understanding variable scope is crucial in scripting, as it determines where a variable can be used within a script.

Example: Variable Scope Error in Bash Script

bashCopy code

```bash
#!/bin/bash function my_function { local local_var="Local
Variable" } my_function echo $local_var
```

In the Bash script above, the variable **local_var** is defined as a local variable within the **my_function** function, making it inaccessible outside the function.

Solution:

To access the **local_var** variable outside the function, you can declare it as a global variable by removing the **local** keyword:

bashCopy code

```bash
#!/bin/bash function my_function { local_var="Local Variable"
} my_function echo $local_var
```

File Not Found Errors

File not found errors occur when a script or a command attempts to access a file or directory that does not exist. These errors can disrupt script execution and lead to unexpected behavior.

Example: File Not Found Error in Bash Script

bashCopy code

```
#!/bin/bash file="non_existent_file.txt" cat $file
```

In the Bash script above, the **cat** command attempts to read the contents of a file named **non_existent_file.txt**, which does not exist.

Solution:

To prevent file not found errors, you can add error handling to check whether the file exists before attempting to access it:

bashCopy code

```
#!/bin/bash file="non_existent_file.txt" if [ -e "$file" ]; then cat "$file" else echo "File not found: $file" fi
```

Permission Denied Errors

Permission denied errors occur when a script or a command does not have the necessary permissions to access or modify a file or directory. These errors are common in scenarios where a script attempts to perform operations on protected files or directories.

Example: Permission Denied Error in Bash Script

bashCopy code

```
#!/bin/bash file="/etc/shadow" cat $file
```

In the Bash script above, the **cat** command attempts to read the contents of the **/etc/shadow** file, which typically requires superuser privileges.

Solution:

To avoid permission denied errors, you can run the script with elevated privileges or modify the script to access files and directories that are within the user's permissions.

Infinite Loops

Infinite loops occur when a script contains a loop that never terminates. These loops can consume system resources and lead to unresponsive scripts or system crashes.

Example: Infinite Loop in Python Script

pythonCopy code

```
#!/usr/bin/env python while True: print("This is an infinite loop")
```

In the Python script above, the **while True** condition always evaluates to true, resulting in an infinite loop.

Solution:

To prevent infinite loops, ensure that the loop condition eventually becomes false or add a break statement to exit the loop when a specific condition is met.

Null Value Errors

Null value errors occur when a script or a command attempts to use a variable that has not been initialized or contains no value (null or empty). Handling null values appropriately is important to avoid unexpected behavior.

Example: Null Value Error in Bash Script

bashCopy code

```
#!/bin/bash unset my_variable echo "Value of my_variable: $my_variable"
```

In the Bash script above, the variable **my_variable** is unset, resulting in a null value when it is referenced in the **echo** command.

Solution:

To avoid null value errors, ensure that variables are initialized with appropriate values before using them in operations or commands.

Errors are an integral part of scripting, and learning how to identify and resolve them is essential for scriptwriters. By understanding common errors and their solutions, you can become a more proficient script developer and create reliable and efficient scripts. Additionally, testing and debugging skills are valuable assets in the world of scripting, helping you troubleshoot issues and improve your scripting capabilities.

Tips for Efficient CLI Usage

Efficiency is a key goal for command-line interface (CLI) users, as it allows them to perform tasks more quickly and effectively in the terminal environment. Next, we will explore a variety of tips and techniques to help users become more efficient when working with the CLI. These tips range from mastering keyboard shortcuts to using powerful commands and scripting.

1. Learn Keyboard Shortcuts

Mastering keyboard shortcuts can significantly boost your CLI efficiency. These shortcuts allow you to perform common tasks quickly, without the need to type out lengthy commands.

Example:

Ctrl + C: Interrupts the current command or process.

Ctrl + D: Exits the current shell session.

Ctrl + L: Clears the terminal screen.

Ctrl + A: Moves the cursor to the beginning of the line.

Ctrl + E: Moves the cursor to the end of the line.

Tab: Auto-completes commands and file paths.

2. Use Command History

Most CLI environments provide command history functionality that allows you to recall and reuse previous commands. This feature is invaluable for avoiding repetitive typing and minimizing errors.

Example:

Use the **Up Arrow** key to cycle through previous commands.

Use the **Ctrl + R** shortcut to search for and execute previously used commands by typing keywords.

3. Create Aliases

Aliases are custom shortcuts for commonly used commands or command combinations. They can save you time and keystrokes by providing concise alternatives to longer commands.

Example:

Create an alias for a frequently used command:

bashCopy code

alias ll= 'ls -l'

Use the alias in place of the full command:

bashCopy code

ll

4. Take Advantage of Wildcards

Wildcards are characters that represent one or more characters in file or directory names. They enable you to perform operations on multiple files or directories simultaneously.

Example:

Use the * wildcard to match multiple characters:

bashCopy code

rm *.txt

This command deletes all files with a **.txt** extension in the current directory.

Use the **?** wildcard to match a single character:

bashCopy code

ls file?.txt

This command lists files like **file1.txt**, **file2.txt**, etc.

5. Use Pipes and Redirection

Pipes (**|**) and redirection (**>**, **>>**, **<**) are powerful tools for manipulating and redirecting data between commands and files. They enable you to create complex data processing pipelines.

Example:

Pipe the output of one command as input to another:

bashCopy code

cat data.txt | grep "pattern"

Redirect command output to a file:

bashCopy code

ls > filelist.txt

6. Combine Commands

You can combine multiple commands on a single line by separating them with **&&** or **;**. This allows you to execute a series of commands sequentially or conditionally.

Example:

Run commands sequentially using **&&**:

bashCopy code

make build && make install

Run commands regardless of the success of previous ones using **;**:

bashCopy code

git commit -m "Commit message" ; git push

7. Use the Man Pages

The **man** command provides access to manual pages for commands and utilities. These pages offer detailed documentation, options, and usage examples for CLI tools.

Example:

View the manual page for the **ls** command:

bashCopy code

man ls

8. Leverage Shell Scripting

Shell scripting allows you to automate repetitive tasks and create custom tools tailored to your needs. By writing scripts, you can simplify complex operations and save time.

Example:

Create a Bash script to automate file backup:

bashCopy code

#!/bin/bash cp -r /source_dir /backup_dir

9. Use SSH for Remote Access

Secure Shell (SSH) is a secure protocol for remote access to remote servers. It enables you to execute commands on remote systems securely, making it a valuable tool for remote administration.

Example:

Connect to a remote server using SSH:

```bash
bashCopy code
ssh username@remote_server
```

10. Keep Software Updated

Regularly updating your CLI tools and software packages is essential for security and performance. Many CLI tools receive updates and bug fixes over time.

Example:

Update package repositories and install available updates:

```bash
bashCopy code
sudo apt update sudo apt upgrade
```

11. Practice and Explore

Efficiency in the CLI comes with practice and exploration. Don't be afraid to experiment with new commands, options, and techniques. Try solving real-world problems with the CLI to gain experience and confidence.

12. Use Online Resources

Online resources such as forums, blogs, and documentation are valuable sources of information for CLI users. They can provide solutions to specific problems and offer insights into best practices and advanced techniques. Efficiency in the CLI is a valuable skill that can save you time and effort when working in a terminal environment. By mastering keyboard shortcuts, using command history, creating aliases, and leveraging various CLI features, you can become a more efficient and productive CLI user. Continuously expanding your CLI knowledge and exploring new tools and techniques will further enhance your proficiency in the command-line world.

BOOK 2
KALI LINUX CLI BOSS
ADVANCED TECHNIQUES AND TRICKS

ROB BOTWRIGHT

Chapter 1: Beyond the Basics: Advanced Command Line Fundamentals

As you advance in your command-line journey, you'll discover that mastering advanced command-line syntax is essential for effectively using the terminal and accomplishing complex tasks. Next, we will delve into advanced command-line syntax, exploring features like command substitution, environment variables, conditional execution, and more.

Command Substitution

Command substitution is a powerful feature that allows you to embed the output of one command into another. You can use command substitution to pass the result of one command as an argument to another, making your commands more dynamic.

Example:

Use the backticks (`) or **$()** to substitute the output of a command into another command:

bashCopy code

```
current_date=$(date +%Y-%m-%d) echo "Today's date is $current_date"
```

In this example, the **date** command's output, which is the current date in the specified format, is stored in the **current_date** variable and then used in the **echo** command.

Variable Expansion

Variable expansion is a feature that allows you to access the values of environment variables and user-defined variables within your commands.

Example:

Access the value of an environment variable using the **$** symbol:

bashCopy code

```
echo "Your home directory is: $HOME"
```

This command prints the value of the **HOME** environment variable, which represents the user's home directory.

Conditional Execution

Conditional execution allows you to run commands based on the success or failure of previous commands. You can use conditional operators like **&&** and **||** to control the flow of execution.

Example:

Use **&&** to run a command only if the preceding command succeeds:

bashCopy code

```
make build && make install
```

This command will execute the **make install** command only if the **make build** command succeeds without errors.

Use **||** to run a command only if the preceding command fails:

bashCopy code

```
compile_code || echo "Compilation failed"
```

Here, the **echo** command will be executed if the **compile_code** command fails.

Redirecting Input and Output

Redirection is a powerful technique for controlling where the input comes from and where the output goes. You can redirect input from files, commands, or user input, and redirect output to files, devices, or other commands.

Example:

Redirect the output of a command to a file using **>**:

bashCopy code

```
ls > file_list.txt
```

This command redirects the list of files in the current directory to a file named **file_list.txt**.

Redirect the input of a command from a file using **<**:

bashCopy code

```
sort < unsorted_data.txt > sorted_data.txt
```

Here, the **sort** command reads data from the **unsorted_data.txt** file and writes the sorted output to **sorted_data.txt**.

Pipes and Filters

Pipes (|) and filters are powerful tools for processing and manipulating data in the command line. You can chain multiple commands together, passing the output of one command as input to the next.

Example:

Use pipes to filter and transform data:

bashCopy code

```
cat access_log.txt | grep "error" | sort | uniq -c
```

This command reads the **access_log.txt** file, searches for lines containing the word "error" using **grep**, sorts the lines, and then uses **uniq -c** to count the unique occurrences of each line.

Command-Line Arguments

Many command-line programs accept arguments or options that modify their behavior. You can pass arguments to a command when invoking it, allowing you to customize its actions.

Example:

Pass arguments to the **ls** command to customize its output:

bashCopy code

```
ls -l -a
```

In this command, **-l** and **-a** are command-line arguments that instruct **ls** to list files in long format and include hidden files.

Brace Expansion

Brace expansion is a feature that allows you to generate a list of strings based on a pattern defined within curly braces.

Example:

Use brace expansion to create a list of files with sequential numbers:

bashCopy code

```
touch file_{1..5}.txt
```

This command creates five files named **file_1.txt**, **file_2.txt**, and so on.

Command-Line Prompts

Command-line prompts are customizable and can provide valuable information to users. You can change the appearance and content of your shell prompt to include details like the current directory, user information, or git branch status.

Example:

Customize the Bash prompt by setting the **PS1** environment variable:

bashCopy code

PS1= "\u@\h:\w\$ "

This prompt displays the current user (**\u**), hostname (**\h**), current directory (**\w**), and a **$** symbol as the prompt.

Environment Variables

Environment variables are values that can be accessed by various programs and scripts. They provide information about the system, user preferences, and configuration settings.

Example:

Use the **PATH** environment variable to specify directories where the shell looks for executable files:

bashCopy code

export PATH= $PATH :/usr/local/bin

This command adds **/usr/local/bin** to the **PATH** variable, allowing the shell to find executables located in that directory.

Regular Expressions

Regular expressions (regex) are powerful patterns used for searching and matching text. They are commonly employed in commands like **grep**, **sed,** and **awk** for complex text manipulation.

Example:

Use regex with **grep** to search for email addresses in a file:

bashCopy code

grep -E "\b[A-Za-z0-9._%+-]+@[A-Za-z0-9.-]+\.[A-Za-z]{2,4}\b" contacts.txt

This command searches for email addresses that match the specified regex pattern.

Working with Remote Servers

The command line is a valuable tool for interacting with remote servers and systems. Commands like **ssh, scp,** and **rsync** allow you to securely access and manage remote resources.

Example:

Use **ssh** to connect to a remote server:

bashCopy code

ssh username@remote_server

This command establishes a secure shell session with the specified remote server.

Advanced command-line syntax opens up a world of possibilities for performing complex tasks, automating processes, and efficiently working in the terminal environment. By mastering features like command substitution, environment variables, redirection, pipes, and filters, you can become a more proficient command-line user. Continuously exploring and experimenting with these advanced techniques will enhance your command-line skills and enable you to tackle a wide range of tasks with confidence.

Command Line Shortcuts and Aliases

Efficiency in the command line is often a matter of knowing the right shortcuts and creating helpful aliases to streamline your workflow. Next, we'll explore various command line shortcuts and the use of aliases to make your command line experience more efficient and productive.

Command Line Shortcuts

Mastering command line shortcuts can significantly speed up your interaction with the terminal. These shortcuts are often a combination of keyboard keys that perform common tasks with ease.

1. Ctrl + C: Pressing Ctrl + C interrupts the currently running command or process, allowing you to regain control of the terminal.

2. Ctrl + D: Pressing Ctrl + D sends an end-of-file (EOF) character to the terminal, which can be used to exit the current shell session.

3. Ctrl + L: Ctrl + L clears the terminal screen, providing a clean workspace to work in.

4. Ctrl + A: Ctrl + A moves the cursor to the beginning of the current command line, making it easy to edit the command.

5. Ctrl + E: Ctrl + E moves the cursor to the end of the current command line.

6. Ctrl + U: Ctrl + U deletes the text from the cursor position to the beginning of the line.

7. Ctrl + K: Ctrl + K deletes the text from the cursor position to the end of the line.

8. Ctrl + W: Ctrl + W deletes the word to the left of the cursor position.

9. Ctrl + R: Ctrl + R initiates a reverse search for previously executed commands, making it easy to recall and reuse commands from history.

10. Tab Completion: Pressing the Tab key auto-completes commands, file names, and directory names, saving you from typing long paths and commands.

11. Up Arrow: Pressing the Up Arrow key allows you to cycle through previously executed commands, making it easy to recall and rerun commands.

12. !!: Typing **!!** and pressing Enter repeats the last executed command, which can be particularly handy for repeating commands with sudo privileges.

13. !$**: Typing **!$ and pressing Enter inserts the last argument from the previous command into the current command.

14. !<command>: Typing **!<command>** and pressing Enter repeats the last command that started with **<command>**.

Aliases

Aliases are custom shortcuts or abbreviations for frequently used commands. They allow you to create concise alternatives to long and complex commands, making your command line experience more efficient.

Creating Aliases

To create an alias, you can use the **alias** command followed by the alias name and the command or series of commands it represents. Here's a simple example:

bashCopy code

```
alias ll='ls -l'
```

In this example, we've created an alias named **ll** that stands for **ls -l**. Now, whenever you type **ll**, it will be equivalent to running **ls -l**.

Persistent Aliases

To make your aliases persistent across sessions, you can add them to your shell's configuration file. For example, in the Bash shell, you can add your aliases to the **~/.bashrc** file:

bashCopy code

```
echo "alias ll='ls -l'" >> ~/.bashrc
```

After adding the alias to your configuration file, it will be available every time you open a new terminal session.

Common Aliases

While you can create aliases for any command or combination of commands, there are some common aliases that users find particularly useful:

alias ls='ls --color=auto': Adds color to the **ls** command's output, making it easier to distinguish file types and permissions.

alias grep='grep --color=auto': Enables color highlighting for the **grep** command's output, making it easier to spot matches.

alias df='df -h': Displays disk usage in a human-readable format, which is easier to understand.

alias du='du -h': Shows the sizes of directories and files in a human-readable format.

alias rm='rm -i': Adds an interactive prompt to the **rm** command to confirm before deleting files.

alias cp='cp -i': Adds an interactive prompt to the **cp** command to confirm before overwriting files.

alias mv='mv -i': Adds an interactive prompt to the **mv** command to confirm before overwriting files.

alias vi='vim': Maps **vi** to the more feature-rich **vim** text editor.

Customizing Aliases

You can customize aliases to suit your preferences and workflow. For example, if you often work with a specific project directory, you can create an alias to navigate to it quickly:

bashCopy code

alias myproject='cd ~/projects/myproject'

With this alias, typing **myproject** in the terminal will take you directly to the **myproject** directory.

Managing Complex Commands

Aliases are particularly useful for managing complex or lengthy commands. For instance, if you frequently connect to a remote server using SSH with specific options and a key file, you can create an alias for it:

bashCopy code

alias   myserver='ssh   -i   ~/.ssh/my_keyfile.pem user@server.example.com'

Now, instead of typing the entire SSH command, you can simply use **myserver** to connect to the remote server.

Command line shortcuts and aliases are powerful tools for enhancing your productivity and efficiency when working in the terminal. By mastering shortcuts and creating custom aliases for frequently used commands, you can streamline your workflow and make your command line experience more pleasant and productive. Experiment with these techniques to find the shortcuts and aliases that work best for your specific needs and tasks.

Chapter 2: Shell Customization and Power Tips

Customizing Your Shell Prompt

The shell prompt, that unassuming text that waits for your commands in the terminal, may seem like a small detail in your command-line environment, but customizing it can significantly enhance your productivity and provide valuable information at a glance. Next, we'll explore the art of customizing your shell prompt to make it uniquely yours.

Understanding the Shell Prompt

Before diving into customization, let's take a moment to understand what the shell prompt is and its role in the command-line interface. The shell prompt is a text string that typically appears at the beginning of a command line in the terminal. It serves as an indicator, providing information about the current environment and waiting for user input.

By default, the shell prompt displays essential information like the username, hostname, and current directory. It often ends with a symbol (commonly $ for regular users and # for superusers) to indicate the user's privilege level (regular or superuser).

Why Customize Your Prompt?

Customizing your shell prompt goes beyond mere aesthetics. It allows you to tailor your command-line environment to your specific needs and workflow. Here are some compelling reasons to customize your prompt:

Efficiency: A well-crafted prompt can provide quick access to valuable information, reducing the need to run additional commands or queries.

Personalization: Your prompt can reflect your personality and preferences, making your command-line environment feel like your own.

Context Awareness: A customized prompt can show information about the current directory, version control status, or virtual environment, helping you stay aware of your surroundings.

Productivity: With the right customizations, you can save time and reduce cognitive load by having essential information readily available.

Basic Customization

Let's start with some basic customizations that can enhance your shell prompt's appearance and functionality. To customize your prompt, you'll typically work with the configuration file for your shell, such as **~/.bashrc** for the Bash shell or **~/.zshrc** for the Zsh shell.

1. Changing the Prompt Text

The simplest customization is changing the text of your prompt. You can set it to display whatever information you find most useful. Here's an example for Bash:

bashCopy code

```
PS1="MyCustomPrompt> "
```

This configuration will change the prompt to display "MyCustomPrompt> " instead of the default.

2. Adding Color

Adding color to your prompt can make it more visually appealing and convey information more effectively. Most shells support ANSI escape codes for color customization. For example, to make your prompt green:

bashCopy code

```
PS1="\[\e[32m\]MyCustomPrompt> \[\e[0m\]"
```

In this example, **\[\e[32m\]** sets the text color to green, and **\[\e[0m\]** resets it to the default color.

Advanced Customization

Beyond the basics, you can customize your shell prompt in more advanced ways, providing additional information and functionality.

1. Displaying Username and Hostname

You can include the username and hostname in your prompt to quickly identify your current session:

bashCopy code

```
PS1="\[\e[32m\]\u@\h \[\e[0m\]MyCustomPrompt> "
```

This configuration will display **username@hostname MyCustomPrompt>** in your prompt.

2. Showing the Current Directory

Including the current directory in your prompt helps you stay aware of your location:

bashCopy code

```
PS1="\[\e[32m\]\u@\h            \[\e[36m\]\w \[\e[0m\]MyCustomPrompt> "
```

With this setup, you'll see something like **username@hostname /path/to/current/directory MyCustomPrompt>** .

3. Version Control Integration

If you use version control systems like Git, you can display information about the current branch and its status in your prompt.

bashCopy code

```
PS1="\[\e[32m\]\u@\h            \[\e[36m\]\w \[\e[33m\]\$(git_branch)\[\e[31m\]\$(git_status) \[\e[0m\]MyCustomPrompt> "
```

In this example, **git_branch** and **git_status** are custom functions that fetch and display Git-related information.

4. Displaying the Date and Time

Including the date and time in your prompt can be useful for tracking when commands were executed.

bashCopy code

```
PS1="\[\e[32m\]\u@\h \[\e[36m\]\w \[\e[33m\]\D{%Y-%m-%d %H:%M:%S} \[\e[0m\]MyCustomPrompt> "
```

This configuration will show the current date and time in the prompt.

5. Virtual Environment Indicator

If you work with Python's virtual environments, you can display an indicator in your prompt to show which environment is active.

bashCopy code

```
PS1="\[\e[32m\]\u@\h                    \[\e[36m\]\w
\[\e[33m\]\$(python_venv) \[\e[0m\]MyCustomPrompt> "
```

Here, **python_venv** is a custom function that checks and displays the virtual environment if one is active.

Customizing your shell prompt is a powerful way to tailor your command-line environment to your preferences and workflow. By displaying essential information, integrating version control status, and adding personal touches, you can create a prompt that enhances your productivity and makes the command line more enjoyable. Experiment with different customizations to find the prompt configuration that works best for you and makes your command-line experience uniquely yours.

Advanced Shell Configuration

In the world of command-line interface (CLI) customization, advanced shell configuration is where you can truly fine-tune your environment to meet your unique needs and preferences. Next, we will explore the intricacies of advanced shell configuration, covering topics like environment variables, shell scripts, and interactive shells.

Environment Variables

Environment variables are an essential part of shell configuration, providing a way to store and access values that influence how commands and programs behave. They can be system-wide or user-specific, and they play a crucial role in customizing your CLI experience.

Setting environment variables can be done using the **export** command in Unix-like systems. For example:

bashCopy code

```
export MY_VARIABLE="This is a custom environment variable"
```

Once defined, you can access the value of **MY_VARIABLE** using the **$** symbol:

bashCopy code

```
echo $MY_VARIABLE
```

Environment variables are used for various purposes, such as configuring the behavior of command-line tools, defining system paths, and storing sensitive information like API keys.

Customizing Your Prompt with Environment Variables

As we explored in the previous chapter, you can use environment variables to customize your shell prompt. By setting environment variables for aspects like color, prompt text, or specific information display, you can create a highly personalized prompt.

For instance, you can define environment variables like:

bashCopy code

```
export        PS1_COLOR= "\[\e[32m\]"        export
PS1_USERNAME="\u"  export  PS1_HOSTNAME="\h"  export
PS1_CURRENT_DIR="\w" export PS1_PROMPT_SYMBOL=">"
```

Then, construct your customized prompt like this:

bashCopy code

```
PS1="$PS1_COLOR$PS1_USERNAME@$PS1_HOSTNAME
$PS1_COLOR$PS1_CURRENT_DIR $PS1_PROMPT_SYMBOL "
```

By using environment variables, you can easily switch between different prompt configurations or share them with others.

Shell Scripts

Shell scripts are an integral part of advanced shell configuration, allowing you to automate tasks, create custom functions, and organize your CLI workflow effectively. Shell scripts are text files containing a sequence of shell commands that are executed one after the other.

To create a simple shell script, you can use any text editor to write your commands. For example, let's create a script named **myscript.sh**:

bashCopy code

```bash
#!/bin/bash  echo "Hello, world!"
```

Here, **#!/bin/bash** is called a shebang line and specifies the shell interpreter to use. After creating the script, make it executable using the **chmod** command:

bashCopy code

```bash
chmod +x myscript.sh
```

Now, you can run the script like any other command:

bashCopy code

```bash
./myscript.sh
```

Shell scripts are versatile and can be used for various purposes, from automating system maintenance tasks to creating complex automation workflows.

Aliases vs. Functions

While aliases are a convenient way to create shortcuts for commands, shell functions offer more flexibility and functionality. Functions can accept arguments, perform complex operations, and interact with the shell environment.

Here's an example of a shell function that calculates the sum of two numbers:

bashCopy code

```bash
add() { result=$(( $1 + $2 )) echo "Sum: $result" }
```

You can call this function and provide arguments:

bashCopy code

```bash
add 5 7
```

The function will calculate the sum and display the result.

Functions are especially useful for creating reusable and modular pieces of code in your shell configuration.

Interactive vs. Non-Interactive Shells

Understanding the distinction between interactive and non-interactive shells is crucial for advanced shell configuration. An interactive shell is the one you use for direct interaction with the command line, where you can run commands and scripts, while a non-interactive shell is typically used for executing scripts or batch processing.

The behavior of your shell configuration can differ between these two types of shells. For example, when you launch a non-interactive shell to execute a script, it may not load certain configuration files or environment variables that are specific to interactive shells.

To account for these differences, you can add conditionals in your shell configuration files. For instance, in your **.bashrc** file, you can use:

bashCopy code

```
if [ -z "$PS1" ]; then  # This is a non-interactive shell  else  # This is an interactive shell  fi
```

This allows you to tailor your shell configuration to behave differently depending on whether it's an interactive or non-interactive shell.

Modular Shell Configuration

As you dive deeper into advanced shell configuration, your configuration files may become complex and difficult to manage. To address this, you can modularize your configuration by breaking it into smaller files or directories.

For example, you can create a directory called **~/.shell-config** and organize your custom scripts, functions, and environment variables within it. Then, source these files from your primary configuration file (e.g., **.bashrc** or **.zshrc**).

bashCopy code

```
# In .bashrc  for file in ~/.shell-config/*; do  source "$file"  done
```

This modular approach makes it easier to maintain and share your shell configuration and allows you to enable or disable specific components as needed.

Advanced Configuration Examples

Advanced shell configuration can lead to powerful enhancements in your CLI experience. Here are a few examples:

Dynamic Prompt: Create a shell function that generates a dynamic prompt based on your current Git branch, virtual environment, and system status.

Aliases for Common Tasks: Define aliases for complex or repetitive commands, making them easier to remember and use.

SSH Key Management: Develop scripts and functions for managing your SSH keys, automating the process of adding, removing, or listing keys.

Workspace Initialization: Write a script that sets up your development environment by creating project directories, initializing Git repositories, and activating virtual environments.

Custom Tab Completions: Extend the shell's tab completion functionality by creating custom completion scripts for your frequently used commands.

Advanced shell configuration is an exploration of the limitless possibilities for customizing your command-line environment. By mastering environment variables, shell scripts, functions, and understanding the differences between interactive and non-interactive shells, you can create a tailored CLI experience that boosts your productivity and aligns with your workflow. Remember that the key to advanced shell configuration is experimentation, learning, and constant refinement to optimize your shell for your specific needs.

Chapter 3: Advanced File System Manipulation

Working with Links and Mount Points
In the world of file systems and data management, links and mount points are powerful tools that allow you to organize and access your files and directories more efficiently. Next, we will delve into the concepts of symbolic links, hard links, and mount points, exploring their uses and advantages.

Symbolic Links
Symbolic links, often referred to as symlinks or soft links, are a type of reference to a file or directory. Unlike hard links, symbolic links are separate files that point to the target file or directory. They are created using the **ln** command with the **-s** option.

For example, to create a symbolic link named **mylink** that points to a file named **myfile.txt**, you can use the following command:

bashCopy code

ln -s myfile.txt mylink

Now, when you access **mylink**, it will transparently redirect you to **myfile.txt**.

One of the key advantages of symbolic links is their flexibility. They can span different file systems and even point to directories. However, if the target file or directory is deleted or moved, the symlink becomes a "dangling" link, pointing to nothing.

Hard Links
Hard links are a different type of reference to a file or directory. In contrast to symbolic links, hard links are multiple directory entries that refer to the same inode on the disk. This means that all hard links to a file or directory are essentially equivalent and refer to the same data on the storage device.

To create a hard link, you can use the **ln** command without the **-s** option. For example, to create a hard link named **myhardlink** for a file named **myfile.txt**, use the following command:
bashCopy code

ln myfile.txt myhardlink

Hard links are particularly useful when you want to create multiple references to the same data without consuming additional storage space. When all hard links to a file are deleted, the data is only released from disk when no references to it remain.

However, hard links come with limitations. They cannot reference directories or span different file systems. Additionally, if you delete the original file, its data is still accessible through any remaining hard links, but it becomes "orphaned" and may eventually be lost when all links are deleted.

Mount Points

Mount points are directories within a file system where other file systems are attached or "mounted." This allows you to access and manage multiple file systems as if they were part of a single directory tree.

For example, you might have a separate file system for your home directory, another for system files, and yet another for external storage devices. By mounting these file systems at specific directories within your primary file system, you can seamlessly access and manage data from multiple sources.

To create a mount point, simply create a directory within your file system. For instance, to create a mount point named **external** where an external storage device will be attached, use the **mkdir** command:
bashCopy code

mkdir external

Once the mount point is created, you can use the **mount** command to attach a file system to it. Assuming the external storage device is **/dev/sdb1**, you can mount it like this:

```bash
bashCopy code
mount /dev/sdb1 /path/to/external
```
Now, all the data on the external storage device is accessible via the **external** directory in your file system.

Mount points enable a variety of use cases, including managing removable media, configuring network shares, and separating data into different partitions or drives. They provide a unified way to access data from various sources without cluttering your root file system.

Unmounting File Systems

When you no longer need access to a mounted file system, you can unmount it using the **umount** command. For example, to unmount the external storage device from the **external** mount point, use:

```bash
bashCopy code
umount /path/to/external
```
Unmounting ensures that any changes made to the mounted file system are saved, and the file system is safely detached. In some cases, you may need superuser privileges (root) to unmount certain file systems.

File System Types and Mount Options

File systems can vary in type and structure, and mounting them often requires specifying the file system type and mount options. For example, you might mount a device with an ext4 file system using the following command:

```bash
bashCopy code
mount -t ext4 /dev/sdc1 /path/to/mount/point
```
Mount options can control various aspects of how a file system is mounted, such as read-write permissions, access control, and error handling. These options are typically specified with the **-o** flag followed by a comma-separated list of options.

For example, to mount an ext4 file system with read-only access, you can use:

```bash
bashCopy code
```

mount -t ext4 -o ro /dev/sdc1 /path/to/mount/point

Understanding the specific requirements of the file system and your use case is crucial for successful mounting.

Bind Mounts

Bind mounts are a type of mount point that allows you to map a directory from one location in your file system to another. This can be useful for creating alternative views of existing data or making data available in multiple locations without duplicating it.

To create a bind mount, use the **mount** command with the -- **bind** option. For example, to bind the **/data** directory to **/mnt/data**, use:

bashCopy code

mount -- bind /data /mnt/data

Now, any changes made in **/data** are reflected in **/mnt/data**, and vice versa.

Bind mounts are commonly used in containerization and virtualization technologies to share data between host and guest environments. They provide a flexible way to organize and access data within your file system.

Links and mount points are essential concepts in the world of file systems and data management, offering versatile ways to organize, access, and share data within your system. Symbolic links and hard links provide different approaches to referencing files and directories, each with its own advantages and limitations. Mount points enable you to manage multiple file systems as if they were part of a single directory tree, simplifying data access and organization. By understanding these concepts and how to use them effectively, you can optimize your data management and file system organization in your command-line environment.

File System Permissions and ACLs

File system permissions are a fundamental aspect of Unix-like operating systems, providing security and access control for files and directories. Next, we'll explore the concepts of file permissions and Access Control Lists (ACLs) and how they govern who can do what with your files and directories.

Understanding File Permissions

At the core of file permissions are three entities: the owner of the file, the group associated with the file, and others (everyone else). For each of these entities, there are three basic permissions:

Read (r): This permission allows reading or viewing the contents of a file or listing the contents of a directory.

Write (w): With write permission, you can modify the contents of a file or create, delete, and rename files within a directory.

Execute (x): Execute permission is essential for running programs, scripts, or changing into directories.

These permissions are represented as a series of nine characters, grouped into three sections:

The first three characters represent the owner's permissions.

The second three characters represent the group's permissions.

The last three characters represent the permissions for others.

For example, in the permission string "rw-r--r--":

The owner has read and write permissions.

The group has read-only permission.

Others have read-only permission.

To view the permissions of a file or directory, you can use the **ls -l** command. For instance:

bashCopy code

ls -l myfile.txt

Changing File Permissions

You can change file permissions using the **chmod** command. To grant read and write permissions to the owner of a file, you can use:

bashCopy code

chmod u+rw myfile.txt

Similarly, to remove execute permissions for others, you can do:

bashCopy code

```
chmod o-x myfile.txt
```

The **chmod** command allows you to specify permissions using symbolic notation (like the examples above) or numeric notation. In numeric notation, each permission is represented by a number:

Read (r) is represented by 4.

Write (w) is represented by 2.

Execute (x) is represented by 1.

To calculate the total permission value, simply add the numbers together. For example, read and write permissions (rw) have a value of 6 (4 for read + 2 for write).

Changing Ownership

Besides changing permissions, you can change the ownership of a file or directory using the **chown** command. For instance, to change the owner of a file to a user named "newowner," you can do:

bashCopy code

```
chown newowner myfile.txt
```

Changing ownership may require superuser (root) privileges, depending on the original owner and the destination user.

Understanding ACLs

While traditional Unix file permissions are powerful, they have limitations. They are based on a simple three-tiered model and do not easily support complex access control scenarios. This is where Access Control Lists (ACLs) come in.

ACLs extend the basic file permissions by allowing you to define fine-grained access rules for multiple users and groups. With ACLs, you can specify not only the owner, group, and others but also additional users and groups and their respective permissions.

Viewing ACLs

To view the ACLs of a file or directory, you can use the **getfacl** command. For example:

bashCopy code

getfacl myfile.txt

This command will display the ACL entries, showing the associated users or groups and their permissions.

Modifying ACLs

To modify ACLs, you can use the **setfacl** command. For example, to add read and write permissions for a user named "user1," you can do:

bashCopy code

setfacl -m u:user1:rw myfile.txt

To add read and execute permissions for a group named "group1," you can do:

bashCopy code

setfacl -m g:group1:rx myfile.txt

ACLs offer greater flexibility and granularity in access control. You can define specific permissions for specific users or groups without affecting the overall file permissions.

Default ACLs

Default ACLs extend the power of ACLs further. They allow you to define default ACLs for directories, ensuring that any new files or directories created within inherit these defaults.

To set a default ACL for a directory, you can use the **-d** option with the **setfacl** command. For example, to set a default ACL for a directory to allow read access to a group "sharedgroup" for all new files and subdirectories, you can do:

bashCopy code

setfacl -m d:g:sharedgroup:r /path/to/directory

Now, any files or directories created within "directory" will inherit this default ACL.

Combining Permissions and ACLs

File permissions and ACLs can coexist on a file or directory, providing a layered security model. When determining access,

106

the system evaluates both the traditional Unix permissions and the ACLs, granting access based on the most permissive setting. For example, if a file has read-only permissions for the owner but a specific ACL entry grants write access to a user, that user will be able to write to the file.

File system permissions and ACLs are vital tools for securing and controlling access to your files and directories in a Unix-like environment. Understanding the basics of file permissions, changing ownership, and using ACLs allows you to configure fine-grained access control and meet your specific security requirements. By combining traditional file permissions with ACLs, you can create a robust security framework that ensures data privacy and integrity in your command-line environment.

Chapter 4: Networking Mastery: Advanced Network Commands

Advanced Network Configuration
In the realm of advanced network configuration, you'll dive deeper into the intricacies of managing and fine-tuning your network settings. This chapter explores topics like network interfaces, routing, firewalls, and network services, providing you with the knowledge to optimize and secure your network connections.

Understanding Network Interfaces
Network interfaces, often referred to as NICs (Network Interface Cards), are the hardware components responsible for connecting your computer to a network. Each interface has a unique identifier known as a MAC (Media Access Control) address, which is used to identify devices on a local network.

To list the network interfaces on your system, you can use the **ifconfig** or **ip** command. For instance:

bashCopy code

```
ifconfig
```

Network interfaces are assigned names like "eth0," "wlan0," or "enp2s0," depending on your system and the type of interface (Ethernet, Wi-Fi, etc.).

Configuring Network Interfaces
Configuring network interfaces involves setting IP addresses, netmasks, and other parameters to enable communication on your network. The primary tool for configuring network interfaces in Unix-like systems is the **/etc/network/interfaces** file.

To edit this file, you can use a text editor like **nano** or **vim**:

bashCopy code

```
sudo nano /etc/network/interfaces
```

Within the file, you can specify the network interface configuration. For example, to configure a static IP address for an Ethernet interface "eth0," you can add:

bashCopy code

```
auto eth0 iface eth0 inet static address 192.168.1.2 netmask 255.255.255.0 gateway 192.168.1.1
```

After making changes, you can apply them by restarting the network service:

bashCopy code

```
sudo service networking restart
```

Routing and Gateways

Routing plays a crucial role in network configuration, determining how data packets are directed between different networks or subnets. A gateway is a device or server responsible for forwarding packets between your local network and external networks, like the internet.

To view the routing table on your system, you can use the **route** or **ip route** command:

bashCopy code

```
route -n
```

By default, your system uses a default gateway to route traffic outside your local network. You can configure the default gateway in the **/etc/network/interfaces** file, as shown in the previous section.

Additionally, you can add custom routes using the **ip route** command. For example, to add a route for the 10.0.0.0/24 subnet through a gateway with IP address 192.168.1.254, you can do:

bashCopy code

```
sudo ip route add 10.0.0.0/24 via 192.168.1.254
```

Firewall Configuration

Firewalls are essential for network security, allowing you to control incoming and outgoing network traffic. In Unix-like systems, the primary firewall tool is **iptables**.

To list the current firewall rules, you can use:

bashCopy code

```
sudo iptables -L
```

You can define rules to permit or deny specific types of traffic based on criteria like source or destination IP addresses, ports, and protocols.

For example, to allow incoming traffic on port 80 (HTTP), you can use:

bashCopy code

```
sudo iptables -A INPUT -p tcp --dport 80 -j ACCEPT
```

And to deny all incoming traffic except established connections:

bashCopy code

```
sudo iptables -A INPUT -m conntrack --ctstate RELATED,ESTABLISHED -j ACCEPT sudo iptables -A INPUT -j DROP
```

Remember to save your firewall rules to ensure they persist across reboots:

bashCopy code

```
sudo service iptables save
```

Network Services and Daemons

Network services and daemons are processes that run in the background, providing various network-related functionalities. Examples of network services include DNS (Domain Name System), DHCP (Dynamic Host Configuration Protocol), and NTP (Network Time Protocol).

You can manage network services using tools like **systemctl** or **service**. For instance, to start the SSH (Secure Shell) service, you can use:

bashCopy code

```
sudo systemctl start ssh
```

To enable it to start at boot:

bashCopy code

```
sudo systemctl enable ssh
```

Network Diagnostics and Troubleshooting

Advanced network configuration also involves diagnosing and troubleshooting network issues. Several command-line tools and utilities are available to help with this.

ping: Use **ping** to test network connectivity to a remote host. For example: **ping google.com**.

traceroute or **traceroute6**: These tools trace the route that packets take to reach a destination, showing the IP addresses of intermediate hops.

netstat: Use **netstat** to display network statistics and information about active network connections.

ss: Similar to **netstat**, **ss** provides socket statistics, including active connections.

tcpdump: This packet analyzer allows you to capture and analyze network traffic. For example: **sudo tcpdump -i eth0 port 80**.

nmap: Nmap is a powerful network scanning tool used for network discovery and security auditing. Be cautious when using it on networks you don't own or have permission to scan.

Advanced network configuration takes your networking skills to the next level, enabling you to fine-tune network interfaces, set up routing and gateways, configure firewalls, and manage network services. By understanding these concepts and mastering the associated commands and tools, you gain greater control over your network connections and the ability to troubleshoot and diagnose network issues effectively. Whether you're configuring a home network or managing a complex enterprise infrastructure, advanced network configuration skills are essential for maintaining a secure and efficient network environment.

Network Troubleshooting Tools
In the world of networking, issues can arise at any time, disrupting communication and causing frustration. When problems occur, it's essential to have a set of reliable network

troubleshooting tools at your disposal to diagnose and resolve these issues efficiently. This chapter explores various command-line tools and utilities that can help you troubleshoot and maintain a healthy network environment.

ping

One of the most fundamental network troubleshooting tools is "ping." The "ping" command sends ICMP (Internet Control Message Protocol) echo requests to a target host and waits for a response. This tool is used to test basic network connectivity and measure response times.

To use "ping," simply open your terminal and type:

bashCopy code

```
ping example.com
```

Replace "example.com" with the domain or IP address you want to test. "Ping" will display information about the packets sent and received, as well as the round-trip time in milliseconds.

traceroute/tracert

"traceroute" (on Unix-like systems) or "tracert" (on Windows) is a tool that traces the route packets take to reach a destination. It displays a list of intermediate hops along with their IP addresses and response times. This information can help you identify network congestion or routing issues.

To use "traceroute" on Unix-like systems:

bashCopy code

```
traceroute example.com
```

On Windows with "tracert":

bashCopy code

```
tracert example.com
```

netstat

"netstat" (network statistics) is a versatile tool that provides information about network connections, routing tables, interface statistics, masquerade connections, and multicast memberships. It allows you to examine active network connections and troubleshoot issues related to ports and services.

To view a list of active network connections and their associated processes, run:

bashCopy code

```
netstat -tuln
```

This command displays open ports, both listening and established connections, and the process IDs associated with each connection.

ss

"ss" (socket statistics) is an alternative to "netstat" that provides socket-level information about network connections. It is considered more efficient and feature-rich than "netstat."

To display listening TCP ports and their states using "ss," you can use:

bashCopy code

```
ss -tuln
```

"ss" is particularly useful for detailed socket analysis and monitoring.

tcpdump

"tcpdump" is a packet analyzer that captures network traffic in real-time. It allows you to examine packets passing through a network interface, making it invaluable for diagnosing network issues and security analysis.

To capture all network traffic on a specific interface (e.g., eth0) and save it to a file called "capture.pcap," use:

bashCopy code

```
sudo tcpdump -i eth0 -w capture.pcap
```

After capturing data, you can analyze it further with tools like Wireshark.

nmap

"Nmap" (Network Mapper) is a powerful open-source network scanning tool used for network discovery, security auditing, and vulnerability assessment. It scans a target network and provides information about open ports, services, and potential security weaknesses.

To scan a target host and display open ports and services, use:
bashCopy code

nmap example.com

"Nmap" offers a wide range of scanning options and scripts for in-depth network reconnaissance.

Wireshark

"Wireshark" is a graphical network protocol analyzer that allows you to capture and dissect network packets. It provides a comprehensive view of network traffic and is invaluable for diagnosing complex network issues.

To start capturing packets using "Wireshark," open the application, select your network interface, and click "Start." You can then analyze the captured packets in real-time or save them for later analysis.

iperf

"iperf" is a tool for measuring network bandwidth and performance. It allows you to test the throughput and quality of a network connection by sending data between two hosts.

To perform a simple bandwidth test between a client and a server, you can run "iperf" as follows:

On the server:
bashCopy code

iperf -s

On the client:
bashCopy code

iperf -c server_ip_address

Replace "server_ip_address" with the actual IP address of the server. "Iperf" can provide valuable insights into network performance and help identify bottlenecks.

dig/nslookup

Both "dig" (Domain Information Groper) and "nslookup" are DNS (Domain Name System) troubleshooting tools. They allow you to query DNS servers for information about domain names and IP addresses.

To perform a DNS query using "dig," use:

bashCopy code

```
dig example.com
```

For "nslookup," simply type:

bashCopy code

```
nslookup example.com
```

These tools provide DNS-related information, including domain records and IP address resolutions.

sshdump

"sshdump" is a utility for monitoring and analyzing SSH (Secure Shell) traffic. It captures and decodes SSH packets, making it useful for troubleshooting SSH connectivity issues and security analysis.

To capture SSH traffic on a specific interface, you can use:

bashCopy code

```
sudo sshdump -i eth0
```

Effective network troubleshooting is essential for maintaining a stable and secure network environment. By familiarizing yourself with these command-line network troubleshooting tools, you can diagnose and resolve a wide range of network issues, from basic connectivity problems to advanced security threats. Whether you're a network administrator or a curious enthusiast, having these tools in your arsenal is invaluable for keeping your network running smoothly.

Chapter 5: User and Group Management Mastery

Advanced User Account Management

In the realm of system administration, managing user accounts is a fundamental and ongoing task. As systems grow in complexity and user populations expand, the need for advanced user account management techniques becomes evident. This chapter delves into advanced aspects of user account management in Unix-like operating systems, exploring user groups, permissions, authentication mechanisms, and security considerations.

User Groups

User groups are a vital component of user account management. Groups allow you to organize users with similar privileges and simplify access control. In Unix-like systems, every user belongs to one or more groups.

To create a new group, you can use the **groupadd** command:

bashCopy code

```
sudo groupadd mygroup
```

To add a user to a group, use the **usermod** command:

bashCopy code

```
sudo usermod -aG mygroup username
```

This command adds the user "username" to the group "mygroup." Groups can be used for permissions, allowing you to grant access to specific files or directories to members of a group.

File Permissions and Groups

Advanced user account management often involves dealing with file permissions and ownership. Unix-like systems use a combination of user ownership and group ownership to control access to files and directories.

To change the group ownership of a file or directory, use the **chown** command:

bashCopy code

sudo chown :mygroup myfile.txt

This command assigns the group "mygroup" as the group owner of "myfile.txt."

You can also change the group ownership of a directory and its contents recursively:

bashCopy code

sudo chown -R :mygroup mydirectory

This recursively changes the group ownership of all files and subdirectories within "mydirectory" to "mygroup."

To set the default group for new files created in a directory, use the **setfacl** command:

bashCopy code

setfacl -d -m group:mygroup:rw mydirectory

This command sets the default group for new files within "mydirectory" to "mygroup" with read and write permissions.

Authentication Mechanisms

Advanced user account management also involves considering various authentication mechanisms. Unix-like systems offer multiple ways to authenticate users, including traditional password authentication, public key authentication, and more.

Public key authentication is a robust and secure authentication method. It involves creating a pair of cryptographic keys: a private key and a public key. The public key is placed on the server, while the private key remains on the client. Users can log in without needing to enter their password, as the server verifies the client's authenticity using the private key.

To generate an SSH key pair for user authentication, use the **ssh-keygen** command:

bashCopy code

ssh-keygen -t rsa -b 4096

This command generates an RSA key pair with a bit length of 4096.

Once the keys are generated, you can copy the public key to the server's **~/.ssh/authorized_keys** file:

bashCopy code

ssh-copy-id username@remote_server

This command adds your public key to the remote server's authorized keys list, allowing passwordless authentication.

User Account Security

Security is a top priority in advanced user account management. Ensuring that user accounts are properly secured and monitored is crucial in preventing unauthorized access and data breaches.

Enforcing strong password policies is a fundamental security measure. You can configure password policies using the **pam_pwquality** module on Unix-like systems.

To configure password policies, edit the **/etc/security/pwquality.conf** file:

bashCopy code

sudo nano /etc/security/pwquality.conf

Here, you can set password complexity requirements, such as minimum length, character classes, and more.

Additionally, you can configure password expiration and account locking policies in the **/etc/security/pwexpire.conf** file.

Account locking can be useful in preventing brute-force attacks. To lock a user's account, you can use the **passwd** command with the **-l** option:

bashCopy code

sudo passwd -l username

This command locks the user account, preventing login with a password. To unlock the account, use the **passwd** command with the **-u** option:

bashCopy code

sudo passwd -u username

Regularly auditing user accounts is another security measure. You can review the **/etc/passwd** and **/etc/shadow** files to ensure that all user accounts are valid and up-to-date. Look for accounts that are no longer needed or have incorrect settings.

User Account Cleanup

Cleaning up user accounts is essential to maintain system security and efficiency. As users come and go, you need to remove accounts that are no longer in use or needed.

To remove a user account, including the user's home directory and files, you can use the **userdel** command with the **-r** option:

bashCopy code

```
sudo userdel -r username
```

This command deletes the user account "username" and removes all associated files.

Before removing a user account, be sure to back up any essential data, as this action is irreversible.

Advanced user account management is a critical aspect of system administration. Managing user groups, configuring file permissions and authentication mechanisms, enforcing security policies, and performing regular account cleanup are essential tasks for maintaining a secure and efficient system. By mastering these advanced techniques, you can effectively manage user accounts in complex Unix-like environments, ensuring the security and stability of your systems.

Group Administration and Policies

In the world of system administration, managing user groups is a fundamental task that plays a crucial role in access control and permissions. As systems grow and evolve, it becomes increasingly important to implement effective group administration and policies to maintain order and security. This chapter delves into the advanced aspects of group management in Unix-like operating systems, exploring group policies, group creation, modification, and troubleshooting.

Understanding Group Policies

Group policies define the rules and guidelines that govern how groups are used and managed within an organization or system. They establish standards for group naming conventions, group membership, and access control. Establishing clear and well-documented group policies is essential for maintaining a structured and secure environment. Group policies typically dictate the following aspects:

Group Naming Conventions: Defining naming conventions for groups helps ensure consistency and clarity in group names. For example, groups for finance personnel might be named "finance-group" or "accounting-team."

Group Membership Criteria: Group policies should specify the criteria for adding or removing users from groups. This could be based on roles, departments, or specific job functions.

Access Control: Clearly defined policies should outline the level of access that each group is granted. For example, an "administrators" group may have full system access, while an "employees" group may have limited access.

Group Creation and Modification: Policies should detail the process for creating new groups, modifying existing groups, and retiring obsolete ones.

Documentation: Effective documentation of group policies ensures that administrators and users understand the rules and guidelines governing group management.

Creating and Modifying Groups

Creating and modifying groups is a routine task in Unix-like operating systems, and it's essential to follow established group policies during these processes.

To create a new group, you can use the **groupadd** command:

bashCopy code

```
sudo groupadd mygroup
```

This command creates a new group named "mygroup."

To add or remove users from a group, use the **usermod** command:

bashCopy code

sudo usermod -aG mygroup username

This command adds the user "username" to the group "mygroup."

To modify group properties, such as the group name, you can use the **groupmod** command:

bashCopy code

sudo groupmod -n newgroupname oldgroupname

This command renames the group from "oldgroupname" to "newgroupname."

Group Troubleshooting

Group troubleshooting is a skill that every system administrator should possess. It involves identifying and resolving issues related to group membership, permissions, and access control. Common group troubleshooting scenarios include:

User Not in the Correct Group: If a user reports that they don't have access to a specific resource, check their group membership to ensure they are in the correct group.

File or Directory Permissions: Verify that the file or directory in question has the appropriate group ownership and permissions to grant access to group members.

Access Denied: If a user is experiencing access denied errors, investigate the group permissions on the resource and verify that the user is a member of the required group.

Group Name Conflicts: Ensure that group names do not conflict with system groups or other user groups, as this can lead to unexpected behavior.

Group Membership Synchronization: Check that group membership changes are synchronized properly across all systems, especially in a networked environment.

Group Policies in Action

Implementing group policies in practice requires a combination of user management tools and careful planning.

For example, imagine a scenario in which an organization wants to ensure that only authorized members of the "dev-team" group can access a development server.

The group policy would dictate that only users explicitly added to the "dev-team" group are allowed access.

To achieve this, administrators would:

Create the "dev-team" group using the **groupadd** command.

Add authorized users to the "dev-team" group using the **usermod** command.

Configure the server to grant access to members of the "dev-team" group by adjusting its permissions and access control settings.

Regularly review group membership to remove users who no longer need access or add new members as necessary.

By following these steps and adhering to the established group policies, the organization can maintain a secure and controlled environment for its development team.

Effective group administration and policies are vital for managing user access, permissions, and security in Unix-like operating systems. Well-defined group policies provide guidelines for naming conventions, group membership criteria, access control, and documentation. By creating and modifying groups in accordance with these policies and troubleshooting group-related issues, system administrators can ensure a secure and well-organized environment. Group policies, when put into action, help organizations maintain control over user access and permissions while enhancing system security and efficiency.

Chapter 6: Advanced Package Management and Repository Handling

Managing Software Repositories

In the realm of system administration and software management, the concept of software repositories plays a pivotal role. Software repositories are central hubs that store and distribute software packages, ensuring the availability, consistency, and security of software installations. This chapter delves into the intricacies of managing software repositories on Unix-like operating systems, exploring repository types, configuration, maintenance, and troubleshooting.

Understanding Software Repositories

A software repository, often referred to as a repo, is a collection of software packages, metadata, and configuration files that enable users and administrators to install, update, and maintain software on a system. Repositories provide a centralized and organized way to distribute software packages and their dependencies.

Unix-like operating systems typically have multiple types of repositories:

Official Distribution Repositories: These repositories are maintained by the OS distribution's maintainers, such as Debian's APT repositories or Red Hat's YUM repositories.

Third-Party Repositories: Independent repositories created and maintained by third-party organizations or individuals. These often provide additional software not included in the official distribution.

Local Repositories: Repositories hosted on the local network, often used by organizations to control software distribution and ensure consistency across multiple systems.

Repository Configuration

To effectively manage software repositories, administrators must configure the system to access the desired repositories. The repository configuration involves specifying the repository URL, repository type, and repository signing keys.

For instance, in Debian-based systems, you can edit the **/etc/apt/sources.list** file to add official distribution repositories:

bashCopy code

```
sudo nano /etc/apt/sources.list
```

You would add lines like:

bashCopy code

```
deb http://archive.debian.org/debian/ stretch main deb-src http://archive.debian.org/debian/ stretch main
```

These lines configure the system to access the Debian stretch main repository.

In Red Hat-based systems, you would configure repositories in files located under **/etc/yum.repos.d/**.

To add a third-party repository, you often need to import the repository's GPG (GNU Privacy Guard) signing key:

bashCopy code

```
sudo rpm --import https://example.com/repo-signing-key.gpg
```

This command imports the GPG key from the specified URL.

Repository Maintenance

Regular maintenance of software repositories is crucial to ensure that software installations and updates proceed smoothly. Maintenance tasks include synchronizing repositories, refreshing metadata, and managing package dependencies.

To synchronize an APT repository, you can use the **apt-get update** command:

bashCopy code

```
sudo apt-get update
```

This command fetches the latest package information from the configured repositories.

In YUM-based systems, use the **yum makecache** command to refresh repository metadata:

bashCopy code

```
sudo yum makecache
```

Refreshing metadata is essential to obtain the latest package listings and verify package authenticity.

Managing package dependencies is another aspect of repository maintenance. When you install or update software, the package manager automatically resolves and installs dependencies from the configured repositories.

Troubleshooting Repositories

Troubleshooting software repositories is a common task for system administrators. Issues can arise due to various reasons, such as network problems, incorrect repository configurations, or missing repository signing keys.

Common repository troubleshooting steps include:

Checking Repository URLs: Ensure that repository URLs in configuration files are correct and accessible.

Verifying GPG Keys: Confirm that the repository's GPG signing key is correctly imported, ensuring the authenticity of packages.

Network Connectivity: Check for network issues, including firewalls or proxy settings that may block repository access.

Repository Mirrors: Consider using alternative repository mirrors if the primary mirror experiences issues.

Package Conflicts: Investigate and resolve package conflicts or dependencies that prevent software installation or updates.

Repository Compatibility: Ensure that repositories are compatible with your system's distribution version.

Repository Removal: If a repository is causing issues, consider removing it from the repository list and retesting.

Repository Security Considerations

Security is a paramount concern when managing software repositories. Compromised or malicious repositories can lead to the installation of compromised software packages, compromising system security.

To enhance repository security:

Use Official Repositories: Whenever possible, rely on official distribution repositories, which are maintained and audited for security.

Verify GPG Signatures: Always ensure that packages are signed with a trusted GPG key to verify their authenticity.

Repository Access Control: Limit access to your local repositories, using authentication and access control mechanisms to prevent unauthorized access.

Periodic Auditing: Regularly audit repository configurations and review the packages available in repositories to detect and address security issues.

Managing software repositories is a critical aspect of system administration and software management on Unix-like operating systems. Understanding the different types of repositories, configuring them, performing maintenance tasks, troubleshooting issues, and implementing security measures are essential skills for administrators. By effectively managing software repositories, administrators can ensure the availability, reliability, and security of software installations and updates, contributing to the stability and security of the overall system environment.

Package Customization and Building

In the realm of system administration and software management, there are instances where the need arises to customize software packages to meet specific requirements. These customizations can include adding or removing features, changing configuration options, or even creating entirely new packages. This chapter delves into the intricacies of package customization and building on Unix-like operating systems, exploring the process, tools, and best practices.

Understanding Package Customization

Package customization is the process of modifying a software package to tailor it to specific needs or preferences. Customization can range from simple adjustments to complex transformations, depending on the desired outcome.

Common scenarios where package customization is beneficial include:

Feature Removal: Removing unnecessary features from a package to reduce its size or minimize attack surface.

Configuration Tweaks: Modifying default configuration settings to align with system requirements or security policies.

Adding Patches: Applying patches or fixes to address specific issues or vulnerabilities in a package.

Rebranding: Customizing the branding or appearance of software to match an organization's identity.

Creating Variants: Building multiple versions of a package with different features or configurations to cater to various use cases.

Customization Process

The customization process typically involves several steps:

Package Extraction: The package is extracted to access its source code and files.

Configuration: Configuration files or build scripts are modified to apply desired changes.

Compilation: The package is recompiled to incorporate the modifications.

Testing: The customized package is tested to ensure it functions correctly and meets the desired objectives.

Packaging: The customized package is packaged into a new package format for distribution.

Repository Integration: If necessary, the customized package is integrated into a repository for deployment.

Customization Tools

To perform package customization, administrators can utilize various tools and utilities.

One common tool for customization is the package management system itself. Package management systems like APT (Advanced Package Tool) and YUM (Yellowdog Updater, Modified) provide mechanisms to build and customize packages from source code.

For instance, Debian-based systems offer the **dpkg-buildpackage** tool to build and customize Debian packages. On Red Hat-based systems, the **rpmbuild** command is used to build and customize RPM (Red Hat Package Manager) packages.

Additionally, administrators can use build automation tools like **autotools**, **CMake**, or **Makefile** to configure and compile packages.

Package Building Best Practices

Effective package customization requires adhering to best practices to ensure that the resulting packages are reliable, maintainable, and secure.

Documentation: Maintain thorough documentation of customization steps, configuration changes, and patches applied to the package.

Versioning: Use consistent versioning practices to differentiate customized packages from their original counterparts.

Patch Management: Keep track of patches applied to packages and ensure they are well-maintained and up to date.

Testing: Rigorously test customized packages to identify and address any issues or regressions introduced during customization.

Security Considerations: Maintain security awareness and regularly monitor security updates for both the original package and customizations.

Creating Custom Repositories

To manage customized packages effectively, administrators can create custom repositories. Custom repositories provide a centralized location to store and distribute customized packages, making it easier to manage and deploy them across multiple systems.

Creating a custom repository involves the following steps:

Package Building: Build and customize packages as needed.

Repository Structure: Organize the packages into a directory structure compatible with repository management tools.

Repository Configuration: Configure repository management tools such as **apt-ftparchive** or **createrepo** to generate repository metadata.

HTTP Server: Set up an HTTP server to serve the repository content to client systems.

Client Configuration: Configure client systems to access the custom repository by adding the repository URL to their package manager configuration.

Package customization and building are valuable skills for system administrators, enabling them to tailor software packages to specific requirements. Understanding the customization process, utilizing the right tools, and following best practices ensure that customized packages are reliable, maintainable, and secure. By creating custom repositories, administrators can efficiently manage and distribute customized packages, contributing to the flexibility and effectiveness of system administration on Unix-like operating systems.

Chapter 7: Process Control: Advanced Techniques and Monitoring Tools

Process Prioritization and Control

In the world of system administration, managing processes is a fundamental task that involves controlling and prioritizing the execution of various tasks and applications. Processes are individual instances of running programs, and ensuring they run efficiently and effectively is crucial for maintaining system performance and stability. This chapter delves into the intricacies of process prioritization and control on Unix-like operating systems, exploring the concepts, tools, and best practices.

Understanding Process Prioritization

Process prioritization is the practice of assigning priority levels to running processes to determine their access to system resources, such as CPU time and memory. It allows administrators to allocate resources appropriately, ensuring that critical processes receive the necessary attention while preventing resource contention.

In Unix-like systems, processes are assigned priority values known as "nice values." A lower nice value indicates higher priority, while a higher nice value means lower priority. Processes with higher priority values may be slowed down to ensure that other processes have access to resources.

Viewing Process Priorities

To view the priority of running processes, you can use the **ps** command with the **o** option:

bashCopy code

```
ps -eo pid, comm , nice
```

This command displays the process ID, command name, and nice value for all running processes.

To change the priority of a running process, you can use the **renice** command:

bashCopy code

renice -n 10 -p 1234

This command changes the nice value of the process with ID 1234 to 10, which lowers its priority.

Process Control

Process control involves managing the lifecycle of processes, including starting, stopping, pausing, and restarting them as needed. System administrators use various tools and commands to control processes effectively.

To start a new process, you can use the **command** command:

bashCopy code

command_name arguments

For example, to start the **top** command, you would simply enter:

bashCopy code

top

To stop a running process, you can use the **kill** command:

bashCopy code

kill PID

Where **PID** is the process ID of the process you want to terminate.

To pause a process, you can use the **kill** command with the **STOP** signal:

bashCopy code

kill -STOP PID

To resume a paused process, you can use the **kill** command with the **CONT** signal:

bashCopy code

kill -CONT PID

Process Prioritization Strategies

Effective process prioritization is essential to ensure that critical tasks receive the necessary resources. Several strategies can be employed to prioritize processes:

Priority Scheduling: Use the operating system's scheduler to assign priority levels to processes based on their importance and resource requirements.

Real-time Scheduling: Employ real-time scheduling policies to ensure that time-sensitive tasks are executed promptly without delays.

Process Grouping: Group related processes together and assign priorities to the entire group, ensuring that they collectively receive adequate resources.

Resource Limitation: Set resource limits for processes to prevent them from consuming excessive CPU time or memory.

Affinity Control: Assign processes to specific CPU cores or affinities to ensure that critical tasks are executed on dedicated resources.

Process Monitoring and Automation

Continuous monitoring of processes is essential to identify resource bottlenecks or potential issues. Administrators can employ various tools, such as **top**, **htop**, or process monitoring systems like **systemd**, to track the performance and resource utilization of running processes.

Automation plays a crucial role in process control and prioritization. Administrators can create scripts or use automation tools like **cron** to schedule tasks, manage processes, and adjust priorities based on predefined criteria or system conditions.

Process Control Best Practices

To effectively manage processes, administrators should follow best practices:

Resource Monitoring: Continuously monitor system resource usage to identify potential bottlenecks or performance issues.

Priority Assessment: Regularly assess the priority of processes to ensure that critical tasks are appropriately prioritized.

Automation: Implement automation scripts or tools to streamline process control and management tasks.

Resource Allocation: Allocate resources based on the importance and requirements of processes, considering CPU, memory, and disk usage.

Security Considerations: Be mindful of security implications when changing process priorities, as this can impact system stability and security.

Process prioritization and control are essential aspects of system administration on Unix-like operating systems. Managing processes efficiently ensures that critical tasks receive the necessary resources while maintaining system stability. Understanding process priorities, using the appropriate commands and tools, and following best practices contribute to effective process management and system performance.

Advanced Process Monitoring
In the realm of system administration, process monitoring is a critical task that involves tracking the performance, resource utilization, and behavior of running processes. Advanced process monitoring goes beyond the basics and provides deeper insights into the system's operation. This chapter delves into the intricacies of advanced process monitoring on Unix-like operating systems, exploring advanced tools, techniques, and best practices.

Advanced Process Monitoring Tools
While basic process monitoring tools like **top** and **ps** offer valuable insights into process behavior, advanced process monitoring often requires specialized tools that provide more in-depth information. Some of these advanced tools include:

htop: **htop** is an enhanced version of **top** that offers a more user-friendly interface with interactive features. It provides detailed information about system resources, CPU usage, memory consumption, and allows processes to be manipulated in real-time.

strace: **strace** is a powerful debugging tool that traces system calls and signals of running processes. It allows administrators to identify system calls made by processes, which is useful for troubleshooting and understanding application behavior.

iotop: **iotop** focuses on monitoring I/O (input/output) activity of processes. It helps identify processes that are reading or writing data to disks and provides insights into disk I/O performance.

nmon: **nmon** is a system performance monitoring tool that offers an extensive range of performance data, including CPU, memory, disk, and network statistics. It presents data in a highly readable format and is particularly useful for analyzing system performance trends over time.

strace: **strace** is a powerful debugging tool that traces system calls and signals of running processes. It allows administrators to identify system calls made by processes, which is useful for troubleshooting and understanding application behavior.

iotop: **iotop** focuses on monitoring I/O (input/output) activity of processes. It helps identify processes that are reading or writing data to disks and provides insights into disk I/O performance.

Resource Utilization Metrics

Advanced process monitoring often involves examining specific resource utilization metrics to identify performance bottlenecks. These metrics can include:

CPU Usage: Monitoring CPU usage helps identify processes that consume excessive CPU resources, causing system slowdowns. Tools like **htop** and **top** display CPU usage in real-time, making it easier to spot resource-intensive processes.

Memory Usage: Tracking memory usage is crucial to identify processes that consume excessive memory or cause memory leaks. Tools like **top** and **htop** provide memory usage statistics, including resident and virtual memory.

Disk I/O: Monitoring disk I/O activity with tools like **iotop** helps identify processes that read or write data to disk. High disk I/O can lead to disk bottlenecks and slow down overall system performance.

Network Activity: Examining network activity with tools like **netstat** or **iftop** helps identify processes that generate significant network traffic. This is crucial for troubleshooting network-related performance issues.

Process Tracing and Debugging

Advanced process monitoring often involves tracing and debugging processes to understand their behavior and diagnose issues. Tools like **strace** and **gdb** (GNU Debugger) provide powerful capabilities for this purpose.

strace allows administrators to trace system calls and signals made by a process. By examining the system calls, administrators can identify issues such as file access problems, socket communication errors, or resource contention.

gdb is a full-featured debugger that allows deep introspection of running processes. It can attach to a running process, inspect its memory, set breakpoints, and step through code execution. This is invaluable for diagnosing complex issues in software applications.

Custom Monitoring Scripts

For highly specialized monitoring needs, administrators can create custom monitoring scripts. These scripts can leverage system utilities and tools to collect specific performance data and trigger alerts or actions based on predefined conditions.

For example, a custom monitoring script could periodically check the free disk space and send an email notification when it falls below a certain threshold. Such scripts allow administrators to tailor monitoring to their unique requirements.

Best Practices in Advanced Process Monitoring

Effective advanced process monitoring relies on the following best practices:

Focus on Relevant Metrics: Concentrate on monitoring metrics that are relevant to your specific objectives and system performance goals.

Use Specialized Tools: Employ specialized monitoring tools when necessary to gather detailed and accurate performance data.

Automation: Automate monitoring tasks and create alerting mechanisms to detect abnormal behavior or resource exhaustion.

Resource Efficiency: Monitor the performance impact of monitoring tools themselves to ensure they don't consume excessive system resources.

Regular Review: Regularly review and analyze monitoring data to identify trends, anomalies, and potential issues.

Documentation: Maintain comprehensive documentation of monitoring procedures, including configuration settings and custom scripts.

Advanced process monitoring is an essential aspect of system administration, enabling administrators to gain deeper insights into system behavior and performance. By using specialized tools, examining resource utilization metrics, tracing and debugging processes, creating custom monitoring scripts, and following best practices, administrators can effectively manage and optimize system performance. Advanced process monitoring empowers administrators to proactively address issues, ensure system stability, and maintain the overall health of Unix-like operating systems.

Chapter 8: Mastering Text Processing and Regular Expressions

Advanced Text Manipulation

In the realm of system administration and data processing, text manipulation plays a pivotal role in managing, analyzing, and transforming textual data. Advanced text manipulation techniques go beyond basic text editing and enable administrators to perform complex tasks, such as parsing log files, extracting specific information, and automating data processing. This chapter delves into the intricacies of advanced text manipulation on Unix-like operating systems, exploring powerful tools, regular expressions, and best practices.

Text Manipulation Tools

Unix-like operating systems provide a wealth of text manipulation tools that empower administrators to manipulate text efficiently. Some of the most commonly used tools include:

sed (Stream Editor): sed is a powerful command-line utility that allows administrators to perform text transformations on an input stream. It can be used to find and replace text, delete lines, and perform various text editing tasks.

awk: awk is a versatile text processing tool that allows administrators to define patterns and actions for processing text files. It is particularly useful for extracting and manipulating structured data.

grep: grep is a text search utility that searches for patterns or regular expressions within text files. It is handy for locating specific data within log files or large text documents.

cut: cut is used to remove sections from each line of files. It is useful for extracting specific columns or fields from structured text data.

tr (Translate): tr is a simple utility for translating, deleting, or squeezing characters. It is often used for character-level substitutions.

paste: **paste** is used to merge lines from multiple files. It is helpful for combining data from different sources.

Regular Expressions

A key component of advanced text manipulation is the use of regular expressions. Regular expressions, often abbreviated as regex or regexp, are powerful patterns that define searches within text. They enable administrators to perform sophisticated searches, replacements, and extractions based on complex patterns.

For example, a regular expression pattern like **\d{3}-\d{2}-\d{4}** can be used to match Social Security numbers in a text document. Understanding regular expressions and their syntax is essential for advanced text manipulation.

Examples of Advanced Text Manipulation

Log File Parsing: Administrators often need to parse log files generated by various applications. Tools like **awk** and **grep** combined with regular expressions can extract specific data, such as error messages or timestamps, from these logs.

Data Extraction: When working with structured data, such as CSV files, **awk** is invaluable for extracting specific columns or fields. For instance, extracting the names and email addresses from a CSV file can be accomplished using **awk** with field delimiters.

Text Transformation: **sed** is commonly used for text transformation tasks. For instance, replacing all occurrences of a word with another word throughout a text document can be done with **sed**.

Data Cleaning: In data processing tasks, text data may contain inconsistencies or errors. Text manipulation tools can help clean and standardize data by removing unwanted characters, fixing formatting issues, and more.

Automating Data Processing Workflows: Combining text manipulation tools with shell scripting enables administrators to automate complex data processing workflows. For example, a shell script can process multiple log files, extract relevant information, and generate summary reports.

Best Practices in Advanced Text Manipulation

Use Regular Expressions Wisely: Regular expressions are powerful but can be complex. Use them judiciously and test thoroughly to ensure they match the intended patterns.

Document Your Work: When performing advanced text manipulation tasks, document the specific commands, regular expressions, and patterns used. This documentation is valuable for reproducing the process or sharing with colleagues.

Backup Data: Before performing extensive text manipulation, especially if it involves data removal or replacement, create backups of the original data. This precaution helps prevent data loss in case of mistakes.

Modularize and Reuse: Create reusable text manipulation scripts or functions to streamline future tasks. This approach saves time and ensures consistency.

Practice Regular Expression Skills: Regular expressions are a skill that improves with practice. Invest time in learning and mastering regex patterns to become proficient in advanced text manipulation.

Advanced text manipulation is a crucial skill for system administrators and data analysts. It empowers them to efficiently manage, analyze, and transform textual data using powerful tools and regular expressions. By mastering advanced text manipulation techniques, administrators can automate data processing workflows, extract valuable insights, and ensure data consistency and accuracy in Unix-like operating systems.

Regular Expressions in Depth

Regular expressions, often abbreviated as regex or regexp, are a versatile and powerful tool for text pattern matching and manipulation. They provide a way to define complex search patterns in text and are used extensively in various fields, including programming, system administration, data analysis, and text processing. Next, we will explore regular expressions in depth, covering their syntax, common use cases, and advanced techniques.

Syntax of Regular Expressions

Regular expressions consist of a combination of literal characters and special metacharacters that define a pattern to be matched within a text. Let's delve into the syntax elements commonly used in regular expressions:

Literal Characters: Literal characters, such as letters and digits, match themselves in the text. For example, the regular expression **abc** will match the string "abc" in the text.

Metacharacters: Metacharacters have special meanings and are used to define more complex patterns. Examples of metacharacters include **.** (dot), ***** (asterisk), **+** (plus), **?** (question mark), and many others.

Character Classes: Character classes, defined within square brackets **[ ]**, match any character from the set. For instance, **[aeiou]** matches any vowel, and **[0-9]** matches any digit.

Quantifiers: Quantifiers specify how many times a character or group should be repeated. Common quantifiers include ***** (zero or more), **+** (one or more), and **?** (zero or one).

Anchors: Anchors define the position in the text where a match should occur. **^** (caret) matches the beginning of a line, while **$** (dollar sign) matches the end of a line.

Grouping and Alternation: Parentheses **( )** are used to group expressions, and the pipe **|** symbol denotes alternation, allowing for multiple options. For example, **(cat|dog)** matches either "cat" or "dog."

Common Use Cases for Regular Expressions

Regular expressions find applications in a wide range of scenarios:

Text Search and Validation: Regular expressions are commonly used for searching text within files, validating user input (e.g., email addresses, phone numbers), and extracting specific data from documents.

Pattern Matching in Programming: Programming languages such as Python, Perl, and JavaScript incorporate regular expressions to facilitate advanced string manipulation and pattern matching.

Log Analysis: System administrators use regular expressions to parse log files, extract relevant information, and identify patterns indicating system issues or security breaches.

Data Extraction and Transformation: In data analysis and ETL (Extract, Transform, Load) processes, regular expressions help extract and transform data from various sources, such as web pages or spreadsheets.

Web Scraping: Web developers employ regular expressions to scrape data from websites by defining patterns that match specific content within HTML or XML documents.

Search and Replace: Text editors and IDEs often support regular expressions for performing complex search-and-replace operations within code or documents.

Advanced Regular Expression Techniques

Beyond the basics, advanced regular expression techniques enable more sophisticated text processing:

Non-Capturing Groups: Non-capturing groups **(?:)** allow grouping without capturing matched text. This is useful when you want to group expressions for quantification but don't need to extract the matched text.

Lookahead and Lookbehind Assertions: Lookahead assertions **(?=)** and lookbehind assertions **(?<=)** are used to define conditions that must be met before or after a match. For example, **x(?=y)** matches "x" only if it is followed by "y."

Backreferences: Backreferences allow you to refer to previously captured groups in the regex pattern. For instance, **(a|b)\1** matches "aa" or "bb," where **\1** refers to the first captured group.

Lazy (Non-Greedy) Matching: By default, quantifiers are greedy and match as much as possible. Adding a **?** after a quantifier, such as ***?** or **+?**, makes it lazy and match as little as possible.

Recursive Patterns: Some regex flavors support recursive patterns, enabling the matching of nested structures. This is particularly useful for parsing complex data formats like JSON or XML.

Best Practices for Using Regular Expressions

Effective use of regular expressions requires adhering to best practices:

Understand Your Data: Familiarize yourself with the data you're working with to create accurate and efficient regex patterns.

Test Thoroughly: Regular expressions can be complex, so thoroughly test them on various inputs to ensure they work as intended.

Optimize for Performance: Complex regex patterns can be resource-intensive. Optimize patterns for efficiency when working with large datasets or processing sensitive systems.

Use Comments: Many regex flavors support comments within patterns to enhance readability. Utilize comments to document the purpose of each part of your pattern.

Escape Metacharacters: When you want to match literal metacharacters, escape them with a backslash (e.g., **\.** matches a period). Regular expressions are a powerful tool for text pattern matching and manipulation, offering a versatile way to define complex patterns in text. By understanding their syntax, common use cases, and advanced techniques, administrators and developers can leverage regular expressions to perform a wide range of tasks efficiently and effectively. Regular expressions are a valuable asset in the toolkit of anyone dealing with textual data and text processing in Unix-like operating systems.

Chapter 9: Scripting Magic: Advanced Automation and Scripting Techniques

Advanced Scripting Languages and Tools

In the world of system administration, scripting is an indispensable skill that allows administrators to automate tasks, perform complex operations, and manage systems efficiently. While basic scripting languages like Bash provide a solid foundation, advanced scripting languages and tools take automation to the next level. This chapter explores the realm of advanced scripting, including languages like Python and Ruby, as well as specialized automation tools.

Advanced Scripting Languages

Python: Python is a versatile, high-level scripting language known for its simplicity and readability. It offers extensive standard libraries and third-party modules that make it suitable for a wide range of tasks, from system administration to web development and data analysis.

Ruby: Ruby Is an elegant and dynamic scripting language with a strong emphasis on simplicity and productivity. It is often used for web development (Ruby on Rails) and offers robust scripting capabilities for automation and system administration tasks.

Perl: Perl, the "Practical Extraction and Reporting Language," is renowned for its text-processing capabilities. It excels at parsing and manipulating text data, making it a favorite for log analysis, data transformation, and report generation.

Lua: Lua is a lightweight, embeddable scripting language often used in applications and games. While less common in system administration, it can be a valuable tool when integrated with other software.

JavaScript: JavaScript is a widely used scripting language for web development. Node.js extends its capabilities to server-side scripting, enabling administrators to build scalable, networked applications.

Key Features of Advanced Scripting Languages

Advanced scripting languages offer several key features that make them well-suited for system administration and automation:

Rich Libraries: These languages come with extensive libraries and modules, simplifying complex tasks such as network communication, file handling, and database interaction.

Cross-Platform Compatibility: Many advanced scripting languages are cross-platform, allowing scripts to run on different operating systems without modification.

Community and Ecosystem: Robust communities and ecosystems exist around these languages, providing access to a wealth of resources, packages, and documentation.

Versatility: Advanced scripting languages are versatile, capable of handling various tasks beyond system administration, including web development, data analysis, and machine learning.

Automation Tools

In addition to advanced scripting languages, several automation tools are specifically designed for system administration:

Ansible: Ansible is an open-source automation tool that focuses on configuration management, application deployment, and task automation. It uses simple YAML-based playbooks to define tasks and automation workflows.

Chef: Chef is a powerful automation platform that uses recipes and cookbooks to manage infrastructure as code. It is particularly useful for configuring and maintaining large-scale server environments.

Puppet: Puppet is an infrastructure-as-code tool that automates the provisioning, configuration, and management of servers. It uses a declarative language to define the desired state of systems.

SaltStack: SaltStack, often referred to as Salt, is a remote execution and configuration management tool. It is known for its speed and scalability, making it suitable for managing large server fleets.

Docker: Docker is a containerization platform that automates application deployment and management. It allows administrators to package applications and their dependencies into containers, ensuring consistent deployment across different environments.

Choosing the Right Tool or Language

Selecting the appropriate scripting language or automation tool depends on the specific needs of the task at hand:

Task Complexity: Consider the complexity of the task and whether a simple script or a full-fledged automation tool is required.

Existing Infrastructure: Evaluate the existing infrastructure and tools in use to ensure compatibility and integration.

Community and Support: Assess the availability of community support, documentation, and resources for the chosen tool or language.

Performance: Depending on the task, performance may be a critical factor in selecting the right tool or language.

Scalability: Consider whether the solution can scale to meet the needs of your environment, especially in larger or rapidly changing systems.

Best Practices in Advanced Scripting and Automation

To maximize the effectiveness of advanced scripting and automation, consider the following best practices:

Version Control: Use version control systems like Git to manage and track changes to your scripts and automation code.

Modularity: Break down scripts and automation workflows into modular components to promote reusability and maintainability.

Error Handling: Implement robust error handling to gracefully handle unexpected issues and failures.

Documentation: Document your scripts, automation processes, and code to facilitate collaboration and troubleshooting.

Testing: Thoroughly test scripts and automation workflows in a controlled environment before deploying them in production.

Security: Pay careful attention to security practices when creating automation scripts, especially when dealing with sensitive data or tasks.

Monitoring and Logging: Implement monitoring and logging in your automation to track its performance and detect potential issues.

Advanced scripting languages and automation tools are essential components of modern system administration, enabling administrators to automate tasks, manage infrastructure, and streamline operations. By choosing the right scripting language or tool for the job, following best practices, and staying updated with the evolving landscape of automation technologies, administrators can enhance their efficiency and effectiveness in managing complex systems and environments.

Scripting for System Automation

Scripting is a fundamental skill for system administrators, allowing them to automate repetitive tasks, manage configurations, and streamline system maintenance. Next, we explore the essential aspects of scripting for system automation, including its importance, scripting languages, and practical applications.

Scripting's Importance in System Administration

Scripting serves as a bridge between manual tasks and automated processes, providing system administrators with a means to simplify and expedite their work. Through scripting, administrators can create reusable solutions for various tasks, reducing the risk of errors and enhancing productivity.

Scripting Languages for System Automation

System administrators have a range of scripting languages to choose from, each with its strengths and applications. Let's explore some of the most commonly used scripting languages in system automation:

1. Bash Scripting: Bash, the Bourne Again Shell, is the default shell on many Unix-like systems. Bash scripting is ideal for automating tasks within the command-line environment, such as file manipulation, process management, and system configuration.

2. Python: Python is a versatile, high-level scripting language known for its readability and extensive standard library. System administrators often use Python for tasks like network automation, log analysis, and web server configuration.

3. PowerShell: PowerShell is a powerful scripting language developed by Microsoft for managing Windows systems. It offers seamless integration with Windows components and is suitable for automating Windows-specific tasks.

4. Ruby: Ruby is an elegant and dynamic scripting language known for its productivity and ease of use. System administrators may use Ruby for tasks like server provisioning and application deployment.

5. Perl: Perl, the "Practical Extraction and Reporting Language," excels at text processing and string manipulation. It is a preferred choice for log analysis, data transformation, and report generation.

6. Shell Scripting (other shells): Apart from Bash, other Unix-like shells, such as Zsh and Fish, offer scripting capabilities. System administrators may choose these shells based on personal preference and system requirements.

Practical Applications of Scripting in System Administration

Scripting plays a crucial role in system administration across a spectrum of practical applications:

1. Configuration Management: System administrators use scripts to automate the configuration of servers and workstations, ensuring consistency and adherence to desired configurations.

2. Backup and Recovery: Scripts automate backup processes, making it possible to schedule regular backups of critical data and streamline recovery procedures.

3. Log Analysis and Monitoring: Scripting facilitates the automated analysis of log files, enabling administrators to detect issues, generate reports, and receive alerts.

4. User Account Management: Tasks like creating, modifying, and deleting user accounts are automated through scripts, ensuring accurate user management.

5. Patch Management: Administrators use scripts to automate the installation of software patches and updates, reducing vulnerabilities and improving system security.

6. Task Scheduling: Scripting languages offer features for task scheduling, enabling the automation of routine maintenance and housekeeping tasks.

7. System Monitoring: Automation scripts can continuously monitor system performance and resource utilization, allowing administrators to take proactive measures.

Best Practices for Scripting in System Administration

To harness the power of scripting effectively in system administration, consider the following best practices:

1. Planning: Before writing scripts, plan the automation process carefully, defining objectives and expected outcomes.

2. Modularity: Break down scripts into modular components, making them easier to maintain and reuse.

3. Error Handling: Implement robust error handling in scripts to gracefully handle unexpected situations and failures.

4. Version Control: Use version control systems like Git to track changes and collaborate with others on script development.

5. Documentation: Document scripts thoroughly, including usage instructions and explanations of key components.

6. Testing: Test scripts thoroughly in controlled environments before deploying them in production.

7. Security: Pay attention to security considerations when scripting, especially when handling sensitive data and privileged operations.

Automation Tools and Frameworks

In addition to scripting languages, administrators can leverage automation tools and frameworks to streamline system administration tasks. Some popular automation tools include:

1. Ansible: Ansible is an open-source automation tool that simplifies configuration management, application deployment, and task automation. It uses YAML-based playbooks to define automation tasks.

2. Puppet: Puppet is an infrastructure-as-code tool designed for automated provisioning, configuration, and management of servers.

3. Chef: Chef is an automation platform that uses recipes and cookbooks to manage infrastructure as code, facilitating configuration management.

4. SaltStack: SaltStack, often referred to as Salt, is a remote execution and configuration management tool known for its speed and scalability.

5. Docker: Docker is a containerization platform that automates application deployment, making it easier to manage and scale applications.

Choosing the right automation tool or framework depends on specific requirements, such as the complexity of tasks, the existing infrastructure, and scalability needs.

Scripting is a cornerstone of system administration, empowering administrators to automate tasks, manage configurations, and improve overall system efficiency. By selecting the appropriate scripting language or automation tool, adhering to best practices, and staying informed about evolving technologies, system administrators can excel in their role and meet the challenges of modern IT environments.

Chapter 10: Troubleshooting and Debugging like a Pro

Advanced Debugging Techniques
Debugging is an essential skill for programmers and system administrators alike, allowing them to identify and resolve issues within software and systems. While basic debugging techniques are crucial, advanced debugging techniques provide additional tools and insights to tackle complex problems. Next, we delve into advanced debugging techniques that can help professionals in various technical fields effectively troubleshoot and resolve issues.

Understanding the Debugging Process
At its core, debugging is a systematic process of identifying and fixing errors or issues within a program or system. The process typically involves the following steps:

Reproduction: First, reproduce the issue to understand its scope and impact. This step often includes collecting relevant data and documenting the problem.

Isolation: Isolate the problematic component, whether it's a piece of code, a hardware component, or a system module. This helps narrow down the root cause of the issue.

Analysis: Analyze the isolated component, inspecting its behavior, data flow, and interactions with other components. Advanced debugging requires a deep understanding of the system and its components.

Testing and Validation: Develop test cases and validation procedures to confirm the presence of the issue and track its progression.

Hypothesis: Formulate hypotheses or theories about the root cause of the issue based on analysis and testing.

Experimentation: Conduct experiments to test hypotheses, gather more data, and validate assumptions.

Resolution: Once the root cause is identified, implement a solution to address the issue. This may involve code changes, system configuration adjustments, or hardware replacements.

Advanced Debugging Techniques

Advanced debugging techniques build upon the foundational process by incorporating additional tools, methods, and strategies:

Logging and Tracing: Implement extensive logging and tracing mechanisms within software or systems. Log files can provide valuable insights into the sequence of events, data values, and error messages leading up to an issue.

Profiling and Performance Analysis: Use profiling tools to measure the performance of software or systems. Profilers identify bottlenecks, memory leaks, and resource usage patterns, helping optimize performance.

Memory Analysis: Memory-related issues, such as leaks and corruption, can be challenging to identify. Advanced memory analysis tools can help detect and resolve these issues by monitoring memory usage and allocation.

Debugging Symbols: Debugging symbols are additional metadata included in compiled code to map machine code back to source code. These symbols enable advanced debuggers to provide more context during debugging sessions.

Remote Debugging: Debugging remote systems or distributed applications may require remote debugging tools and techniques. These tools allow developers to debug code running on remote servers or devices.

Dynamic Analysis: Dynamic analysis tools intercept code execution and modify it in real-time to observe behavior. This approach is valuable for understanding complex, runtime issues.

Static Analysis: Static analysis tools analyze source code or compiled binaries without executing them. These tools can identify potential issues, such as code vulnerabilities, even before execution.

Core Dumps: In Unix-like systems, core dumps capture the state of a crashed or misbehaving process. Analyzing core dumps can reveal the cause of application crashes.

Reverse Debugging: Reverse debugging allows developers to step backward through code execution, helping identify issues that occurred earlier in the program's lifecycle.

Fault Injection: In controlled environments, introduce faults or errors intentionally to observe how a system or application reacts. This technique can help uncover vulnerabilities and improve resilience.

Troubleshooting Complex Issues

Advanced debugging techniques are particularly useful when dealing with complex, elusive issues that evade conventional approaches. These issues may involve intricate interactions between software components, subtle timing-related problems, or race conditions.

To troubleshoot such issues effectively, consider the following strategies:

Replication: If possible, replicate the issue in a controlled environment to gain a deeper understanding of its behavior.

Regression Testing: Use regression testing to ensure that changes made during debugging do not introduce new issues.

Collaboration: Collaborate with colleagues, community forums, or support channels to tap into collective expertise.

Documentation: Keep detailed records of debugging steps, findings, and outcomes for reference and knowledge sharing.

Thorough Testing: Test the proposed solution thoroughly to confirm that it effectively resolves the issue without introducing unintended consequences.

Iterative Approach: Debugging often involves an iterative process of hypothesis, testing, and refinement. Be prepared to revisit earlier steps as new insights emerge.

Debugging in Various Domains

Advanced debugging techniques are applicable across a range of domains:

Software Development: Developers use advanced debugging to identify and fix software bugs, performance bottlenecks, and security vulnerabilities.

System Administration: System administrators rely on debugging to troubleshoot system failures, configuration issues, and network problems.

Embedded Systems: Debugging embedded systems involves specialized tools and techniques to diagnose issues in constrained environments.

Web Development: Web developers debug web applications to resolve issues related to frontend and backend code, database interactions, and network communication.

Data Analysis: Data analysts debug data processing pipelines and analytics scripts to ensure the accuracy and reliability of results.

Advanced debugging techniques are invaluable tools for professionals across various technical disciplines. They enable the identification and resolution of complex issues that may otherwise remain elusive. By mastering advanced debugging tools and strategies, professionals can enhance their troubleshooting capabilities and contribute to more robust and reliable systems and software.

Troubleshooting Complex Issues

In the realm of IT and technical support, troubleshooting complex issues is an art and science that demands a deep understanding of systems, analytical thinking, and patience. Complex issues can manifest in a multitude of ways, from elusive software bugs to intricate hardware failures, network anomalies, and beyond. Next, we embark on a journey into the world of troubleshooting complex issues, exploring strategies, techniques, and best practices that can help unravel even the most perplexing problems.

The Nature of Complex Issues

Complex issues are characterized by their multifaceted nature, often involving a web of interconnected components and dependencies. These issues may remain hidden until a critical moment, when they disrupt operations and challenge the expertise of IT professionals. The complexity can arise from various sources:

Interactions: Complex issues frequently result from interactions between different elements of a system, where the combined effect creates unexpected behaviors.

Dependencies: Systems often rely on numerous dependencies, such as libraries, services, and external components. When one of these dependencies behaves unexpectedly, it can cascade into complex problems.

Scale: In large-scale environments, issues can be magnified due to the sheer number of components and interactions. This complexity makes diagnosis and resolution more challenging.

Emergent Behavior: Complex issues can exhibit emergent behavior, where the outcome is not readily apparent from examining individual components.

Effective Troubleshooting Strategies

Effectively troubleshooting complex issues requires a structured and systematic approach. While each problem is unique, the following strategies can serve as a roadmap:

Define the Problem: Begin by clearly defining the problem, including its symptoms, impact on operations, and any recent changes or events that may have triggered it.

Reproduce the Issue: Attempt to reproduce the issue in a controlled environment. Reproduction helps validate the problem's existence and provides a consistent testing ground.

Isolate Components: Identify and isolate the components or systems involved in the issue. Determine which part of the infrastructure is affected and which remains unaffected.

Gather Data: Collect data, logs, and diagnostic information from relevant components. Comprehensive data gathering helps uncover patterns and anomalies.

Analyze Logs and Metrics: Scrutinize logs, metrics, and system outputs to identify patterns, errors, or deviations from expected behavior. Advanced analysis tools can assist in uncovering subtle issues.

Consider Interactions: Examine how different components interact with each other. A change in one area may have unintended consequences elsewhere.

Hypothesize: Formulate hypotheses about the root cause of the issue based on available data and analysis. Hypotheses guide the investigative process.

Experiment: Conduct experiments to test hypotheses and gather additional data. Experiments may involve changing configurations, isolating components, or applying patches.

Document Findings: Keep detailed records of findings, experiments, and outcomes. Documentation aids in knowledge sharing and prevents redundancy.

Collaborate: Engage with colleagues, experts, or online communities to seek insights and alternative perspectives. Collaboration can lead to breakthroughs.

Iterate: Be prepared for an iterative process, where each investigation cycle refines the understanding of the issue and narrows down possible causes.

Tools and Techniques

Effective troubleshooting often involves a range of tools and techniques tailored to the specific problem:

Packet Capture and Analysis: Network issues may require packet capture tools like Wireshark to examine network traffic and pinpoint anomalies.

Memory Analysis: Memory analysis tools can detect memory leaks, corruption, or excessive resource usage in software.

Log Analysis Tools: Log analysis tools like ELK Stack (Elasticsearch, Logstash, Kibana) help centralize and analyze log data.

Performance Profiling: Profiling tools identify performance bottlenecks in applications and systems.

Scripting and Automation: Automate data collection and analysis using scripts to expedite troubleshooting.

Reverse Engineering: In cases involving proprietary or closed-source components, reverse engineering techniques may be necessary to understand behavior.

Configuration Management: Configuration management tools help track and manage changes, aiding in identifying configuration-related issues.

Dealing with Emergencies

In some instances, complex issues may evolve into emergencies, where immediate action is necessary to minimize disruption. When faced with emergencies:

Stay Calm: Maintain composure and focus on identifying and mitigating the immediate impact.

Invoke Incident Response Plans: If available, follow incident response plans and procedures to address the emergency.

Communicate: Keep stakeholders informed about the situation, progress, and actions being taken.

Prioritize: Prioritize actions based on their impact on service availability and data integrity.

Documentation: Even in emergencies, document actions taken and their outcomes for post-incident analysis.

Post-Incident Analysis and Prevention

Once an issue is resolved, it is essential to conduct a post-incident analysis to understand its root cause fully. This analysis informs preventive measures to reduce the likelihood of recurrence.

Root Cause Analysis: Delve deep into the incident to identify the exact root cause. This may involve reviewing logs, conducting forensic analysis, and verifying hypotheses.

Corrective Actions: Implement corrective actions to address the root cause, whether it involves software patches, configuration changes, or process improvements.

Preventive Measures: Develop and implement preventive measures to reduce the likelihood of similar issues occurring in the future. This may include better monitoring, redundancy, and improved testing.

Documentation and Knowledge Sharing: Document the incident, its resolution, and preventive measures. Share this knowledge with the team to enhance collective expertise.

Troubleshooting complex issues is a demanding but rewarding endeavor that requires a blend of technical expertise, critical thinking, and persistence. With a structured approach, effective tools, and a commitment to continuous improvement, IT professionals can conquer even the most intricate challenges. In the ever-evolving landscape of technology, mastering the art of troubleshooting is a skill that remains indispensable.

BOOK 3
KALI LINUX CLI BOSS
EXPERT-LEVEL SCRIPTING AND AUTOMATION

ROB BOTWRIGHT

Chapter 1: Harnessing the Power of Scripting Languages

Introduction to Scripting Languages
Scripting languages are the backbone of automation and customization in the world of computing, enabling users to instruct computers to perform specific tasks through a series of commands. These languages have played a pivotal role in simplifying complex processes, improving productivity, and providing versatility in software development, system administration, and various other domains.

The Purpose of Scripting Languages
At their core, scripting languages are designed to automate repetitive or time-consuming tasks, allowing users to create efficient and tailored solutions to specific problems. Whether it's automating data processing, managing system configurations, or building web applications, scripting languages serve as a bridge between human intent and computer execution.

Scripting vs. Traditional Programming Languages
Scripting languages are often contrasted with traditional programming languages like C++, Java, or Python. While traditional languages are compiled into machine code before execution, scripting languages are typically interpreted line by line, making them more accessible and flexible for certain tasks.

Interpreted vs. Compiled
An interpreted language, such as Python or JavaScript, executes code directly from the source, which can be advantageous for rapid development and debugging. On the other hand, compiled languages like C or C++ translate code into machine-readable binary files, resulting in faster execution but longer development cycles.

Ease of Learning

One of the key advantages of scripting languages is their relatively low learning curve. Their syntax is often more forgiving, making them accessible to beginners and experienced programmers alike. This ease of learning has contributed to the popularity of scripting languages in fields such as web development and system administration.

Versatility

Scripting languages find applications across a wide spectrum of domains:

Web Development: Languages like JavaScript, PHP, and Ruby are essential for creating dynamic web applications and websites.

System Administration: Shell scripting languages like Bash automate system tasks, such as backups, software installations, and log analysis.

Data Analysis: Python and R are widely used for data analysis, machine learning, and statistical modeling.

Automation: Scripting languages are the backbone of automation frameworks like Ansible and Puppet, used for configuration management and provisioning.

Game Development: Lua is commonly used in the gaming industry for scripting game behavior and interactions.

Common Characteristics

While scripting languages can vary significantly in terms of syntax and purpose, they share some common characteristics:

Dynamic Typing: Scripting languages typically use dynamic typing, allowing variables to change types during runtime, which simplifies development but can introduce errors.

Garbage Collection: Many scripting languages include automatic memory management, simplifying memory allocation and reducing the risk of memory leaks.

High-Level Abstractions: Scripting languages often provide high-level abstractions that simplify complex tasks, such as working with data structures or handling file I/O.

Popular Scripting Languages

Numerous scripting languages have gained popularity over the years, each catering to specific needs and preferences:

Python: Known for its simplicity and versatility, Python is a favorite for web development, data analysis, and automation.

JavaScript: As the primary language for web browsers, JavaScript is essential for web development, enabling interactivity and dynamic content.

Ruby: Ruby's elegant syntax and focus on developer happiness have made it a popular choice for web development, especially with the Ruby on Rails framework.

Perl: Renowned for its text-processing capabilities, Perl is commonly used for tasks like log analysis, data transformation, and report generation.

PHP: PHP is a server-side scripting language widely used for web development, particularly for creating dynamic websites and web applications.

Lua: Lua's lightweight design and embeddability make it a preferred choice for scripting within video games and applications.

Shell Scripting (Bash, PowerShell): Shell scripting languages, such as Bash for Unix-like systems and PowerShell for Windows, are crucial for system administration and automation.

Scripting in Action

To illustrate the power of scripting languages, let's consider a common scenario: automating the process of renaming a batch of files with a specific naming convention. In Python, this task can be accomplished with the following script:

pythonCopy code

```
import os # Define the source directory and naming
convention source_directory = '/path/to/source/files'
naming_convention = 'file_prefix_{}.ext' # Iterate through files
in the source directory for index, filename in
enumerate(os.listdir(source_directory)): # Generate the new
```

filename based on the naming convention new_filename = naming_convention. format (index + 1) # Rename the file os.rename(os.path.join(source_directory, filename), os.path.join(source_directory, new_filename))

This Python script leverages the language's simplicity and the **os** module to automate a task that would be time-consuming if performed manually.

Scripting languages are invaluable tools in modern computing, offering automation, customization, and versatility in various domains. As you explore the world of scripting, you'll discover how these languages empower you to streamline processes, solve complex problems, and create innovative solutions. Whether you're a developer, system administrator, data analyst, or web designer, scripting languages are an essential part of your toolkit, enabling you to turn your ideas into reality with efficiency and ease.

Selecting the Right Scripting Language
Choosing the right scripting language is a critical decision that can significantly impact your ability to solve problems efficiently and effectively in the world of computing. The vast landscape of scripting languages offers a plethora of choices, each with its own strengths, weaknesses, and ideal use cases. To make an informed decision, it's essential to consider several factors and weigh the trade-offs associated with each scripting language.

Understanding Your Requirements
The first step in selecting the right scripting language is understanding your project's requirements and goals. Take the time to identify the specific tasks and challenges you need to address. Consider the following questions:
What is the nature of the project? Is it web development, data analysis, system administration, or something else?

Are there any existing technologies or frameworks that you must work with or integrate into your project?

What are the performance and scalability requirements?

Do you have a team with expertise in a particular language?

Programming Paradigm

Different scripting languages are designed to work within specific programming paradigms. Some languages are well-suited for procedural programming, where you define a series of steps to execute sequentially. Others excel at object-oriented programming, organizing code around objects and their interactions. Functional programming languages emphasize immutability and functions as first-class citizens.

Consider which programming paradigm aligns with your project's needs. For example, if you're developing a complex web application, a language with strong support for object-oriented programming might be a good fit. On the other hand, if you're working on data analysis tasks, a language that excels at functional programming could be advantageous.

Ecosystem and Libraries

The availability of libraries, frameworks, and third-party packages can greatly impact your productivity. A rich ecosystem provides pre-built solutions for common tasks, reducing the need to reinvent the wheel. Consider the availability and maturity of libraries in your chosen language for the specific domain you're working in.

For web development, languages like Python and JavaScript have extensive libraries and frameworks, such as Django, Flask, and React. If data science is your focus, Python's data science ecosystem, including libraries like NumPy, pandas, and scikit-learn, is unmatched. In the realm of system administration and automation, languages like Python and PowerShell offer powerful libraries and modules for various tasks.

Community and Support

The strength of a scripting language's community and support system can significantly impact your ability to overcome challenges. A vibrant community provides forums, tutorials, documentation, and a wealth of knowledge to tap into. Consider the size and engagement of the community around your chosen language.

Languages like Python and JavaScript have large and active communities, making it easy to find help, share experiences, and stay up-to-date with best practices. Smaller or specialized languages may have more niche communities, which can still be valuable if they align with your project's requirements.

Learning Curve

The learning curve associated with a scripting language is an important consideration, especially if you or your team are new to it. Some languages are known for their ease of learning, with simple and intuitive syntax. Others may require more time and effort to master.

Languages like Python and Ruby are often praised for their readability and learnability, making them accessible to beginners. In contrast, languages like C++ or Rust may have steeper learning curves due to their complex features and strict type systems.

Performance and Efficiency

The performance requirements of your project can influence your choice of scripting language. Some languages, like Python, are known for their simplicity and ease of use but may have performance limitations. Others, like C++ or Go, prioritize performance and efficiency but may require more development time.

Consider whether your project demands high performance, low latency, or efficient resource usage. In scenarios where milliseconds matter, a language with a strong emphasis on performance may be a better fit. However, for many projects, the perceived performance impact of the language may not be critical, and other factors may take precedence.

Portability and Compatibility

If your project needs to run on multiple platforms or integrate with existing systems, consider the portability and compatibility of your chosen scripting language. Some languages have excellent cross-platform support, making it easier to write code that works on different operating systems. Others may be more tightly coupled to specific platforms.

For example, Python is known for its portability and can run on various operating systems with minimal modifications. JavaScript, as the language of the web, enjoys broad compatibility across web browsers and platforms.

Scalability

Scalability is a crucial factor for projects that need to handle increasing workloads or user demands. Consider whether your chosen scripting language is well-suited for scaling your application or system.

Languages like Python have been used successfully in web applications and data analysis at scale. However, if your project's scalability requirements are exceptionally high, languages like Go or Erlang, known for their concurrency and parallelism support, may be more appropriate.

Security

Security is a paramount concern for any software project. Different scripting languages have varying levels of built-in security features and community practices. Consider the security requirements of your project and whether your chosen language aligns with best security practices.

Languages like Python and JavaScript have robust security communities and established practices for addressing common vulnerabilities. However, the security of your application ultimately depends on how you write and configure your code, regardless of the language.

Long-Term Viability

Think about the long-term viability of your chosen scripting language. Is it actively maintained, and does it have a clear roadmap for future development? Obsolete or unsupported

languages can pose risks as your project evolves and new challenges arise.
Languages like Python, JavaScript, and Ruby have demonstrated long-term viability and continue to evolve with the changing needs of the software development landscape. When considering a less-known language, assess its stability and the commitment of its community to ensure its relevance in the years to come.

Selecting the right scripting language is a crucial decision that can significantly impact the success of your project. By carefully considering your project's requirements, programming paradigms, ecosystems, communities, and other factors, you can make an informed choice that aligns with your goals and objectives. Remember that there is no one-size-fits-all answer, and the best scripting language for your project depends on your unique circumstances and priorities.

Chapter 2: Advanced Bash Scripting Techniques

Bash Script Optimization
Optimizing Bash scripts is a critical skill for any system administrator or developer who regularly works with Unix-like systems. Bash, the Bourne-Again Shell, is a powerful and versatile scripting language commonly used for automating tasks, managing system configurations, and processing data. While Bash is known for its simplicity and ease of use, inefficient or poorly optimized scripts can lead to performance bottlenecks, increased resource consumption, and maintenance challenges. Next, we explore strategies and techniques for optimizing Bash scripts to enhance their efficiency, reliability, and maintainability.

The Importance of Optimization
Before diving into optimization techniques, it's essential to understand why optimization matters. Optimized Bash scripts can significantly impact your system's performance, especially when dealing with repetitive or resource-intensive tasks. Some of the key reasons to prioritize optimization include:

Faster Execution: Well-optimized scripts run faster, reducing the time required to complete tasks.

Resource Efficiency: Efficient scripts consume fewer system resources, such as CPU and memory, making better use of available hardware.

Reduced Costs: Optimized scripts can lead to cost savings in cloud or server environments, where resource consumption directly affects expenses.

Improved Responsiveness: Responsive systems ensure smooth user experiences and reduce the risk of system downtime.

Enhanced Scalability: Optimized scripts scale better when faced with increasing workloads.

Easier Maintenance: Cleaner and more efficient code is easier to understand, maintain, and troubleshoot.

Optimization Techniques

Let's explore some optimization techniques that can help you get the most out of your Bash scripts:

Avoid Unnecessary Forks: Minimize the use of unnecessary subshells and external processes. Each fork (creating a new process) introduces overhead. Use variables and built-in Bash functions whenever possible.

Use Efficient Data Structures: Associative arrays (also known as dictionaries) introduced in Bash 4 provide efficient ways to store and manipulate data. Use them when managing structured data, as they can be faster than iterating through flat arrays.

Reduce Disk I/O: Minimize file read and write operations, as disk I/O is typically slower than in-memory operations. Store frequently accessed data in variables rather than repeatedly reading from files.

Batch Operations: When processing multiple files or data items, batch operations are more efficient than processing each item individually. Use loops and commands like **find** to operate on multiple items in a single pass.

Avoid Redundant Commands: Repeating the same command with identical arguments in a loop is inefficient. Store the command's output in a variable and use it within the loop.

Optimize Loops: Loop efficiency is crucial. Use **for** loops with the **in** clause for iterating over arrays or lists. Minimize the number of loops, especially nested ones.

Use Built-In Commands: Bash provides many built-in commands and features that are more efficient than external utilities. For example, use **read** to process text lines instead of using **sed** or **awk** for simple text manipulation.

Caching: Implement caching mechanisms when applicable to avoid redundant computations. Cached results can significantly reduce script execution time.

Parallelization: When processing large datasets or performing time-consuming tasks, consider parallelizing operations using tools like GNU Parallel or by running background processes.

Error Handling: Implement efficient error handling to avoid unnecessary resource consumption in case of failures. Use **trap** to clean up resources and ensure proper script termination.

Limit Resource Usage: Set resource limits using **ulimit** to prevent scripts from consuming excessive CPU, memory, or file handles.

Profile and Benchmark: Profile your scripts using tools like **time** and **bash -x** to identify performance bottlenecks. Benchmark different approaches to find the most efficient solutions.

Example of Optimization

To illustrate optimization techniques, let's consider a simple example: searching for a specific word in multiple text files and counting its occurrences. A basic Bash script to accomplish this task might look like this:

bashCopy code

```
#!/bin/bash search_word="example" file_list="file1.txt
file2.txt filc3.txt" for file in $file_list; do count=$(grep -o
"$search_word" "$file" | wc -l) echo "Occurrences of
'$search_word' in $file: $count" done
```

While this script achieves the desired outcome, it can be optimized for efficiency. Here's an optimized version:

bashCopy code

```
#!/bin/bash search_word="example" file_list="file1.txt
file2.txt file3.txt" for file in $file_list; do if [[ -f "$file" ]];
then count=0 while IFS= read -r line; do words=($line) for
word in "${words[@]}"; do if [[ "$word" == "$search_word"
]]; then ((count++)) fi done done < "$file" echo
"Occurrences of '$search_word' in $file: $count" else echo
"File $file does not exist." fi done
```

This optimized script avoids unnecessary external commands (**grep** and **wc**) and minimizes file I/O. It counts word occurrences directly within the script, resulting in improved performance, especially for a large number of files or large files.

Testing and Profiling

After optimizing your Bash scripts, it's crucial to test and profile them thoroughly. Ensure that the optimized version produces correct results and doesn't introduce new bugs. Use tools like **time** and **bash -x** to measure execution time and identify any remaining performance bottlenecks.

Bash script optimization is a valuable skill that can significantly enhance the performance and efficiency of your scripts. By following optimization techniques and continually refining your code, you can reduce resource consumption, decrease execution time, and improve the overall reliability and maintainability of your Bash scripts. Remember that optimization is an ongoing process, and as your scripts evolve and new requirements arise, there may be opportunities for further improvement.

Error Handling in Bash Scripts

Error handling is a critical aspect of writing robust and reliable Bash scripts. In the world of scripting, errors can occur for various reasons, including invalid input, file not found, permission issues, or unexpected failures. A well-designed error-handling mechanism ensures that your scripts gracefully handle these situations, providing informative feedback to users and preventing unexpected script termination.

Understanding Errors

Before delving into error handling, it's important to understand the types of errors that can occur in Bash scripts. Errors can broadly be categorized into two main types:

Syntax Errors: These errors occur when the script violates the syntax rules of the Bash language. Common syntax errors include missing semicolons, incorrect variable assignments, or mismatched quotes. Bash typically identifies and reports syntax errors during script execution, making them relatively easy to spot and fix.

Runtime Errors: Runtime errors occur while the script is executing and can result from various issues, such as invalid user input, missing files, or unexpected behavior of external commands. Handling runtime errors requires proactive measures in your script to detect and respond to these situations.

Detecting and Reporting Errors

In Bash, you can detect errors by examining the exit status (also known as the return code) of commands and operations. The exit status is a numeric value that indicates the success or failure of a command. By convention, an exit status of 0 signifies success, while any non-zero value indicates an error.

To check the exit status of a command, you can use the **$?** variable immediately after the command's execution. For example, consider a simple script that attempts to open a non-existent file and checks the exit status:

bashCopy code

```
#!/bin/bash file="nonexistent.txt" if [[ ! -f "$file" ]]; then
echo "Error: File '$file' not found." fi
```

In this script, the **[[! -f "$file"]]** condition checks if the file does not exist, and if so, it reports an error. However, handling errors in this manner is rudimentary and lacks sophistication.

Exit Codes

Commands in Bash return specific exit codes to convey the nature of the error. While the exact codes can vary between commands, it's common for a non-zero exit code to indicate an error, with specific codes representing different error conditions. For example, the **ls** command uses exit codes to indicate various errors, such as:

0: Success (no error)

1: General error (unspecified error)

2: Missing or invalid argument

126: Permission denied

127: Command not found

128: Invalid exit argument

130: Script terminated by interrupt (e.g., Ctrl+C)

By understanding exit codes, you can tailor your error-handling logic to respond to specific error conditions.

The set -e Option

Bash provides the **set -e** option, also known as the "errexit" option, which causes the script to exit immediately when any command returns a non-zero exit status. While this option can simplify error handling, it may also lead to unexpected script termination, especially when dealing with commands that return non-zero codes under normal circumstances.

For example, consider a script that checks if a directory exists and then removes it:

bashCopy code

```
#!/bin/bash directory="mydir" if [[ -d "$directory" ]]; then
rmdir "$directory" fi echo "Script completed."
```

With **set -e** enabled, if the directory does not exist, the **rmdir** command will return a non-zero exit code, causing the script to terminate abruptly. In such cases, it's important to use the **set +e** option to temporarily disable **errexit** for specific commands or sections of code where you expect non-zero exit codes.

Custom Error Messages

To provide meaningful feedback to users, it's essential to craft custom error messages that explain the nature of the error. Rather than relying solely on standard error messages generated by commands, you can use **echo** or **printf** statements to display informative messages to the user.

For example, consider a script that attempts to read a configuration file:

bashCopy code

```bash
#!/bin/bash config_file="config.conf" if [[ -f "$config_file" ]];
```
then # Process the configuration file echo "Configuration file
'$config_file' found and processed." else # Display a custom
error message echo "Error: Configuration file '$config_file' not
found." fi

Custom error messages not only enhance user experience but
also assist in troubleshooting and debugging.

Logging Errors

In addition to displaying error messages to the user, it's a good
practice to log errors to a file for future reference. Logging
errors helps you analyze issues, track patterns, and monitor
script behavior over time. You can use redirection (**>>**) to
append error messages to a log file within your script.

For example, a script that processes data might log errors like
this:

bashCopy code

```bash
#!/bin/bash data_file="data.txt" log_file="error.log" if [[ -f
```
"$data_file"]]; then # Process the data echo "Data
processing completed." else # Log the error and display a
custom message error_message="Error: Data file '$data_file'
not found." echo "$error_message" >> "$log_file" echo
"$error_message" fi

By maintaining a separate error log, you can review errors
systematically and ensure that critical issues do not go
unnoticed.

Handling Different Error Conditions

To handle different error conditions gracefully, you can use
conditional statements to branch your error-handling logic. For
example, you might want to take different actions based on
whether a file is missing or if a command fails due to a
permissions issue.

Consider a script that attempts to execute a command with
elevated privileges using **sudo**:

bashCopy code

```bash
#!/bin/bash command="some_command" # Attempt to
execute the command with sudo if sudo "$command"; then
echo "Command executed successfully." else # Check the exit
code to determine the cause of the error case $? in 1) echo
"Error: Insufficient privileges to run '$command'." ;; 127) echo
"Error: Command '$command' not found." ;; *) echo "Error:
An unspecified error occurred." ;; esac fi
```

In this script, we use a **case** statement to examine the exit code
of the **sudo** command and provide specific error messages
accordingly. This approach allows for fine-grained error
handling tailored to different error conditions.

Handling Errors in Functions

When writing Bash functions, it's essential to handle errors
within the function itself. Functions can use the **return**
statement to indicate success or failure, with the convention of
returning 0 for success and non-zero values for errors.

Consider a function that performs a file backup operation:
bashCopy code

```bash
#!/bin/bash backup_file() { local source_file="$1" local
destination_dir="$2" if [[ -f "$source_file" ]]; then # Perform
backup operation cp "$source_file" "$destination_dir"
return 0 # Success else echo "Error: Source file '$source_file'
not found." return 1 # Error fi } # Example usage of the
function                         source="important_file.txt"
destination="backup_dir/"      if      backup_file      "$source"
"$destination"; then echo "Backup completed successfully."
else echo "Backup failed." fi
```

In this example, the **backup_file** function returns a 0 exit status
on success and 1 on error, allowing the caller to handle the
outcome appropriately.

Effective error handling is a fundamental aspect of writing
reliable and user-friendly Bash scripts. By understanding the

types of errors, checking exit codes, crafting custom error messages, logging errors, and using conditional statements, you can create scripts that gracefully respond to unexpected situations. Well-designed error-handling mechanisms not only enhance the reliability of your scripts but also improve the overall user experience and simplify troubleshooting.

Python Libraries for Automation

In the world of automation, Python stands out as one of the most versatile and widely used programming languages. Python's simplicity, readability, and extensive ecosystem of libraries make it an ideal choice for automating a wide range of tasks, from web scraping to system administration. Next, we'll explore some of the essential Python libraries that empower developers and system administrators to streamline their automation efforts.

Requests: HTTP for Humans

When it comes to web automation and data retrieval, the **requests** library is indispensable. It simplifies HTTP requests, making it easy to interact with web services, APIs, and websites. With **requests**, you can send GET and POST requests, handle cookies, and manage sessions effortlessly. Here's an example of fetching data from a web API using **requests**:

pythonCopy code

```
import requests response = requests.get('https://api.example.com/data') if response.status_code == 200: data = response.json() # Process the retrieved data else: print(f'Error: Failed to fetch data (Status code: {response.status_code})')
```

Beautiful Soup: HTML Parsing Made Easy

For web scraping and parsing HTML and XML documents, the **Beautiful Soup** library is a valuable asset. It provides a convenient way to navigate and extract data from web pages. You can search for specific elements, extract text, and manipulate the document's structure. Here's an example of using **Beautiful Soup** to scrape data from a web page:

pythonCopy code

```python
from bs4 import BeautifulSoup import requests url =
'https://example.com' response = requests.get(url) if
response.status_code == 200: soup =
BeautifulSoup(response.text, 'html.parser') # Extract data
from the parsed HTML else: print(f'Error: Failed to fetch web
page (Status code: {response.status_code})')
```

Selenium: Browser Automation

When automation requires interacting with web browsers,
Selenium is the go-to library. It allows you to automate actions
like clicking buttons, filling out forms, and navigating websites
just as a human would. Selenium supports various browsers,
making it versatile for different use cases. Here's an example of
using Selenium to automate a web browser:

pythonCopy code

```python
from selenium import webdriver # Create a new instance of
the Firefox driver driver = webdriver.Firefox() # Open a
website driver.get('https://example.com') # Interact with the
web page, e.g., clicking buttons or filling forms # ... # Close the
browser when done driver.quit()
```

Paramiko: SSH Automation

For automating tasks on remote servers over SSH, **Paramiko** is
an essential library. It provides a Pythonic interface to SSH
protocol, enabling secure and seamless automation of remote
server management tasks. With **Paramiko**, you can connect to
remote servers, execute commands, transfer files, and more.
Here's an example of using **Paramiko** to automate SSH
commands:

pythonCopy code

```python
import paramiko # Create an SSH client ssh_client =
paramiko.SSHClient() # Connect to a remote server
ssh_client.connect('example.com', username='username',
password='password') # Execute a remote command stdin,
```

```
stdout, stderr = ssh_client.exec_command('ls -l') # Read and
process the command output output =
stdout.read().decode('utf-8') print(output) # Close the SSH
connection ssh_client.close()
```

psutil: System Monitoring and Control

When automating system administration tasks, the **psutil**
library is a valuable companion. It provides an interface to
monitor and control various aspects of system resources, such
as CPU, memory, disks, and network. With **psutil**, you can
gather system information, manage processes, and perform
system-related tasks. Here's an example of using **psutil** to
monitor system resources:

pythonCopy code

```
import psutil # Get CPU usage cpu_percent =
psutil.cpu_percent(interval=1) print(f'CPU Usage:
{cpu_percent}%') # Get memory usage memory =
psutil.virtual_memory() print(f'Memory Usage:
Total={memory.total}B, Used={memory.used}B') # List running
processes process_list = psutil.process_iter() for process in
process_list: print(f'Process: {process.name()} (PID:
{process.pid})')
```

OpenPyXL: Working with Excel Files

For automating tasks involving Excel spreadsheets, the
OpenPyXL library is a powerful tool. It allows you to read,
write, and manipulate Excel files (both **.xlsx** and **.xlsm** formats)
programmatically. With **OpenPyXL**, you can automate tasks like
data extraction, report generation, and data analysis. Here's an
example of using **OpenPyXL** to read data from an Excel file:

pythonCopy code

```
import openpyxl # Load an Excel workbook workbook =
openpyxl.load_workbook('example.xlsx') # Select a specific
worksheet worksheet = workbook['Sheet1'] # Access cell
```

values cell_value = worksheet['A1'].value print(f'Cell A1 contains: {cell_value}') # Iterate through rows for row in worksheet.iter_rows(min_row=2, values_only=True): # Process data in each row pass # Save changes to the workbook workbook.save('modified_example.xlsx')

Schedule: Task Scheduling

When automation requires scheduling tasks at specific times or intervals, the **schedule** library can be a handy addition. It provides a straightforward way to create and manage scheduled jobs within your Python scripts. With **schedule**, you can automate tasks like data backups, report generation, or data retrieval at predefined times. Here's an example of using **schedule** to automate a task:

pythonCopy code

```
import schedule import time def my_task(): print('Task executed at:', time.strftime('%Y-%m-%d %H:%M:%S')) # Schedule the task to run every day at 3:00 PM schedule.every().day.at('15:00').do(my_task) # Keep the script running while True: schedule.run_pending() time.sleep(60) # Sleep for one minute
```

Python's rich ecosystem of libraries makes it a formidable tool for automation tasks. Whether you're working with web data, remote servers, system resources, or office documents, Python offers libraries to simplify the automation process. By leveraging these libraries, developers and system administrators can streamline their workflow, save time, and reduce the potential for errors in their automation efforts. Automation with Python has never been more accessible and powerful, making it an invaluable skill in today's technology-driven world.

Exception Handling in Python Scripts

Exception handling is a crucial aspect of writing reliable and robust Python scripts. In the world of programming, exceptions are unexpected events or errors that can occur during the execution of a script. These events can range from simple issues like dividing by zero to more complex problems like file not found errors. Next, we will explore how to effectively handle exceptions in Python scripts to ensure graceful and controlled error management.

Understanding Exceptions

Before diving into exception handling, it's essential to grasp the concept of exceptions. In Python, an exception is a signal that an error or an unusual condition has occurred during the execution of a program. When an exception occurs, Python generates an exception object that contains information about the error, such as its type and a description.

Basic Exception Handling

Python provides a straightforward way to handle exceptions using **try** and **except** blocks. In a **try** block, you place the code that you suspect might raise an exception. In the corresponding **except** block, you specify how to handle the exception if it occurs.

pythonCopy code

```
try: # Code that may raise an exception result = 10 / 0 # Division by zero  except ZeroDivisionError: # Handle the exception  print("Error: Division by zero")
```

In this example, the **ZeroDivisionError** exception is caught, and an error message is displayed. By using **try** and **except**, you prevent the script from abruptly terminating when an exception occurs.

Handling Multiple Exceptions

Python allows you to handle multiple exceptions using multiple **except** blocks. This approach enables you to tailor your error-handling logic to different types of exceptions.

pythonCopy code

```
try: file = open("nonexistent_file.txt", "r") data = file.read()
except FileNotFoundError: print("Error: File not found")
except IOError: print("Error: Input/output error")
```

Here, we catch both **FileNotFoundError** and **IOError** exceptions and provide specific error messages for each.

Handling All Exceptions

In some cases, you may want to catch any exception that occurs without specifying a particular type. To do this, you can use a generic **except** block without specifying an exception type.

pythonCopy code

```
try: result = 10 / 0  # Division by zero  except: print("An error occurred")
```

While catching all exceptions can be convenient, it may make it harder to diagnose and fix specific issues, so it's generally recommended to catch only the exceptions you expect.

The else and finally Blocks

Python provides two additional blocks that can enhance your exception-handling capabilities: **else** and **finally**. The **else** block is executed when no exceptions occur in the **try** block. This can be useful for performing actions that should only happen if the script runs without errors.

pythonCopy code

```
try: result = 10 / 2  except ZeroDivisionError: print("Error: Division by zero") else: print("Division successful. Result:", result)
```

The **finally** block is always executed, whether an exception occurs or not. It is often used for cleanup tasks like closing files or network connections.

pythonCopy code

```
file = None try: file = open("data.txt", "r") data = file.read()
except FileNotFoundError: print("Error: File not found")
finally: if file is not None: file.close()
```

In this example, the **finally** block ensures that the file is closed, even if an exception occurs while opening or reading it.

Raising Exceptions

In addition to handling exceptions, Python allows you to raise exceptions explicitly using the **raise** statement. You can raise built-in exceptions or create custom exceptions by defining your own exception classes.

pythonCopy code

```python
def divide(x, y): if y == 0: raise ZeroDivisionError("Division by zero is not allowed") return x / y try: result = divide(10, 0) except ZeroDivisionError as e: print("Error:", e)
```

Here, we define a custom **ZeroDivisionError** exception and raise it when dividing by zero.

Custom Exception Classes

Creating custom exception classes can make your code more expressive and help differentiate between different types of errors. To define a custom exception, you can inherit from the **Exception** class or one of its subclasses.

pythonCopy code

```python
class MyCustomError(Exception): def __init__(self, message): super().__init__(message) def perform_critical_operation(): try: # Some critical operation that might fail result = 1 / 0 # Simulate a critical error except ZeroDivisionError: raise MyCustomError("Critical operation failed: Division by zero") try: perform_critical_operation() except MyCustomError as e: print("Custom error:", e)
```

In this example, we define **MyCustomError** as a subclass of **Exception** and raise it in the **perform_critical_operation** function.

Logging Exceptions

To maintain a record of exceptions that occur during script execution, it's a good practice to log them. The Python **logging** module provides a flexible and powerful way to log exceptions and other information.

pythonCopy code

```
import logging try: # Code that may raise an exception result = 10 / 0 # Division by zero except ZeroDivisionError as e: # Log the exception logging.exception("An error occurred: %s", e)
```

By configuring the **logging** module, you can control where and how exceptions are logged, making it easier to troubleshoot issues. Exception handling is a fundamental aspect of writing reliable Python scripts. By using **try** and **except** blocks, you can gracefully handle errors and prevent script termination. Additionally, **else** and **finally** blocks provide further control over exception handling and resource cleanup. Custom exceptions allow you to create meaningful error messages and differentiate between various types of errors. Logging exceptions helps you maintain a record of issues and simplifies debugging. Understanding and effectively implementing exception handling can significantly improve the reliability and maintainability of your Python scripts, ensuring they continue to perform as expected, even in the face of unexpected errors.

Creating Modular Shell Scripts
Modularization is a key concept in software development that promotes code reusability, maintainability, and readability. In the world of shell scripting, creating modular scripts can greatly enhance your productivity and make your scripts more organized. Next, we'll explore the principles of creating modular shell scripts and demonstrate how to implement them effectively.

Why Modularity Matters
Modularity is the practice of breaking down a large program or script into smaller, self-contained modules or functions. These modules can then be developed, tested, and maintained independently, making the overall script easier to understand and manage.

In the context of shell scripting, modularity offers several advantages:

Code Reusability: You can reuse modules in multiple scripts, reducing redundancy and saving time.

Maintainability: Smaller, well-defined modules are easier to maintain and troubleshoot.

Collaboration: Multiple developers can work on different modules simultaneously, enhancing team productivity.

Testing: Isolating modules simplifies testing and debugging, as you can focus on individual components.

Defining Functions in Shell Scripts
In shell scripting, functions serve as the building blocks of modularity. You can define a function using the **function** keyword or by simply providing its name followed by parentheses.

bashCopy code

Using the 'function' keyword (optional) function greet() { echo "Hello, World!" } # Defining a function without 'function' keyword say_hello() { echo "Hello, World!" }

To call a function, you use its name followed by parentheses.

bashCopy code

greet # Calling the 'greet' function say_hello # Calling the 'say_hello' function

Functions can accept arguments just like regular shell scripts. You can access the arguments inside the function using the **$1**, **$2**, etc., syntax.

bashCopy code

greet_person() { echo "Hello, $1!" } greet_person "Alice" # Calling the function with an argument greet_person "Bob" # Calling the function with a different argument

Returning Values from Functions

Shell functions can also return values using the **return** statement. The return value is stored in the special variable **$?**.

bashCopy code

calculate_sum() { local result=$(($1 + $2)) # Perform the calculation return $result # Return the result } calculate_sum 5 3 # Calling the function sum=$? # Storing the return value echo "The sum is: $sum"

In this example, the **calculate_sum** function computes the sum of two numbers and returns the result.

Local Variables

To avoid conflicts between variables in different parts of your script, it's a good practice to declare variables as **local** within functions. Local variables are only accessible within the function scope.

bashCopy code

global_variable="I'm global" print_variable() { local local_variable="I'm local" echo "Inside function: $local_variable" echo "Inside function: $global_variable" } print_variable echo "Outside function: $local_variable" echo "Outside function: $global_variable"

Here, the **local_variable** is accessible only inside the **print_variable** function, while the **global_variable** is accessible throughout the script.

Including External Files

Another way to create modular shell scripts is by including external files or script modules. You can use the **source** or . command to load functions and variables from an external file into your main script.

bashCopy code

Module file: utils.sh # Define a function print_message () { echo "This is a message from the module." } # Main script: main.sh # Include the module source utils.sh # Call the function from the module print_message

By splitting your script into multiple files, you can keep related functions and code organized, making it easier to manage larger projects.

Organizing Your Project

When working on more extensive shell scripting projects, consider organizing your project into directories and subdirectories. Each subdirectory can contain related modules and scripts.

Copy code

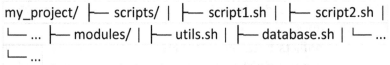

my_project/ ├── scripts/ | ├── script1.sh | ├── script2.sh | └── ... ├── modules/ | ├── utils.sh | ├── database.sh | └── ... └── ...

This structure helps maintain a clean and logical separation of code, making it easier for you and your team to collaborate and manage the project.

Documentation and Comments

To make your modular shell scripts more accessible to others and to your future self, it's essential to provide clear documentation and comments. Document the purpose of each function, list its arguments, and describe the expected return values. Use comments to explain complex logic and provide context for future readers.

bashCopy code

```
# Function: greet_person  # Description: Greets a person by name.  # Arguments:  # $1: Name of the person to greet  # Returns:  # None  greet_person() { echo "Hello, $1!" }
```

By following this practice, you create scripts that are easier to understand and maintain.

Testing and Debugging

Modularization simplifies the process of testing and debugging your shell scripts. You can test each function independently, ensuring that it behaves as expected. When issues arise, you can isolate and focus on the problematic module, making debugging more efficient.

Creating modular shell scripts is a valuable practice that improves code organization, reusability, and maintainability. Functions serve as the building blocks of modularity, allowing you to encapsulate logic and handle arguments and return values. Incorporating external modules and organizing your project's structure further enhances your ability to manage larger scripts and collaborate with others. By documenting your code and practicing good commenting, you make your scripts more accessible and understandable. Testing and debugging become more straightforward when you can isolate and focus on individual modules. Overall, embracing modularity in shell scripting empowers you to write more efficient, organized, and maintainable code.

Advanced Shell Scripting Patterns

As you advance in your shell scripting journey, you'll encounter complex tasks and scenarios that demand more than basic script structures. Next, we'll explore advanced shell scripting patterns and techniques that will enable you to tackle intricate challenges and create robust and efficient scripts.

Conditionals and Decision Making

Conditionals are a fundamental part of scripting, allowing you to make decisions based on various conditions. The **if** statement is your primary tool for implementing conditional logic in shell scripts.

bashCopy code

```
if [ condition ]; then  # Code to execute if the condition is true
fi
```

You can use various comparison operators in your conditions, such as **-eq** for equality, **-lt** for less than, and **-gt** for greater than.

bashCopy code

```
age=25 if [ "$age" -lt 18 ]; then  echo  "You are under 18 years old." else  echo  "You are 18 or older."  fi
```

The **if-else** construct allows you to execute different code blocks depending on the outcome of the condition.

Nested Conditionals

For more complex decision-making scenarios, you can nest **if** statements within each other.

bashCopy code

```
if [ condition1 ]; then  # Code to execute if condition1 is true  if [ condition2 ]; then  # Code to execute if both condition1 and condition2 are true  fi  fi
```

Nested conditionals enable you to handle intricate logic and make your scripts more versatile.

Case Statements

Another way to implement decision making is through **case** statements, which are particularly useful when dealing with multiple possible values for a variable.

bashCopy code

```
case "$variable" in "value1") # Code to execute if variable is equal to value1 ;; "value2") # Code to execute if variable is
```

equal to value2 ;; *) # Default code to execute if no match is found ;; esac

The **case** statement simplifies code readability in scenarios with numerous branching options.

Loops

Loops allow you to execute a block of code repeatedly until a specified condition is met. Shell scripts support several types of loops, including **for, while**, and **until**.

bashCopy code

```
# For loop for item in "${array[@]}"; do # Code to execute for each item in the array done
```

bashCopy code

```
# While loop while [ condition ]; do # Code to execute as long as the condition is true done
```

bashCopy code

```
# Until loop until [ condition ]; do # Code to execute until the condition becomes true done
```

Loops are invaluable for iterating through arrays, processing files, and performing repetitive tasks.

Function Recursion

Shell scripts support function recursion, allowing a function to call itself.

bashCopy code

```
factorial () { if [ "$1" -eq 0 ]; then echo 1 else local temp=$(( "$1" - 1 )) local result=$(factorial "$temp") echo $(( "$1" * "$result" )) fi } result=$(factorial 5) echo "Factorial of 5 is $result"
```

Recursion can be powerful for solving problems that involve recursive patterns or algorithms.

File Operations

Shell scripts often deal with files, whether it's reading, writing, or manipulating them. Advanced file handling techniques include appending data to files, checking if a file exists, and creating directories as needed.

bashCopy code

```
# Appending data to a file echo "New data" >> file.txt
```

bashCopy code

```
# Checking if a file exists if [ -e "file.txt" ]; then echo "File exists." else echo "File does not exist." fi
```

bashCopy code

```
# Creating directories as needed mkdir -p "/path/to/new/directory"
```

These operations enhance your ability to work with files and directories efficiently.

Error Handling and Debugging

Advanced scripts should include mechanisms for error handling and debugging. You can set the script to exit on the first error using **set -e**.

bashCopy code

```
#!/bin/bash set -e # Script commands
```

Additionally, you can use the **trap** command to define custom error handling functions.

bashCopy code

```
#!/bin/bash trap 'cleanup' EXIT cleanup() { # Code to run on script exit echo "Script is exiting." }
```

This ensures that your script cleans up resources and handles errors gracefully.

Regular Expressions

Regular expressions (regex) are powerful tools for pattern matching and text manipulation. You can use them to search, extract, or replace specific patterns within text data.

bashCopy code

```
# Using regex to match an email address if [[ "$email" =~ ^[A-Za-z0-9._%+-]+@[A-Za-z0-9.-]+\.[A-Za-z]{2,4}$ ]]; then echo "Valid email address." else echo "Invalid email address." fi
```

Regular expressions are invaluable for tasks like data validation and log file parsing.

Command Line Arguments

Advanced shell scripts often accept command line arguments to customize their behavior. You can access these arguments using the special variables **$1, $2**, and so on.

bashCopy code

```bash
#!/bin/bash if [ "$1" = "-v" ]; then verbose_mode=true fi if [ "$verbose_mode" = true ]; then echo "Verbose mode is enabled." fi
```

Command line arguments make scripts more versatile and user-friendly.

Working with External Commands

Shell scripts frequently interact with external commands and programs. You can capture the output of external commands using command substitution.

bashCopy code

```bash
current_date=$(date) echo "Current date and time: $current_date"
```

Shell scripts can also pass arguments to external commands.

bashCopy code

```bash
filename="file.txt" word_count=$(wc -w "$filename") echo "Word count of $filename: $word_count"
```

These techniques allow you to integrate external tools seamlessly.

Parallel Execution

To improve script performance, you can run tasks in parallel using background processes and job control.

bashCopy code

```bash
#!/bin/bash # Run tasks in parallel task1 & task2 & task3 & # Wait for all background tasks to complete wait
```

Parallel execution can significantly speed up tasks that involve multiple independent operations.

Advanced shell scripting patterns and techniques empower you to tackle complex scripting challenges with confidence. You can implement conditional logic, loops, and recursion to handle intricate decision-making scenarios. File operations, error handling, and debugging mechanisms enhance your script's reliability and maintainability. Regular expressions enable powerful text manipulation, and command line arguments provide flexibility and customization options. Working with external commands and parallel execution further extends the capabilities of your shell scripts. By mastering these advanced patterns, you become a proficient shell script developer capable of crafting efficient and versatile scripts to automate tasks and solve real-world problems.

Database integration is a crucial aspect of scripting when dealing with data-driven applications and automation. Next, we will explore various techniques and considerations for integrating databases into your shell scripts.

Selecting the Right Database

The first step in integrating a database into your script is selecting the appropriate database management system (DBMS) that suits your requirements. Common choices for shell scripting include SQLite, MySQL, PostgreSQL, and Oracle Database, among others.

SQLite: A Lightweight Option

SQLite is a popular choice for simple database integration in shell scripts due to its lightweight nature. It is a self-contained, serverless, and zero-configuration SQL database engine that stores data in a single file.

bashCopy code

```
# Create an SQLite database sqlite3 mydatabase.db # Run SQL commands interactively sqlite3 mydatabase.db # Execute SQL commands from a script sqlite3 mydatabase.db < script.sql
```

SQLite is ideal for smaller projects, prototyping, and situations where you need a database without the complexities of a full-fledged DBMS.

Interacting with MySQL

For more extensive database needs, MySQL is a robust open-source relational database management system. You can interact with MySQL databases from shell scripts using the **mysql** command-line client.

bashCopy code

```bash
# Connect to a MySQL database mysql -u username -p #
Execute SQL commands from a script mysql -u username -p <
script.sql
```

MySQL offers advanced features, scalability, and performance for larger-scale applications.

Utilizing PostgreSQL

PostgreSQL is another powerful open-source relational database system known for its extensibility and SQL compliance. You can work with PostgreSQL databases in shell scripts using the **psql** command-line utility.

bashCopy code

```bash
# Connect to a PostgreSQL database psql -U username -d
dbname # Execute SQL commands from a script psql -U
username -d dbname -f script.sql
```

PostgreSQL is an excellent choice for projects that require advanced features, such as support for JSON and spatial data.

Oracle Database Integration

When dealing with enterprise-level applications, Oracle Database is a prominent choice. You can interact with Oracle databases from shell scripts using tools like **sqlplus**.

bashCopy code

```bash
# Connect to an Oracle Database sqlplus
username/password@TNS_ALIAS # Execute SQL commands
from a script sqlplus username/password@TNS_ALIAS
@script.sql
```

Oracle Database offers extensive capabilities for handling complex business requirements.

Establishing Database Connections

Regardless of the DBMS you choose, establishing a database connection is a critical step. You need to provide connection parameters such as the database host, port, username, and password.

bashCopy code

Define database connection parameters db_host= "localhost" db_port= "3306" db_username= "myuser" db_password= "mypassword" db_name= "mydatabase"

These parameters will be used to connect to the database within your script.

Executing SQL Queries

Once you've established a database connection, you can execute SQL queries from your shell script. You can use command substitution to capture the results of a SQL query.

bashCopy code

```
# Execute a SELECT query and capture the result result=$(mysql -h "$db_host" -P "$db_port" -u "$db_username" -p "$db_password" -D "$db_name" -e "SELECT * FROM mytable")
```

The **result** variable now holds the output of the SQL query, which you can further process within your script.

Handling SQL Errors

It's essential to handle SQL errors gracefully in your shell scripts. You can check the exit status of the database command to determine If an error occurred.

bashCopy code

```
# Execute a SQL command and check for errors mysql -h "$db_host" -P "$db_port" -u "$db_username" -p "$db_password" -D "$db_name" -e "INSERT INTO mytable (name) VALUES ('John')" || echo "Error: SQL command failed."
```

By using **||** to execute the echo command when the SQL command fails, you can implement error handling in your script.

Using Prepared Statements

Prepared statements can help protect your shell scripts from SQL injection attacks. They allow you to parameterize your queries and bind values securely.

bashCopy code

```
# Using a prepared statement with MySQL statement="INSERT INTO mytable (name) VALUES (?)" mysql -h "$db_host" -P "$db_port" -u "$db_username" -p"$db_password" -D "$db_name" -e "$statement" --bind-variables "John"
```

Using prepared statements is a recommended practice for database integration in scripts.

Working with Data

Once you retrieve data from the database, you can process it within your script. Common tasks include parsing, formatting, and transforming the data to meet your application's needs.

bashCopy code

```
# Process data retrieved from the database while read -r row; do # Perform data processing here done <<< "$result"
```

This loop processes each row of data obtained from the database query.

Automating Database Backups

Shell scripts are excellent tools for automating routine database backups. You can create a script that connects to the database, exports the data, and stores it securely.

bashCopy code

```
# Automated database backup script backup_filename="backup-$(date +'%Y%m%d%H%M%S').sql" mysqldump -h "$db_host" -P "$db_port" -u "$db_username" -p"$db_password" "$db_name" > "$backup_filename"
```

This script generates a backup file with a timestamp in its name.

Logging and Monitoring

When integrating databases into your scripts, it's vital to implement logging and monitoring mechanisms. You can use standard Unix utilities like **logger** to log script activities and error messages.

bashCopy code

Logging script activity logger "Script execution started."

Monitoring scripts' execution and logging can help you troubleshoot issues and track the performance of your database-related tasks.

Security Considerations

Security is a paramount concern when dealing with databases in scripts. Ensure that you protect sensitive information like database credentials by using environment variables or configuration files.

bashCopy code

```
# Store database credentials in a separate configuration file
db_host="localhost"                        db_port="3306"
db_username="myuser"        db_password="mypassword"
db_name="mydatabase"
```

By separating credentials from your script code, you reduce the risk of accidental exposure. Database integration in shell scripts allows you to leverage the power of relational databases to enhance automation and data-driven tasks. Selecting the right database management system, establishing connections, executing SQL queries, and handling data are fundamental aspects of this integration. Security, logging, and monitoring should always be considered to ensure the reliability and safety of your scripts. By mastering these techniques, you can create shell scripts that efficiently interact with databases, enabling you to build robust and data-driven automation solutions. SQL (Structured Query Language) is a powerful tool for managing and retrieving data from relational databases, making it an essential component of automation in various applications. Next, we'll explore the role of SQL queries in automation, focusing on how you can leverage SQL to streamline data-related tasks within your scripts.

Understanding SQL Queries

SQL queries are commands used to interact with databases, allowing you to perform actions like retrieving, updating, inserting, or deleting data. SQL queries are structured statements that follow a specific syntax and are executed by the database management system.

sqlCopy code

-- Example SQL SELECT query SELECT column1, column2 FROM mytable WHERE condition;

SQL queries provide a standardized and efficient way to communicate with databases, regardless of the DBMS in use.

Automating Data Retrieval

One of the primary uses of SQL queries in automation is data retrieval. You can use SQL SELECT queries to extract specific information from a database and incorporate it into your scripts.

bashCopy code

```
#!/bin/bash # Database connection parameters db_host="localhost" db_port="3306" db_username="myuser" db_password="mypassword" db_name="mydatabase" # Execute an SQL SELECT query result=$(mysql -h "$db_host" -P "$db_port" -u "$db_username" -p"$db_password" -D "$db_name" -e "SELECT name, age FROM users WHERE status='active'") # Process the retrieved data while read -r row; do # Perform data processing here done <<< "$result"
```

By executing SQL queries from your scripts, you can automate the retrieval of specific data sets, enabling you to work with up-to-date information.

Automating Data Insertion and Updates

SQL queries also facilitate automation for data insertion and updates. You can use SQL INSERT and UPDATE statements to add new records or modify existing ones in your database.

bashCopy code

```
#!/bin/bash # Database connection parameters db_host="localhost" db_port="3306"
```

```
db_username="myuser"          db_password="mypassword"
db_name="mydatabase"  # Define  data  to  insert
new_name="John"  new_age=30  # Execute an SQL INSERT
query mysql -h "$db_host" -P "$db_port" -u "$db_username"
-p "$db_password" -D "$db_name" -e "INSERT INTO users
(name, age) VALUES ('$new_name', $new_age)"
```

bashCopy code

```
#!/bin/bash      #  Database   connection   parameters
db_host="localhost"                    db_port="3306"
db_username="myuser"          db_password="mypassword"
db_name="mydatabase"  # Define  data  for  the  update
user_id=123 new_status="inactive"  # Execute an SQL UPDATE
query mysql -h "$db_host" -P "$db_port" -u "$db_username"
-p "$db_password" -D "$db_name" -e "UPDATE users SET
status='$new_status' WHERE id=$user_id"
```

Automating data insertion and updates with SQL queries simplifies the process of maintaining your database.

Database Cleanup and Deletion

In automation scenarios, you may also need to delete records or perform cleanup tasks in your database. SQL DELETE statements provide a straightforward way to automate these actions.

bashCopy code

```
#!/bin/bash      #  Database   connection   parameters
db_host="localhost"                    db_port="3306"
db_username="myuser"          db_password="mypassword"
db_name="mydatabase"  # Define conditions for deletion
threshold_age=60 # Execute an SQL DELETE query mysql -h
"$db_host"  -P  "$db_port"  -u  "$db_username"  -
p "$db_password" -D "$db_name" -e "DELETE FROM users
WHERE age > $threshold_age"
```

Automating data deletion based on specific conditions helps keep your database tidy and optimized.

Scheduling Database Tasks

Automation often involves scheduling tasks to run at specific intervals. You can use tools like cron jobs or systemd timers in combination with your scripts to automate database-related activities, such as data backups or regular maintenance.

bashCopy code

```
# Example cron job to run a database backup script daily at 2 AM 0 2 * * * /path/to/backup-script.sh
```

By scheduling database-related tasks, you ensure that critical operations occur automatically and on time.

Error Handling and Logging

When automating SQL queries, it's essential to implement robust error handling and logging mechanisms. SQL queries can fail due to various reasons, such as connection issues or incorrect syntax.

bashCopy code

```
#!/bin/bash  # Database connection parameters db_host="localhost"  db_port="3306" db_username="myuser"  db_password="mypassword" db_name="mydatabase"  # Execute an SQL query and check for errors mysql -h "$db_host" -P "$db_port" -u "$db_username" -p"$db_password" -D "$db_name" -e "SELECT * FROM mytable" || echo "Error: SQL query failed."
```

Incorporating error handling ensures that your scripts can gracefully recover from unexpected issues.

SQL Transactions

When performing multiple SQL operations as part of an automated process, you may want to use SQL transactions. Transactions provide a way to group several SQL statements into a single unit of work, ensuring that either all statements succeed or none do.

```bash
bashCopy code
#!/bin/bash   #   Database   connection   parameters
db_host="localhost"                      db_port="3306"
db_username="myuser"        db_password="mypassword"
db_name="mydatabase"  # Start a transaction mysql -h
"$db_host"   -P   "$db_port"   -u   "$db_username"   -
p"$db_password" -D "$db_name" -e "START TRANSACTION"
# Execute multiple SQL statements within the transaction
mysql -h "$db_host" -P "$db_port" -u "$db_username" -
p"$db_password" -D "$db_name" -e "UPDATE table1 SET
column1=value1"  mysql -h "$db_host" -P "$db_port" -u
"$db_username"  -p"$db_password"  -D  "$db_name"  -e
"INSERT INTO table2 (column2) VALUES (value2)" # Commit
the  transaction  mysql -h  "$db_host"  -P  "$db_port"  -u
"$db_username"   -p"$db_password"   -D   "$db_name"   -e
"COMMIT"
```

Using transactions ensures data consistency and integrity when
automating complex database operations.

SQL Queries and Security

Security should always be a top priority when automating SQL
queries. Avoid using user input directly in your SQL statements
to prevent SQL injection attacks.

```bash
bashCopy code
#!/bin/bash   #   Database   connection   parameters
db_host="localhost"                      db_port="3306"
db_username="myuser"        db_password="mypassword"
db_name="mydatabase"  # User input (potentially vulnerable
to SQL injection) user_input="John'; DROP TABLE users; --" #
Execute an SQL query with user input (unsafe) mysql -h
"$db_host"   -P   "$db_port"   -u   "$db_username"   -
p"$db_password" -D "$db_name" -e "SELECT * FROM users
WHERE name='$user_input'"
```

Instead, use prepared statements or parameterized queries to safely handle user input.

bashCopy code

```
#!/bin/bash   #   Database   connection   parameters
db_host="localhost"                      db_port="3306"
db_username="myuser"        db_password="mypassword"
db_name="mydatabase"  # User input (potentially vulnerable
to SQL injection) user_input="John'; DROP TABLE users; --"  #
Execute an SQL query with prepared statement (safe) mysql -h
"$db_host"   -P   "$db_port"   -u   "$db_username"   -
p"$db_password" -D "$db_name" -e "PREPARE stmt FROM
'SELECT   *   FROM   users   WHERE   name=?';   SET
@name='$user_input';   EXECUTE   stmt   USING   @name;
DEALLOCATE PREPARE stmt;"
```

By following best practices for SQL query execution and security, you can ensure that your automated scripts are robust and safe from potential vulnerabilities.

SQL queries play a crucial role in automation, allowing you to interact with databases efficiently and securely. Automating data retrieval, insertion, updates, and deletion tasks simplifies data management and ensures that your scripts work with up-to-date information. Scheduling and error handling mechanisms enhance the reliability and effectiveness of your automation efforts. Remember to prioritize security by using prepared statements and avoiding direct user input in your SQL queries. By mastering SQL queries in automation, you can build powerful and data-driven scripts that streamline complex tasks in various applications.

Advanced Script Architecture
Advanced script architecture is a critical aspect of creating maintainable, efficient, and scalable scripts. Next, we will explore various techniques and principles for designing scripts that are well-structured, modular, and easy to manage.

Modular Script Design
Modular design is the foundation of advanced script architecture. Breaking your script into smaller, reusable modules or functions allows you to organize code logically and promote code reusability.
bashCopy code

```
#!/bin/bash  # Function to calculate the square of a number calculate_square() { local num="$1" local result=$((num * num)) echo "$result" } # Usage example result=$(calculate_square 5) echo "The square of 5 is $result."
```

In this example, the **calculate_square** function encapsulates a specific task, making the script more modular and easier to maintain.

Separation of Concerns
Another essential principle in advanced script architecture is the separation of concerns. Each part of your script should have a clear and distinct responsibility.
bashCopy code

```
#!/bin/bash  # Function to retrieve data from a database retrieve_data() { # Database retrieval code here } # Function to process data process_data() { # Data processing code here } # Function to generate a report generate_report() { # Report generation code here } # Main script data=$(retrieve_data) processed_data=$(process_data "$data") generate_report "$processed_data"
```

By separating data retrieval, processing, and report generation into distinct functions, you improve script readability and maintainability.

Configuration Management

Advanced scripts often require configuration management to handle settings, parameters, or options. Storing configuration values in a separate configuration file or using environment variables can make your script more flexible and adaptable.

bashCopy code

```
#!/bin/bash  # Load configuration from a separate file  source config.sh  # Access configuration variables  echo "Database host: $db_host"  echo "Database port: $db_port"  echo "API key: $api_key"
```

Separating configuration from the main script code simplifies updates and allows you to reuse the same script with different configurations.

Error Handling and Logging

Robust error handling and logging are crucial components of advanced script architecture. You should anticipate potential issues, handle errors gracefully, and log relevant information for troubleshooting.

bashCopy code

```
#!/bin/bash  # Function to perform a risky operation  perform_operation() { # Risky operation code here  if [ $? -ne 0 ]; then  echo "Error: Operation failed." >&2  exit 1  fi  }  # Main script  perform_operation || { # Log error message  echo "Error occurred: $(date) - Operation failed" >> error.log  exit 1  }
```

In this example, the **perform_operation** function includes error handling, and the script logs error messages to an error log file.

Documentation and Comments

Clear and concise documentation, including comments within your script, is essential for advanced script architecture.

Documentation helps you and others understand the script's purpose, usage, and inner workings.

bashCopy code

```bash
#!/bin/bash # Script: data_processing.sh # Description: This script retrieves data, processes it, and generates a report. # Function to retrieve data from a database retrieve_data() { # Database retrieval code here } # Function to process data process_data() { # Data processing code here } # Function to generate a report generate_report() { # Report generation code here } # Main script data=$(retrieve_data) processed_data=$(process_data "$data") generate_report "$processed_data"
```

A well-documented script is easier to maintain and troubleshoot, especially when revisiting it after some time.

Testing and Validation

Advanced script architecture involves thorough testing and validation to ensure script reliability. You can use testing frameworks or write custom test cases to verify that your script functions as intended.

bashCopy code

```bash
#!/bin/bash # Function to add two numbers add() { local result=$((num1 + num2)) echo "$result" } # Test cases assert_equal() { local expected="$1" local actual="$2" if [ "$expected" != "$actual" ]; then echo "Test failed: expected $expected but got $actual" >&2 exit 1 fi } num1=5 num2=7 result=$(add "$num1" "$num2") assert_equal 12 "$result"
```

By writing and running tests, you can catch issues early in the development process and ensure that changes do not introduce regressions.

Version Control

Version control systems, such as Git, play a vital role in advanced script architecture. Using version control allows you to track changes, collaborate with others, and revert to previous versions if needed.

bashCopy code

```
# Initialize a Git repository git init # Add script files to the repository git add script.sh # Commit changes with a meaningful message git commit -m "Initial script version" # Collaborate with others, track changes, and more
```

Version control provides a structured and organized approach to script development, making it easier to manage and maintain.

Code Reviews

In advanced script architecture, code reviews by peers or team members are valuable. Code reviews help identify potential issues, improve code quality, and ensure adherence to coding standards.

bashCopy code

```
# Request a code review on a feature branch git checkout -b feature-branch git push origin feature-branch # Collaborator reviews and provides feedback # Collaborator approves and merges the feature branch
```

Code reviews foster collaboration, knowledge sharing, and the continuous improvement of your script codebase.

Performance Optimization

Efficient script performance is another consideration in advanced script architecture. You can optimize your script by identifying bottlenecks, reducing resource consumption, and improving execution speed.

bashCopy code

```
#!/bin/bash # Use optimized data structures and algorithms # Minimize resource-intensive operations # Implement parallel processing when applicable # Optimize data retrieval and storage mechanisms
```

Performance optimization is especially important for scripts that handle large volumes of data or require real-time processing.

Security Measures

Security is a critical aspect of advanced script architecture, especially when dealing with sensitive data or privileged operations. Implement security best practices, such as input validation, access controls, and encryption, to protect your script and its data.

bashCopy code

```
#!/bin/bash  # Validate user input to prevent potential vulnerabilities  # Implement role-based access controls (RBAC)  # Use encryption for sensitive data storage and transmission  # Regularly update and patch dependencies and libraries
```

Security measures ensure that your scripts are resistant to unauthorized access and data breaches.

Advanced script architecture encompasses various principles and techniques to create robust, maintainable, and efficient scripts. Modular design, separation of concerns, configuration management, error handling, and documentation are essential components of advanced scripts. Testing, version control, code reviews, performance optimization, and security measures further enhance script quality and reliability. By following these principles and best practices, you can develop scripts that meet the demands of complex automation tasks and maintain them effectively over time.

Logging and Reporting in Automation Scripts

Logging and reporting are crucial aspects of automation scripts, ensuring that you have visibility into the script's execution and can track its performance and errors.

The Importance of Logging

Logging serves multiple purposes in automation scripts, such as providing a record of script activities, diagnosing issues, and auditing script behavior. Without proper logging, it can be challenging to identify the root causes of problems or monitor the script's progress.

bashCopy code

```bash
#!/bin/bash # Log file location log_file="script.log" # Function to log messages log() { local message="$1" local timestamp=$(date +"%Y-%m-%d %H:%M:%S") echo "[$timestamp] $message" >> "$log_file" } # Log a message log "Script execution started."
```

In this example, a simple **log** function records messages to a log file with a timestamp, helping you track when specific events occurred during script execution.

Types of Logs

Automation scripts typically generate different types of logs, including informational, warning, and error logs. Informational logs document normal script activities, while warning and error logs highlight issues that require attention.

bashCopy code

```bash
#!/bin/bash # Log file locations info_log="info.log" warning_log="warning.log" error_log="error.log" # Function to log messages with different levels log_info() { local message="$1" local timestamp=$(date +"%Y-%m-%d %H:%M:%S") echo "[$timestamp] INFO: $message" >> "$info_log" } log_warning() { local message="$1" local timestamp=$(date +"%Y-%m-%d %H:%M:%S") echo "[$timestamp] WARNING: $message" >> "$warning_log" } log_error() { local message="$1" local timestamp=$(date +"%Y-%m-%d %H:%M:%S") echo "[$timestamp] ERROR: $message" >> "$error_log" } # Log messages with different levels log_info "Script execution started." log_warning "Low disk space detected." log_error "Database connection failed."
```

Maintaining logs at various levels allows you to categorize and prioritize issues for effective troubleshooting.

Log Rotation

Over time, log files can become large and consume disk space. Log rotation is a technique used to manage log files by creating new log files periodically and compressing or deleting old ones.

bashCopy code

```
#!/bin/bash # Log file locations log_file="script.log" max_log_size=10M # Function to rotate logs when they reach the maximum size rotate_log() { if [ -f "$log_file" ] && [ "$(du -m "$log_file" | cut -f1)" -gt "$max_log_size" ]; then mv "$log_file" "$log_file.1" touch "$log_file" fi } # Rotate logs before logging rotate_log log "Script execution started."
```

In this example, the **rotate_log** function checks if the log file exceeds a specified size limit and renames it with a numeric suffix before creating a new log file.

Reporting

Reporting in automation scripts involves summarizing the results of script execution, often in a structured format. Reports can include information on successful operations, errors, and performance metrics.

bashCopy code

```
#!/bin/bash # Report file location report_file="script_report.txt" # Function to generate a report generate_report() { local timestamp=$(date +"%Y-%m-%d %H:%M:%S") local success_message="Script executed successfully." local error_message="Script encountered errors. Please check the log." echo "Report generated on $timestamp" > "$report_file" echo "" >> "$report_file" if grep -q "ERROR:" "$log_file"; then echo "$error_message" >> "$report_file" else echo "$success_message" >>
```

"$report_file" fi } # Generate a report after script execution generate_report

The **generate_report** function creates a report file and includes a timestamp, along with a success or error message based on the presence of error logs in the log file.

Integration with Monitoring Systems

Automation scripts can be integrated with monitoring systems that collect and analyze log and report data. Monitoring systems can alert administrators to issues, track script performance over time, and trigger automated responses.

bashCopy code

```
#!/bin/bash # Function to send log messages to a monitoring system send_to_monitoring() { local message="$1" # Send message to monitoring system (e.g., via API call) } # Log a message and send it to the monitoring system log "Script execution started." send_to_monitoring "Script execution started."
```

Integration with monitoring systems enhances proactive error detection and incident response capabilities.

Security Considerations

When handling sensitive data or executing privileged operations, security is paramount in logging and reporting. Ensure that log files are protected from unauthorized access, and consider encrypting log data if necessary.

bashCopy code

```
#!/bin/bash # Secure log file permissions chmod 600 "$log_file" # Function to log sensitive data log_sensitive_data() { local data="$1" # Log sensitive data securely echo "$data" | gpg -e -r admin@example.com >> "$log_file" } # Log sensitive data securely log_sensitive_data "Password: mysecretpassword"
```

In this example, the **log_sensitive_data** function logs sensitive information using GPG encryption to protect it from unauthorized access.

Summary

Logging and reporting are essential components of automation scripts, providing visibility, troubleshooting capabilities, and performance tracking. Different types of logs, log rotation, and structured reporting contribute to effective script management. Integration with monitoring systems enhances proactive error detection and response. Security considerations are vital when handling sensitive data in logs.

By implementing robust logging and reporting mechanisms and considering security best practices, you can create automation scripts that are reliable, maintainable, and secure.

Network Automation with Scripts
Network automation with scripts has become an integral part of managing and maintaining modern computer networks. In today's interconnected world, networks play a critical role in delivering services, and automating network tasks can streamline operations, improve efficiency, and enhance overall network performance.

The Need for Network Automation

Networks are constantly evolving, with new devices, services, and security threats emerging regularly. As networks grow in complexity, manual configuration and management of network devices become time-consuming, error-prone, and challenging to scale.

bashCopy code

```
#!/bin/bash  # Script to automate network device configuration configure_device()  {  local  device="$1"  local configuration_file="$2"  ssh "$device" < "$configuration_file" }  # Automate  configuration  of  a  network  router configure_device "router1.example.com" "router_config.txt"
```

In this example, a simple Bash script automates the configuration of a network router by providing a configuration file to the device via SSH.

Common Network Automation Tasks

Network automation scripts can address various common tasks, such as:

Configuration Management: Automating the configuration of network devices, including routers, switches, and firewalls, to ensure consistency and reduce manual errors.

bashCopy code

```bash
#!/bin/bash # Script to backup router configurations
backup_config() { local device="$1" ssh "$device" "show
running-config" > "$device-config.txt" } # Backup
configurations of multiple routers
devices=("router1.example.com" "router2.example.com") for
device in "${devices[@]}"; do backup_config "$device" done
```

This script backs up the configurations of multiple routers,
simplifying routine maintenance and disaster recovery.

Monitoring and Alerts: Monitoring network performance,
detecting anomalies, and sending alerts when issues arise.

bashCopy code

```bash
#!/bin/bash # Script to monitor network latency and send
alerts monitor_latency() { local target_ip="$1" local
threshold=100 # Set latency threshold in milliseconds local
current_latency=$(ping -c 4 "$target_ip" | grep "rtt" | cut -d
'/' -f 5) if [ "$current_latency" -gt "$threshold" ]; then
send_alert "High latency detected on $target_ip." fi } # Send
an alert (e.g., via email or SMS) send_alert() { local
message="$1" echo "$message" | mail -s "Network Alert"
admin@example.com } # Monitor latency for a specIfIc IP
address monitor_latency "8.8.8.8"
```

In this script, network latency is monitored, and an alert is sent
if latency exceeds a predefined threshold.

Security and Access Control: Enforcing security policies,
managing access control lists (ACLs), and detecting
unauthorized network access.

bashCopy code

```bash
#!/bin/bash # Script to manage firewall rules
configure_firewall() { local device="$1" local rule_file="$2"
scp "$rule_file" "$device:/tmp/firewall_rules" ssh "$device"
"apply_firewall_rules.sh /tmp/firewall_rules" } # Configure
firewall rules on multiple devices
```

```
devices=("firewall1.example.com"  "firewall2.example.com")
rule_file="firewall_rules.txt" for device in "${devices[@]}";
do configure_firewall "$device" "$rule_file" done
```
This script pushes firewall rule updates to multiple devices, ensuring that security policies are consistently applied.

Advantages of Network Automation

Network automation offers several advantages, including:

Time Savings: Automation reduces the time required to perform repetitive network tasks, allowing network administrators to focus on more strategic activities.

Consistency: Automation ensures that network configurations are consistent across devices, reducing the risk of misconfigurations.

Error Reduction: Automation eliminates human errors that can occur during manual configuration and reduces the likelihood of network outages.

Scalability: Automated scripts can scale to manage a large number of network devices and services efficiently.

Compliance: Automation helps enforce security and compliance policies, ensuring that networks adhere to industry standards and regulations.

Challenges and Considerations

While network automation offers significant benefits, it also presents challenges and considerations:

Script Complexity: Managing and maintaining complex automation scripts can be challenging, and documentation is crucial to understand script logic and functionality.

Testing: Rigorous testing of automation scripts is essential to ensure they perform as expected and do not introduce vulnerabilities.

Security: Automation scripts should follow security best practices to prevent unauthorized access and protect sensitive data.

Version Control: Using version control systems like Git helps manage and track changes to automation scripts.

Monitoring: Continuous monitoring of network automation processes is necessary to detect failures or anomalies.

Education and Training: Network administrators may require training to develop scripting skills and understand automation tools.

Network automation with scripts has become indispensable for network administrators and organizations seeking to manage and optimize their networks effectively. By automating common network tasks, administrators can reduce errors, improve efficiency, and enhance network security. However, it's essential to address challenges, maintain documentation, and follow best practices to ensure successful network automation implementations. In an era where networks continue to evolve and grow in complexity, automation is a key enabler for managing modern network infrastructures.

System Configuration Automation

System configuration automation is the process of using scripts and tools to manage and maintain the configuration of computer systems, ensuring that they operate efficiently, securely, and consistently. Automation plays a pivotal role in modern IT operations, as it enables administrators to streamline repetitive tasks, reduce human errors, and scale their infrastructure with ease.

In the world of system administration and IT management, configuring and maintaining computer systems is a fundamental task. This task involves setting up hardware, installing software, configuring network settings, and managing user accounts and permissions, among other responsibilities.

Traditionally, system administrators performed these tasks manually, which was time-consuming and prone to human errors. As systems grew in complexity and organizations expanded, the need for automation became evident.

Automation scripts and tools empower system administrators to define and deploy configurations programmatically. By scripting configuration tasks, administrators can ensure that systems are set up consistently and quickly, reducing the risk of configuration drift and discrepancies.

bashCopy code

```bash
#!/bin/bash  # Example of automating software installation install_software() { local package_name="$1" local installation_command="apt-get install -y $package_name" $installation_command } # Automate the installation of essential software packages software_packages=("nginx" "mysql-server" "php-fpm") for package in
```

```bash
"${software_packages[@]}"; do install_software "$package"
done
```

In this example, a Bash script automates the installation of essential software packages using the **apt-get** package manager on a Debian-based system.

System configuration automation extends beyond software installation and encompasses tasks such as setting up system users, configuring security policies, managing network settings, and more. By scripting these tasks, administrators can achieve consistent and repeatable results across multiple systems.

bashCopy code

```bash
#!/bin/bash  # Example of automating user account creation
create_user() { local username="$1" local password="$2"
useradd "$username" -m -p "$password" } # Automate the
creation of user accounts user_data=("alice:password123"
"bob:securepass" "eve:strongpassword") for data in
"${user_data[@]}"; do IFS=":" read -r username password
<<< "$data" create_user "$username" "$password" done
```

In this script, user accounts are created with specific usernames and passwords, ensuring that user management is consistent across systems.

Automation tools such as Ansible, Puppet, and Chef have gained popularity for managing system configurations at scale. These tools provide a higher level of abstraction and offer features like idempotency, which ensures that applying configurations multiple times has the same result as applying them once.

yamlCopy code

```yaml
--- - name: Ensure NTP is installed and running hosts: all
become: yes tasks: - name: Install NTP package apt:
name: ntp state: present - name: Start NTP service
service: name: ntp state: started
```

In this Ansible playbook example, the desired state of the NTP (Network Time Protocol) service is defined. Ansible ensures that the NTP package is installed and the NTP service is running on all specified hosts.

System configuration automation also plays a critical role in infrastructure as code (IAC) and cloud computing. When provisioning virtual machines or cloud resources, automation scripts define the configuration and state of these resources, allowing for dynamic and scalable infrastructure.

terraformCopy code

```
resource "aws_instance" "example" { ami = "ami-0c55b159cbfafe1f0" instance_type = "t2.micro" tags = { Name = "example-instance" } }
```

In this Terraform configuration, an AWS EC2 instance is defined, specifying its Amazon Machine Image (AMI), instance type, and tags. Terraform automates the provisioning and configuration of this instance when applied.

Security is a paramount consideration in system configuration automation. Automation scripts must adhere to security best practices and follow least privilege principles. Sensitive information, such as passwords and API tokens, should be stored securely and not hard-coded in scripts.

bashCopy code

```
#!/bin/bash # Example of securely handling sensitive data api_token="your-api-token-here" # Use environment variables to store sensitive data export API_TOKEN="$api_token" # Script logic here
```

In this example, sensitive data (an API token) is stored in an environment variable, which is a more secure approach than hard-coding it in the script.

System configuration automation is an ongoing process. As systems evolve, configurations may need to change, security patches must be applied, and new software may be introduced. Automation allows for the rapid and consistent implementation of these changes.

Documentation and version control are essential aspects of system configuration automation. Scripts and configuration files should be well-documented, making it easy for administrators to understand their purpose and functionality. Version control systems like Git enable teams to collaborate on automation code, track changes, and roll back to previous configurations if needed.

In summary, system configuration automation is a foundational practice in modern IT operations. By scripting and automating tasks related to system configuration, administrators can achieve consistency, efficiency, and scalability in managing computer systems. Automation tools provide advanced capabilities for managing configurations at scale, while security considerations and documentation ensure that automation is performed securely and reliably. As organizations continue to embrace automation, system configuration automation remains a critical skill for IT professionals.

Web Scraping Techniques

Web scraping is the process of automatically extracting data from websites, turning unstructured information on the web into structured data that can be used for various purposes. This technique has gained immense popularity for its ability to collect, analyze, and store data from the vast expanse of the internet.

Web scraping is often used for data mining, market research, competitive analysis, news aggregation, and more. It allows businesses and individuals to gather valuable insights from publicly available web content.

Web Scraping Fundamentals

At its core, web scraping involves sending HTTP requests to a website's server, retrieving the HTML content of web pages, and then parsing and extracting the desired data. The extracted data can be saved in various formats, such as CSV, JSON, or a database, for further analysis.

pythonCopy code

```
import requests from bs4 import BeautifulSoup # Send an
HTTP GET request to a website response =
requests.get("https://example.com") # Parse the HTML
content using BeautifulSoup soup =
BeautifulSoup(response.text, "html.parser") # Extract data
from the parsed HTML title = soup.title.text print("Title:",
title)
```

In this Python code snippet, the **requests** library is used to send
an HTTP GET request to a website, and **BeautifulSoup** is used
to parse and extract the title of the web page.

Selecting Elements

Web pages are comprised of various HTML elements such as
headings, paragraphs, links, and tables. To extract specific data,
web scrapers must identify and select the relevant elements
using CSS selectors or XPath expressions.

pythonCopy code

```
# Extract all the links from a web page links = soup.select("a")
for link in links: print("Link:", link["href"])
```

In this example, the **select** method is used to find all anchor
(**<a>**) elements on the page and extract their **href** attributes,
which contain the URLs of the links.

Handling Pagination

Many websites display data across multiple pages, requiring
web scrapers to navigate through pagination. This can be
achieved by sending requests to subsequent pages and
extracting data until all pages have been processed.

pythonCopy code

```
# Scrape data from multiple pages with pagination for
page_number in range(1, 6): url =
f"https://example.com/page/{page_number}" response =
requests.get(url) soup = BeautifulSoup(response.text,
"html.parser") # Extract and process data from each page
```

In this loop, the code iterates through page numbers and sends requests to each page to scrape data from a paginated website.

Handling Dynamic Content

Some websites load content dynamically using JavaScript, making it challenging to scrape data directly from the initial HTML source. To handle such websites, headless browsers like Selenium or tools like Puppeteer can be used to automate interactions with the web page and retrieve data.

pythonCopy code

```
from selenium import webdriver # Create a headless Chrome browser instance options = webdriver.ChromeOptions() options.add_argument("--headless") browser = webdriver.Chrome(options=options) # Navigate to a website and scrape data browser.get("https://example.com") # Extract data using browser automation
```

In this example, Selenium is used to create a headless Chrome browser, navigate to a website, and interact with it to retrieve data from dynamically loaded content.

Respecting Robots.txt

Web scraping should be done ethically and responsibly, respecting a website's **robots.txt** file, which provides guidelines on what can and cannot be scraped. Adhering to these rules is essential to avoid legal issues and maintain a positive web scraping reputation.

Rate Limiting and IP Rotation

Web scraping can place a heavy load on a website's server, potentially causing disruptions. To mitigate this, it's good practice to implement rate limiting by adding delays between requests to avoid overloading the server.

Additionally, rotating IP addresses using proxies or VPNs can help distribute the scraping workload and prevent IP bans from websites that may limit access.

Data Cleaning and Transformation

Extracted data may require cleaning and transformation to remove unwanted characters, format dates, or convert data types. Data cleaning is an essential step in preparing the scraped data for analysis.

pythonCopy code

```
# Clean and transform scraped data raw_data = "Price: $1,250.00" price = float(raw_data.split("$")[1].replace(",", "")) print("Cleaned Price:", price)
```

In this code, the raw price data is cleaned and transformed into a numeric format by removing the dollar sign and commas.

Handling CAPTCHAs and Anti-Scraping Measures

Some websites implement CAPTCHAs or employ anti-scraping techniques to deter automated scraping. Solving CAPTCHAs programmatically can be challenging, and scraping such websites may require manual intervention or alternative data sources.

Web Scraping Tools and Libraries

Several libraries and tools are available for web scraping in various programming languages. Popular choices include Python libraries like BeautifulSoup, Scrapy, and Selenium, as well as Node.js-based tools like Puppeteer.

Legal and Ethical Considerations

While web scraping is a powerful tool for data collection, it's essential to be aware of legal and ethical considerations. Some websites explicitly prohibit scraping in their terms of service, and scraping personal or sensitive data may violate privacy laws.

Web scraping techniques have revolutionized the way data is collected from the internet. By automating the process of data extraction, web scrapers enable businesses and individuals to gather valuable insights, track market trends, and make informed decisions.

However, web scraping should be conducted responsibly, adhering to ethical standards, respecting website policies, and avoiding disruptive scraping practices.

As data on the internet continues to grow, web scraping remains a vital skill for data analysts, researchers, and businesses seeking to harness the vast wealth of information available online.

Chapter 9: Security Automation and Incident Response

Automating Security Vulnerability Scanning

In today's digital landscape, security vulnerabilities pose a significant threat to organizations and individuals alike. Hackers and cybercriminals continually seek to exploit weaknesses in software, networks, and systems to gain unauthorized access, steal sensitive data, or disrupt operations.

Security vulnerability scanning is a crucial practice that helps identify and mitigate potential security weaknesses. It involves the systematic examination of software, hardware, and network infrastructure to uncover vulnerabilities that could be exploited by attackers.

The Importance of Vulnerability Scanning

The consequences of security breaches can be severe, leading to financial losses, reputation damage, and legal liabilities. To safeguard their assets and data, organizations must proactively assess and address vulnerabilities in their IT environments.

Vulnerability scanning is a proactive security measure that provides the following benefits:

Early Detection: Identifying vulnerabilities before attackers do allows organizations to take action to fix or mitigate them.

Risk Reduction: By addressing vulnerabilities promptly, organizations reduce the likelihood of successful attacks.

Compliance: Many regulatory standards and industry best practices require regular vulnerability assessments.

Resource Optimization: Automated scanning tools can efficiently assess large and complex environments, saving time and resources.

Automating Vulnerability Scanning

Automating vulnerability scanning is a best practice for organizations seeking to maintain a strong security posture. Manual scanning processes can be time-consuming and error-prone, making automation a more efficient and accurate approach.

One widely used tool for automating vulnerability scanning is **OpenVAS (Open Vulnerability Assessment System)**. OpenVAS is an open-source framework that provides a comprehensive vulnerability scanning and management solution.

To use OpenVAS, you can start with the installation of the tool:

bashCopy code

```
# Install OpenVAS on a Linux system sudo apt-get install openvas
```

After installation, the next step is to configure OpenVAS and update its vulnerability database:

bashCopy code

```
# Start the OpenVAS setup sudo openvas-setup # Update the vulnerability database sudo greenbone-feed-sync
```

Once configured, you can run a vulnerability scan on your target systems:

bashCopy code

```
# Run a vulnerability scan on a target host sudo openvas-scan target_Ip_or_hostname
```

The scan results will include a list of identified vulnerabilities, their severity ratings, and recommended actions for mitigation.

Scheduling Scans

Automated vulnerability scanning becomes even more powerful when scans are scheduled to run regularly. This ensures that your organization's systems are continuously monitored for new vulnerabilities.

Scheduling a scan with OpenVAS can be done using the **cron** scheduler in Linux:

bashCopy code

```
# Schedule a weekly vulnerability scan using cron 0 0 * * 0 sudo openvas-scan target_ip_or_hostname
```

This example schedules a scan to run every Sunday at midnight.

Integration with Security Information and Event Management (SIEM) Systems

To enhance security monitoring, organizations often integrate vulnerability scanning tools like OpenVAS with their SIEM systems. This integration allows security teams to correlate vulnerability data with other security events and alerts, providing a holistic view of the threat landscape.

For example, you can use the **gmp** (Greenbone Management Protocol) to retrieve scan results from OpenVAS and forward them to a SIEM system for analysis and alerting.

Remediation Workflow

Identifying vulnerabilities is only the first step in the security vulnerability scanning process. Effective remediation is essential to address and mitigate the identified vulnerabilities.

Automation can also play a role in the remediation workflow. For instance, you can create automated scripts or workflows that trigger specific actions based on the severity and criticality of the vulnerabilities detected.

bashCopy code

```bash
# Example of an automated remediation script #!/bin/bash # Define a threshold for critical vulnerabilities critical_threshold=5 # Run the OpenVAS scan and parse the results scan_results=$(sudo openvas-scan target_ip_or_hostname) # Extract the number of critical vulnerabilities critical_count=$(echo "$scan_results" | grep "Critical" | wc -l) # If critical vulnerabilities exceed the threshold, trigger an automated response if [ "$critical_count" -gt "$critical_threshold" ]; then # Take remediation actions, such as isolating the affected system or applying patches echo "Critical vulnerabilities detected. Taking remediation actions." else echo "No critical vulnerabilities detected." fi
```

In this example, the script checks for critical vulnerabilities and takes predefined remediation actions if the threshold is exceeded.

Continuous Improvement

Automating security vulnerability scanning is not a one-time effort but an ongoing practice. To stay ahead of evolving threats, organizations should continuously assess, update, and refine their scanning processes and tools.

Regularly updating vulnerability databases, adjusting scan schedules, and fine-tuning scan parameters are essential steps in maintaining an effective vulnerability scanning program.

Furthermore, organizations should stay informed about emerging vulnerabilities and security trends to adapt their scanning strategies accordingly.

In summary, automating security vulnerability scanning is a critical component of modern cybersecurity. It helps organizations identify and address vulnerabilities proactively, reducing the risk of security breaches and their associated consequences.

By integrating automated scanning tools, scheduling regular scans, and implementing remediation workflows, organizations can enhance their security posture and protect their digital assets from evolving threats in an ever-changing threat landscape.

Chapter 10: Scaling Up: Advanced Automation for Large Environments

Managing Large-Scale Automation

As organizations grow and evolve, so does the complexity of their IT environments and the need for automation. While automation can greatly enhance efficiency and productivity, managing it at a large scale presents unique challenges and considerations.

The Complexity of Large-Scale Automation

Large organizations often rely on extensive automation to manage their IT infrastructure, applications, and workflows. These automation systems can encompass a wide range of tasks, from provisioning and scaling cloud resources to deploying software updates and managing network configurations.

At a large scale, automation can involve thousands or even millions of tasks, scripts, and workflows. Managing this complexity requires careful planning, coordination, and the right tools and practices.

Challenges of Large-Scale Automation

Managing large-scale automation comes with several challenges:

Scalability: As automation systems grow, they need to scale seamlessly to handle increased workloads and tasks.

Integration: Integrating automation across different platforms, tools, and systems can be challenging.

Orchestration: Coordinating and orchestrating complex workflows involving multiple automation components is crucial.

Visibility: Maintaining visibility into the status and performance of automated tasks across the organization can be difficult.

Security: Ensuring the security of automated processes and access controls is paramount.

Compliance: Meeting regulatory and compliance requirements while automating processes is essential.

Error Handling: Dealing with errors and exceptions in large-scale automation systems can be complex.

Strategies for Managing Large-Scale Automation

To effectively manage large-scale automation, organizations can adopt several strategies and best practices:

Centralized Automation Management: Establish a centralized automation management platform that provides a unified view and control over all automation tasks and processes.

Scalable Architecture: Design automation systems with scalability in mind, ensuring that they can handle increased loads and tasks without degradation in performance.

Modularization: Break down automation tasks into modular components that can be managed independently, making it easier to scale and maintain.

Version Control: Implement version control for automation scripts and workflows to track changes, facilitate collaboration, and rollback in case of issues.

Monitoring and Alerting: Implement robust monitoring and alerting solutions to provide real-time visibility into the status and performance of automated tasks.

Logging and Auditing: Maintain detailed logs and audit trails of automated activities to ensure accountability and meet compliance requirements.

Error Handling and Recovery: Develop comprehensive error-handling mechanisms and recovery procedures to handle issues gracefully and minimize disruptions.

Security Framework: Establish a robust security framework for automation, including access controls, encryption, and regular security assessments.

Documentation: Document all automation processes, scripts, and workflows to ensure that knowledge is shared and transferable within the organization.

Testing and Validation: Implement automated testing and validation procedures to verify the correctness and reliability of automation tasks.

Automation Tools and Platforms

Managing large-scale automation often involves using specialized automation tools and platforms. These tools can provide features such as workflow orchestration, job scheduling, and automation script management.

Some popular automation tools for large-scale environments include:

Ansible: Ansible is an open-source automation platform that allows organizations to automate tasks, orchestrate workflows, and manage configuration at scale.

Jenkins: Jenkins is an open-source automation server that supports building, deploying, and automating projects. It offers a wide range of plugins for different automation tasks.

SaltStack: SaltStack is a configuration management and automation platform that can manage and automate complex infrastructures.

Puppet: Puppet is an infrastructure automation platform that helps organizations manage and enforce configurations across their systems.

Chef: Chef is an automation platform that allows organizations to define infrastructure as code and automate the provisioning and configuration of systems.

Case Study: Large-Scale Cloud Automation

Consider a large enterprise that operates in a multi-cloud environment, using multiple cloud providers for various services. To manage large-scale automation in this scenario, the organization adopts a cloud management and orchestration platform.

This platform enables the organization to:

Provision and scale cloud resources dynamically based on demand.

Automate the deployment and configuration of applications across multiple cloud environments.

Monitor the performance and cost of cloud resources in real-time.

Implement policy-based governance and compliance checks across all cloud deployments.

Integrate with existing tools and platforms, including CI/CD pipelines and configuration management systems.

Provide self-service portals for different teams within the organization to request and manage cloud resources.

By centralizing and automating cloud management at scale, the organization gains greater efficiency, agility, and cost control while reducing the complexity of managing multiple cloud environments manually.

Large-scale automation is a critical component of modern IT operations, enabling organizations to achieve efficiency, scalability, and agility. While it presents challenges in terms of complexity and management, adopting the right strategies, tools, and best practices can help organizations effectively navigate and harness the power of automation at scale.

As technology continues to evolve and organizations increasingly rely on automation to drive their operations, mastering large-scale automation becomes an essential skill for IT professionals and organizations looking to stay competitive and resilient in the digital age.

Scalability and Performance Optimization

In the world of IT and software development, scalability and performance optimization are fundamental concepts that play a crucial role in the success of any application or system. As businesses grow and user demands increase, the ability of software and infrastructure to scale and perform efficiently becomes paramount.

Scalability refers to a system's capacity to handle growing workloads and adapt to increased demands without sacrificing performance. It is a measure of how well a system can grow both vertically (by adding more resources to a single component) and horizontally (by adding more components or nodes to a distributed system) to meet the needs of users and business operations.

Performance optimization, on the other hand, focuses on enhancing the efficiency and responsiveness of a system to ensure it delivers the best possible user experience. It involves identifying and addressing bottlenecks, inefficiencies, and resource constraints that may hinder a system's performance.

Why Scalability Matters

Scalability is crucial for various reasons:

Business Growth: As a business expands, its user base and data processing requirements grow. A scalable system can accommodate this growth seamlessly.

Seasonal Demand: Some businesses experience seasonal spikes in user activity. Scalability allows them to handle peak loads without downtime or degraded performance.

Cost Efficiency: Scaling resources up or down as needed can optimize infrastructure costs. Paying for only what is required helps control expenses.

Competitive Advantage: Scalability can be a competitive advantage. Organizations that can scale rapidly in response to market demands have an edge.

User Satisfaction: A scalable system ensures that users experience consistent and reliable performance, leading to higher satisfaction and retention.

Strategies for Scalability

Achieving scalability involves strategic planning, architecture design, and the use of appropriate technologies. Here are some strategies to consider:

Load Balancing: Implement load balancers to evenly distribute incoming requests across multiple servers or instances, ensuring optimal resource utilization.

Horizontal Scaling: Add more servers or nodes to a distributed system to handle increased traffic and workloads.

Vertical Scaling: Upgrade hardware resources, such as CPU, RAM, or storage, in a single server or instance to enhance its performance.

Stateless Architecture: Design applications to be stateless, where each request contains all the information needed to process it. This allows for easy horizontal scaling.

Caching: Implement caching mechanisms to store frequently accessed data or responses, reducing the load on backend servers.

Microservices: Adopt a microservices architecture, where complex applications are broken down into smaller, independently scalable services.

Elastic Scaling: Use cloud services that offer elastic scaling capabilities, allowing you to automatically adjust resources based on demand.

Performance Optimization

Performance optimization complements scalability by ensuring that a system operates efficiently even under heavy loads. Here are some key aspects to consider:

Profiling and Monitoring: Regularly monitor the performance of your application using profiling tools and monitoring solutions to identify bottlenecks.

Code Efficiency: Optimize your code for efficiency by reducing redundant operations, improving algorithms, and minimizing resource consumption.

Database Optimization: Optimize database queries, use indexing, and employ caching to reduce database load and query times.

Content Delivery: Utilize content delivery networks (CDNs) to cache and serve static assets, reducing server load and latency.

Compression: Enable data compression for network transfers and responses to reduce bandwidth usage and improve load times.

Asynchronous Processing: Implement asynchronous processing for tasks that don't require immediate responses, freeing up resources for critical tasks.

Resource Cleanup: Ensure proper resource management, including closing database connections, releasing memory, and disposing of resources when they are no longer needed.

Tools and Technologies

To support scalability and performance optimization efforts, various tools and technologies are available:

Load Balancers: Tools like Nginx, HAProxy, and Amazon ELB distribute incoming traffic to backend servers efficiently.

Profiling Tools: Profilers like New Relic, Blackfire, and Xdebug help analyze code performance and identify bottlenecks.

Content Delivery Networks (CDNs): CDNs such as Cloudflare, Akamai, and Amazon CloudFront cache and serve content closer to users.

Caching Solutions: Tools like Redis, Memcached, and Varnish Cache provide in-memory caching capabilities.

Database Performance Tools: Database optimization tools like MySQLTuner and pgBadger help improve database performance.

Cloud Services: Cloud providers like AWS, Azure, and Google Cloud offer scalable infrastructure and autoscaling options.

Load Testing Tools: Tools like Apache JMeter and Gatling enable load testing to assess system performance under heavy loads.

Case Study: E-Commerce Scalability

Consider an e-commerce platform that experiences seasonal spikes in user traffic during holiday shopping seasons. To ensure scalability and performance, the platform adopts the following strategies:

Utilizes a cloud-based infrastructure that allows for elastic scaling to accommodate increased user demand.

Implements a microservices architecture, where different components, such as product catalog, shopping cart, and user authentication, are decoupled and independently scalable.

Leverages a content delivery network (CDN) to cache and serve product images, reducing the load on the origin server and improving load times.

Regularly monitors application performance and uses profiling tools to identify and optimize slow-performing code.

Implements load balancing to distribute incoming traffic across multiple servers, ensuring high availability and reliability during peak shopping periods.

By implementing these strategies and technologies, the e-commerce platform can handle increased traffic, provide a seamless shopping experience for users, and capitalize on the seasonal surge in demand.

Scalability and performance optimization are indispensable aspects of modern IT and software development. Organizations that prioritize these principles can adapt to changing demands, maintain high-quality user experiences, and remain competitive in today's digital landscape.

Whether it's an e-commerce platform handling holiday shopping traffic or a cloud-based application serving millions of users worldwide, scalability and performance optimization are key drivers of success in the ever-evolving world of technology.

BOOK 4
KALI LINUX CLI BOSS
NAVIGATING THE DEPTHS OF PENETRATION TESTING

ROB BOTWRIGHT

Chapter 1: Introduction to Penetration Testing and Kali Linux

Penetration Testing Defined

Penetration testing, often referred to as "pen testing" or "ethical hacking," is a proactive and systematic approach to evaluating the security of computer systems, networks, and applications. It involves simulating cyberattacks on a target system to identify vulnerabilities and weaknesses that malicious hackers could exploit.

At its core, penetration testing seeks to answer one fundamental question: "How secure is our system, and can it withstand real-world threats?"

The Purpose of Penetration Testing

The primary purpose of penetration testing is to assess the security posture of an organization's digital assets, including servers, applications, databases, and network infrastructure. By conducting controlled and authorized tests, organizations aim to:

Identify Vulnerabilities: Discover security weaknesses and vulnerabilities before malicious actors can exploit them.

Assess Defense Mechanisms: Evaluate the effectiveness of existing security controls, such as firewalls, intrusion detection systems, and access controls.

Validate Compliance: Ensure that the organization complies with industry regulations and security standards.

Strengthen Security: Implement measures to mitigate identified vulnerabilities and enhance overall security.

Raise Awareness: Educate employees and stakeholders about potential security risks and the importance of cybersecurity.

Build Confidence: Demonstrate to clients, partners, and customers that the organization takes security seriously and is committed to protecting sensitive data.

The Penetration Testing Process

Penetration testing is a systematic process that involves several key phases:

Preparation: Define the scope of the test, establish objectives, and gather information about the target system or environment.

Reconnaissance: Collect publicly available information about the target, such as domain names, IP addresses, and employee names, to prepare for further testing.

Enumeration: Identify active hosts, services, and open ports on the target network, helping testers understand the attack surface.

Vulnerability Analysis: Use scanning tools and manual testing techniques to discover vulnerabilities, misconfigurations, and weaknesses.

Exploitation: Attempt to exploit the identified vulnerabilities to gain unauthorized access to systems or sensitive data. This phase replicates the actions of malicious hackers but with authorization.

Post-Exploitation: Assess the impact of successful exploits, including the potential for further compromise or lateral movement within the network.

Reporting: Document findings, including vulnerabilities, the level of risk they pose, and recommended remediation steps. The report is usually presented to stakeholders and management.

Remediation: Work with the organization's IT and security teams to address and fix identified vulnerabilities and weaknesses.

Verification: Re-test the system after remediation to confirm that vulnerabilities have been successfully addressed.

Reporting (Again): Provide a final report outlining the results of post-remediation testing and any remaining issues.

Types of Penetration Testing

Penetration testing can take various forms, depending on the target and the objectives. Some common types include:

External Penetration Testing: Focuses on assessing the security of external-facing systems, such as web servers, email servers, and firewalls.

Internal Penetration Testing: Simulates attacks from within the organization's network, assessing the security of internal systems and data.

Web Application Penetration Testing: Concentrates on identifying vulnerabilities in web applications, including SQL injection, cross-site scripting (XSS), and authentication issues.

Mobile Application Penetration Testing: Evaluates the security of mobile applications on various platforms, including iOS and Android.

Wireless Network Penetration Testing: Assesses the security of wireless networks, including Wi-Fi, and identifies vulnerabilities that could lead to unauthorized access.

Cloud Penetration Testing: Evaluates the security of cloud-based infrastructure and services, such as AWS, Azure, or Google Cloud.

Challenges in Penetration Testing

Penetration testing is not without its challenges:

Scope Limitations: Defining the scope of testing can be challenging, as some vulnerabilities may exist outside the defined scope.

Resource Intensity: Penetration testing requires skilled professionals, tools, and resources, which can be costly.

False Positives/Negatives: Test results may include false positives (indicating vulnerabilities that don't exist) or false negatives (missing actual vulnerabilities).

Risk of Impact: There is a risk that penetration testing could disrupt production systems or cause unintended consequences.

Testing Legality and Authorization: Penetration testing must be authorized and conducted within legal and ethical boundaries to avoid legal consequences.

The Ethical Hacker's Role

Ethical hackers, often referred to as penetration testers or white-hat hackers, play a crucial role in conducting authorized and controlled cyberattacks. Their goal is to identify vulnerabilities and weaknesses in a system without causing harm or unauthorized damage.

To become an effective ethical hacker, one must possess a deep understanding of computer systems, networks, programming, and security. Ethical hackers use a wide range of tools and techniques to uncover vulnerabilities, assess security controls, and provide organizations with valuable insights into their security posture.

Penetration testing is a critical component of modern cybersecurity, helping organizations proactively identify and mitigate security risks. By simulating real-world attacks, organizations can strengthen their defenses, protect sensitive data, and build trust with clients and stakeholders.

In a rapidly evolving threat landscape, penetration testing remains a vital practice for organizations seeking to stay one step ahead of cybercriminals and safeguard their digital assets.

Kali Linux Essentials for Penetration Testing

In the realm of cybersecurity, Kali Linux has emerged as an indispensable tool for professionals engaged in penetration testing and ethical hacking. Kali Linux, a Debian-based distribution, is renowned for its robust set of pre-installed security tools, making it a go-to choice for cybersecurity practitioners.

Understanding the Role of Kali Linux

Kali Linux is designed to be a versatile and comprehensive platform that provides security professionals with the necessary tools and resources to conduct penetration testing and vulnerability assessments effectively. Its purpose is to identify weaknesses in computer systems, networks, and applications before malicious actors can exploit them.

Installation and Setup

Before delving into the essentials of Kali Linux, it's crucial to address the installation and setup process. To get started, one can download the latest version of Kali Linux from the official website or set up a virtual machine if preferred. For installation, the following command is used:

arduinoCopy code

```
sudo apt-get install kali-linux
```

Once Kali Linux is up and running, the user is prompted to create a non-root user with administrative privileges, enhancing security.

Navigating the Kali Linux Interface

Kali Linux provides a user-friendly interface that allows users to access its vast array of security tools and utilities. The default desktop environment for Kali Linux is GNOME, but other environments such as Xfce and KDE are available as well.

Upon logging in, users can explore the Kali Linux menu, which categorizes tools into various sections, including Information Gathering, Vulnerability Analysis, Password Attacks, Wireless Attacks, and more.

The Power of the Terminal

The command-line interface, or terminal, is at the heart of Kali Linux's power and flexibility. It enables users to interact directly with the operating system, execute commands, and leverage the full potential of its tools.

The terminal is opened by pressing **Ctrl+Alt+T** or by searching for "Terminal" in the application menu. Here, users can navigate the file system, run security tools, and execute administrative tasks.

Conducting Information Gathering

Information gathering is a crucial phase in penetration testing, as it lays the foundation for further analysis and assessment. Kali Linux offers an extensive range of tools for this purpose, including tools for network scanning, DNS enumeration, and OS fingerprinting.

For instance, the **nmap** command is widely used for network scanning, allowing users to discover open ports and services on target hosts. Here is an example of how to use **nmap**:

Copy code

```
nmap -sV target_ip
```

The **-sV** flag instructs **nmap** to perform version detection, providing additional information about the detected services.

Vulnerability Analysis

Identifying vulnerabilities is a key objective of penetration testing, and Kali Linux excels in this regard. Tools like **Nessus** and **OpenVAS** are used to scan systems for known vulnerabilities and assess their risk levels.

To use Nessus, one can access it through the web interface after installation:

arduinoCopy code

```
https://localhost:8834
```

This opens the Nessus web interface, allowing users to configure scans, select target hosts, and generate vulnerability reports.

Password Attacks

Password attacks are a common tactic used by malicious actors to gain unauthorized access to systems. Kali Linux includes a variety of tools for testing password strength and attempting brute-force attacks.

One such tool is **Hydra**, a versatile password-cracking tool that supports multiple protocols. Here is an example of using Hydra to perform a brute-force attack on an SSH server:

bashCopy code

```
hydra -l username -P /path/to/wordlist.txt ssh://target_ip
```

In this command, **-l** specifies the username, **-P** points to a wordlist of possible passwords, and **ssh://target_ip** specifies the SSH service to target.

Wireless Attacks

Wireless networks are susceptible to attacks, and Kali Linux offers tools to assess and secure them. **Aircrack-ng** is a popular tool for wireless security testing, allowing users to crack WEP and WPA/WPA2 encryption keys.

To use Aircrack-ng, one can follow these steps:

Put the wireless interface into monitor mode: **airmon-ng start wlan0**

Capture packets: **airodump-ng -c channel --bssid target_bssid -w capture_file mon0**

Perform the actual attack: **aircrack-ng -w wordlist.txt capture_file-01.cap**

Reporting and Documentation

After conducting penetration tests, it is essential to provide detailed reports to clients or stakeholders. Kali Linux assists in this process by allowing users to generate and customize reports using tools like **Dradis** or simply by using Markdown.

The **Dradis** framework streamlines the reporting process by enabling users to import findings, organize them, and generate professional-looking reports. Markdown, a lightweight markup language, can be used to create documentation in a structured and easily readable format.

Staying Updated

Cybersecurity is an ever-evolving field, and it is crucial to stay up-to-date with the latest vulnerabilities, exploits, and security techniques. Kali Linux provides tools and resources for this purpose, including package management tools like **apt** and the ability to access the Kali Linux blog and forums.

Regularly updating Kali Linux ensures that security tools and libraries are current and effective in addressing emerging threats.

Kali Linux is a potent toolset that equips penetration testers and ethical hackers with the essential resources needed to assess and secure digital assets. From information gathering to vulnerability analysis, password attacks, and wireless security testing, Kali Linux offers a comprehensive platform for conducting thorough penetration tests.

Moreover, the ability to generate professional reports and stay updated with the latest cybersecurity developments makes Kali Linux an indispensable tool in the arsenal of cybersecurity professionals dedicated to safeguarding digital environments from potential threats.

Chapter 2: Setting Up a Penetration Testing Environment

Building a Virtual Lab for Testing

In the realm of cybersecurity, hands-on experience is invaluable, and one effective way to gain this experience is by creating a virtual lab for testing. A virtual lab is a safe and controlled environment where individuals can experiment, test security tools, and practice their skills without the risk of compromising real-world systems.

The Importance of a Virtual Lab

A virtual lab serves as a playground for cybersecurity enthusiasts, students, and professionals. It offers a controlled space where they can simulate attacks, explore vulnerabilities, and experiment with security solutions. Creating a virtual lab has numerous benefits, such as:

Risk-Free Learning: It allows individuals to learn and make mistakes in a safe, isolated environment.

Practical Experience: Hands-on practice reinforces theoretical knowledge and builds practical skills.

Testing Scenarios: It enables testing of security tools, techniques, and strategies under different scenarios.

Real-World Simulations: Users can replicate real-world scenarios, such as network configurations and application setups.

Resource Efficiency: It saves time and resources compared to setting up physical hardware labs.

Selecting a Virtualization Platform

To build a virtual lab, one must choose a suitable virtualization platform. Two popular options are VMware Workstation and Oracle VirtualBox, both of which offer robust virtualization capabilities.

Setting Up VMware Workstation

VMware Workstation is a commercial virtualization software that provides a feature-rich environment for creating virtual machines (VMs). Here's how to set up a virtual lab using VMware Workstation:

Download and Install VMware Workstation: Visit the VMware website, download the software, and follow the installation instructions.

Create a New Virtual Machine: Open VMware Workstation and click on "File" > "New Virtual Machine." Follow the wizard to configure the VM's settings, such as OS type and hardware resources.

Install the Guest OS: Boot the VM and install the desired guest operating system, such as Kali Linux or Windows.

Network Configuration: Configure the network settings for the VM, including bridged, NAT, or host-only networking options.

Repeat for Additional VMs: Create additional VMs as needed for your virtual lab environment.

Setting Up Oracle VirtualBox

Oracle VirtualBox is a free, open-source virtualization platform that offers similar functionality to VMware Workstation. Here's how to create a virtual lab using Oracle VirtualBox:

Download and Install VirtualBox: Download VirtualBox from the official website and install it on your host machine.

Create a New Virtual Machine: Open VirtualBox, click on "New," and follow the wizard to create a new VM, specifying OS type and resources.

Install the Guest OS: Start the VM and install the guest OS of your choice.

Network Configuration: Configure networking options for the VM, including NAT, bridged, or host-only networking.

Repeat for Additional VMs: Create additional VMs within VirtualBox to expand your virtual lab.

Lab Topology and Design

Designing the virtual lab topology is a critical step. Consider the following aspects:

Network Segmentation: Create separate networks for different types of experiments, such as a DMZ, internal network, and isolated testing networks.

Firewalls and Routers: Implement virtual routers and firewalls to control traffic flow and simulate real-world network scenarios.

Server and Client VMs: Deploy server and client VMs to mimic common network configurations.

Security Tools: Install security tools like intrusion detection systems (IDS), intrusion prevention systems (IPS), and network monitoring tools.

Data Sets: Use realistic data sets for testing and analysis.

Security Best Practices

When building a virtual lab for testing, it's crucial to follow security best practices to maintain the integrity of the lab and protect the host system:

Isolation: Keep the virtual lab isolated from the host network to prevent accidental security breaches.

Snapshot and Backup: Regularly take snapshots of VMs and back up critical data to restore lab configurations in case of errors or failures.

Update and Patch: Keep guest OS and virtualization software up to date with the latest security patches.

Access Control: Restrict access to the virtual lab to authorized users only.

Monitoring: Implement monitoring tools to track network traffic, system performance, and security events within the lab.

Use Cases for a Virtual Lab

A virtual lab can be used for various cybersecurity scenarios, including:

Penetration Testing: Simulate attacks on vulnerable systems to assess security weaknesses.

Malware Analysis: Analyze malware samples in a controlled environment.

Security Research: Conduct research on new vulnerabilities, exploits, and security technologies.

Forensics Analysis: Investigate incidents and perform digital forensics on compromised systems.

Training and Education: Provide hands-on training for cybersecurity professionals and students.

Development and Testing: Develop and test security tools, scripts, and applications.

Building a virtual lab for testing is a valuable investment for anyone interested in cybersecurity. It offers a secure and flexible environment for learning, experimentation, and honing cybersecurity skills. By selecting the right virtualization platform, designing an effective lab topology, and adhering to security best practices, individuals can create a powerful and safe space to explore the ever-evolving field of cybersecurity.

Top of Form

Chapter 3: Information Gathering and Reconnaissance

Passive Reconnaissance Techniques

In the world of cybersecurity, reconnaissance plays a crucial role in understanding and assessing potential targets. While reconnaissance techniques are often associated with active scanning and probing, passive reconnaissance offers an alternative approach that is less intrusive and can provide valuable information without directly interacting with the target.

Passive reconnaissance, also known as passive information gathering or passive footprinting, involves collecting data from publicly available sources and analyzing it to gather intelligence about a target, such as a network or organization. This approach is particularly useful for ethical hackers, security professionals, and cybersecurity enthusiasts who want to gather information legally and discreetly.

Understanding Passive Reconnaissance

The primary goal of passive reconnaissance is to gather as much information as possible about a target without alerting the target to the fact that it is under investigation. Unlike active reconnaissance, which involves sending probes or queries directly to the target, passive reconnaissance relies on the information that is already publicly accessible or discoverable through open sources.

Passive reconnaissance encompasses a wide range of techniques and tools, all aimed at collecting data that can be valuable for assessing the security posture of a target. The types of information gathered through passive reconnaissance can include:

Domain names and subdomains: Identifying web domains and subdomains associated with the target.

Email addresses: Discovering email addresses of individuals or departments within the organization.

IP addresses: Finding the IP addresses and ranges used by the target's network infrastructure.

Publicly available documents: Accessing documents such as PDFs, reports, or manuals that provide insights into the target's operations.

Social media profiles: Examining the online presence of individuals associated with the target, including employees and key personnel.

DNS records: Analyzing Domain Name System (DNS) records to understand the target's network topology.

WHOIS information: Gathering details about the registered owner of a domain, including contact information.

Passive Reconnaissance Tools and Techniques

Passive reconnaissance relies heavily on open-source intelligence (OSINT) and various tools and techniques that facilitate the collection and analysis of publicly available information. Some common tools and techniques used in passive reconnaissance include:

WHOIS lookup: The **whois** command is used to retrieve information about domain registrations, including the owner's name, email, and contact details.

DNS queries: Running DNS queries, such as **nslookup** or **dig**, to discover subdomains, IP addresses, and mail servers associated with the target.

Search engines: Utilizing popular search engines like Google, Bing, and DuckDuckGo to search for information about the target, including website pages, documents, and indexed content.

Social media mining: Examining social media profiles, posts, and connections to gather information about employees, their roles, and relationships.

Email analysis: Using tools like **theHarvester** to search for email addresses associated with the target's domain in public sources.

Metadata analysis: Extracting metadata from documents, images, or files to uncover hidden information such as author names, timestamps, and locations.

Job boards and forums: Scanning job boards and industry-specific forums for job postings, employee discussions, or insider information.

Archived web pages: Accessing archived versions of websites through services like the Wayback Machine to gather historical data and changes over time.

Ethical Considerations in Passive Reconnaissance

While passive reconnaissance is generally considered legal and ethical because it relies on publicly available information, it is essential to operate within ethical boundaries. Unauthorized access to restricted or private data, hacking into systems, or engaging in any activities that violate laws or regulations is strictly unethical and illegal.

Additionally, it is crucial to respect the privacy of individuals and organizations during the reconnaissance process. Avoid collecting sensitive personal information without consent or engaging in activities that could harm the reputation or security of the target.

Limitations and Challenges

Passive reconnaissance has its limitations and challenges. One of the primary limitations is that it relies solely on publicly available information, which may not always provide a comprehensive view of the target's security posture.

Furthermore, passive reconnaissance may not uncover vulnerabilities or weaknesses in the target's systems or networks. It primarily provides intelligence that can guide further assessment and analysis.

Another challenge is the constant evolution of online information. Websites, domains, and social media profiles change, and data that was once publicly available may become inaccessible or outdated.

Passive reconnaissance is a valuable technique in the arsenal of cybersecurity professionals and ethical hackers. By collecting and analyzing publicly available information, individuals can gain valuable insights into potential targets without alerting them to the investigation.

Understanding the principles of passive reconnaissance, utilizing appropriate tools and techniques, and adhering to ethical guidelines are essential for conducting effective and responsible information gathering. When used in conjunction with other cybersecurity methodologies, passive reconnaissance can contribute significantly to the assessment and protection of digital assets and organizations in an increasingly interconnected world.

Active Reconnaissance and Footprinting

In the realm of cybersecurity, active reconnaissance and footprinting represent a more direct and intrusive approach to gathering information about a target. Unlike passive reconnaissance, which relies on publicly available data and open sources, active reconnaissance involves actively probing and interacting with the target to collect intelligence.

Active reconnaissance serves as a crucial phase in the overall process of ethical hacking and penetration testing. It allows cybersecurity professionals and ethical hackers to assess the security posture of a target, identify vulnerabilities, and gain insights into potential attack vectors.

Understanding Active Reconnaissance

Active reconnaissance, also known as active information gathering, encompasses a range of techniques and tools used to interact with a target system, network, or organization actively. The primary goal is to extract information and data that may not be publicly available and to assess the target's defenses against intrusion.

Unlike passive reconnaissance, which is discreet and unobtrusive, active reconnaissance carries the risk of detection by the target's security measures. Therefore, it requires careful planning and execution to avoid triggering alarms or alerting the target to the probing activities.

Types of Active Reconnaissance Techniques

Active reconnaissance techniques encompass various methodologies and tools, each with its specific purpose and approach. Some common types of active reconnaissance techniques include:

Port Scanning: Port scanning involves sending packets to target ports to identify open ports and services running on them. Popular tools for port scanning include **nmap** and **Masscan**. The following command demonstrates a basic port scan using **nmap**:

cssCopy code

```
nmap -p 1-65535 target_ip
```

Network Scanning: Network scanning involves exploring the network topology, identifying hosts, and discovering the relationships between network devices. Tools like **NetDiscover** and **Angry IP Scanner** are used for network scanning.

Banner Grabbing: Banner grabbing is the process of retrieving banner information from network services. This data often includes the service version and sometimes even vulnerabilities. Telnet and **nc** (netcat) are commonly used for banner grabbing.

Operating System Fingerprinting: Fingerprinting involves identifying the target's operating system. Tools like **nmap** and **p0f** can help determine the OS based on network responses and behavior.

Vulnerability Scanning: Vulnerability scanning involves scanning for known vulnerabilities and weaknesses in target systems. Tools like **OpenVAS** and **Nessus** automate vulnerability scanning and reporting.

Web Application Scanning: Scanning web applications for vulnerabilities, such as SQL injection or cross-site scripting (XSS), using tools like **Burp Suite** and **OWASP ZAP**.

Ethical Considerations in Active Reconnaissance

Active reconnaissance techniques come with ethical and legal considerations. It's essential to obtain proper authorization before conducting active reconnaissance on a target system or network. Unauthorized probing can be considered a breach of privacy and may lead to legal consequences.

Ethical hackers and cybersecurity professionals must also adhere to a code of conduct that emphasizes responsible disclosure and ethical behavior. The goal of active reconnaissance is to improve security, not compromise it.

Challenges and Risks

Active reconnaissance carries certain challenges and risks. The most significant risk is the potential for detection by the target's security measures. Firewalls, intrusion detection systems (IDS), and intrusion prevention systems (IPS) are designed to detect and respond to unusual or suspicious activities, including active reconnaissance.

Another challenge is the potential for false positives and negatives. Active reconnaissance may produce inaccurate results, leading to incorrect s about the target's security posture. For example, an IDS may trigger a false positive alarm, leading to unnecessary investigation and disruption. Active reconnaissance and footprinting are critical phases in the ethical hacking and penetration testing process. They allow cybersecurity professionals to gather valuable information about a target and assess its security defenses.

To conduct active reconnaissance effectively and responsibly, it is essential to obtain proper authorization, use appropriate tools and techniques, and adhere to ethical guidelines. By combining active and passive reconnaissance methodologies, cybersecurity experts can gain a comprehensive understanding of a target's security posture and help organizations better protect their digital assets.

Chapter 4: Vulnerability Scanning and Analysis

Vulnerability Assessment and Analysis

In the ever-evolving landscape of cybersecurity, vulnerability assessment and analysis play a pivotal role in identifying weaknesses and potential points of exploitation in computer systems, networks, and applications. A vulnerability assessment is a systematic process that involves scanning and analyzing a target environment to uncover vulnerabilities that could be exploited by malicious actors.

Understanding Vulnerability Assessment

Vulnerability assessment aims to provide organizations with a comprehensive understanding of their security posture by identifying vulnerabilities and weaknesses in their systems, software, and configurations. The process involves a combination of automated tools and manual analysis to uncover potential security flaws.

One of the fundamental principles of vulnerability assessment is to prioritize vulnerabilities based on their severity and potential impact on the organization. This allows security professionals to focus their efforts on addressing the most critical vulnerabilities first.

Types of Vulnerability Assessments

There are several types of vulnerability assessments, each tailored to specific objectives and scopes. Some common types of vulnerability assessments include:

Network Vulnerability Assessment: This assessment focuses on identifying vulnerabilities within a network infrastructure, including routers, switches, firewalls, and servers. It often involves the use of scanning tools like **Nessus** and **Qualys**.

Web Application Vulnerability Assessment: This assessment targets vulnerabilities in web applications and services. Tools like **Burp Suite** and **OWASP ZAP** are commonly used to assess web applications for issues like SQL injection, cross-site scripting (XSS), and insecure authentication.

Host Vulnerability Assessment: This assessment evaluates the security of individual hosts or devices within a network. It involves scanning and analyzing specific systems for known vulnerabilities.

Cloud Security Assessment: As organizations increasingly migrate to cloud environments, assessing the security of cloud-based resources and configurations becomes crucial. Tools like **AWS Inspector** and **Azure Security Center** help identify cloud-specific vulnerabilities.

Wireless Network Vulnerability Assessment: Focused on identifying vulnerabilities in wireless networks, this assessment examines the security of Wi-Fi networks and access points. Tools like **Aircrack-ng** and **Wireshark** can aid in this assessment.

The Vulnerability Assessment Process

The vulnerability assessment process typically consists of the following steps:

Scope Definition: Determine the scope of the assessment, including the assets, systems, or applications to be assessed.

Asset Discovery: Identify all assets within the defined scope, including servers, workstations, and network devices.

Vulnerability Scanning: Use automated scanning tools to identify known vulnerabilities in the target environment.

bashCopy code

Example vulnerability scanning command : nmap -p 1-65535 - T4 -A -v target_ip

Manual Verification: Security professionals perform manual verification to confirm the existence and severity of identified vulnerabilities.

Risk Assessment: Evaluate the impact and likelihood of exploitation for each identified vulnerability.

Prioritization: Prioritize vulnerabilities based on their criticality to the organization's security posture.

Reporting: Generate comprehensive reports that include a list of vulnerabilities, their severity, and recommended remediation steps.

Challenges and Considerations

Vulnerability assessment is not without its challenges and considerations. Organizations may face the following issues:

False Positives and Negatives: Vulnerability scanners may produce false positive or false negative results, leading to inaccurate assessments.

Patch Management: Identifying vulnerabilities is only the first step; organizations must also have effective patch management processes in place to remediate them.

Comprehensive Coverage: Ensuring comprehensive coverage of all assets, including new and transient ones, can be challenging.

Resource Intensiveness: Vulnerability assessments can be resource-intensive, particularly in large and complex environments.

Continuous Monitoring: Security is an ongoing process, and organizations should conduct regular assessments to stay ahead of emerging threats.

Vulnerability assessment and analysis are critical components of an organization's cybersecurity strategy. By identifying and prioritizing vulnerabilities, organizations can take proactive steps to mitigate risks and enhance their security posture.

Effective vulnerability assessment requires a combination of automated scanning tools, manual analysis, and a well-defined process for reporting and remediation. By addressing vulnerabilities systematically and continuously, organizations can reduce their exposure to cyber threats and protect their digital assets effectively.

Chapter 5: Exploitation and Post-Exploitation Techniques

Exploitation Frameworks and Methods
In the realm of cybersecurity and penetration testing, exploitation is a critical phase that involves taking advantage of vulnerabilities discovered during reconnaissance and vulnerability assessment. Exploitation, when conducted within the boundaries of ethical hacking, is a means to demonstrate the potential risks and consequences of unpatched vulnerabilities.

Understanding Exploitation

Exploitation involves the act of using identified vulnerabilities to gain unauthorized access to a system, network, or application. This phase is where an ethical hacker or penetration tester attempts to leverage weaknesses for various purposes, such as data theft, privilege escalation, or the execution of arbitrary code.

Exploitation typically follows a sequence of steps, including:

Target Selection: Choosing a specific system or application to target based on reconnaissance and vulnerability assessment results.

Exploit Selection: Selecting an appropriate exploit or technique to exploit the identified vulnerability. Exploits can vary widely in complexity, from simple scripts to sophisticated attacks.

Payload Preparation: Preparing a payload that will be delivered to the target system to achieve the desired outcome. Payloads can include shellcode, reverse shells, or other malicious code.

Delivery: Delivering the payload to the target system through various means, such as network communication, email attachments, or web requests.

Execution: Triggering the exploit to execute the payload on the target system.

Post-Exploitation: Once access is gained, ethical hackers often conduct post-exploitation activities to maintain access, escalate privileges, and perform further reconnaissance.

Exploitation Frameworks

Exploitation is often facilitated by the use of exploitation frameworks and tools. These frameworks provide a structured environment for conducting attacks and automating various stages of exploitation. Some popular exploitation frameworks include:

Metasploit: Metasploit is one of the most widely used exploitation frameworks in the cybersecurity community. It offers a vast collection of exploits, payloads, and post-exploitation modules.

ExploitDB: ExploitDB is an online platform that hosts a large database of exploits, making it a valuable resource for ethical hackers and penetration testers.

Canvas: Canvas is a commercial exploitation framework known for its robustness and advanced features. It is used by cybersecurity professionals and organizations for penetration testing and vulnerability assessment.

Core Impact: Core Impact is another commercial exploitation framework that offers a wide range of features for penetration testers, including vulnerability scanning and reporting.

Ethical Considerations in Exploitation

It's crucial to emphasize that exploitation should only be conducted within the boundaries of ethical hacking, with proper authorization and a clear understanding of the rules of engagement. Unauthorized exploitation can lead to legal and ethical consequences, including criminal charges.

Ethical hackers and penetration testers must also adhere to responsible disclosure practices. When vulnerabilities are exploited and demonstrated, they should be reported to the affected parties or vendors promptly to facilitate remediation.

Challenges and Risks

Exploitation carries several challenges and risks, even in ethical hacking scenarios. Some of these challenges include:

Detectability: Exploitation activities may trigger intrusion detection systems (IDS) or other security measures, leading to detection and potentially blocking the attacker.

Mitigations: Some vulnerabilities may have mitigations or compensating controls in place that make successful exploitation more difficult.

Payload Delivery: Delivering payloads to the target system can be challenging, particularly when dealing with well-defended networks.

Variability: Exploits may not work consistently across all target systems due to differences in configurations and patch levels.

Impact: Successful exploitation can lead to system compromise, data loss, or unauthorized access, potentially causing significant harm.

Exploitation is a critical phase in ethical hacking and penetration testing. When conducted responsibly and ethically, it helps organizations identify vulnerabilities and assess the potential risks associated with them.

Ethical hackers use exploitation to demonstrate the real-world consequences of unpatched vulnerabilities, helping organizations prioritize remediation efforts. However, it's essential to conduct exploitation with proper authorization, adhere to responsible disclosure practices, and prioritize the security and privacy of affected systems and data.

By understanding the methods and frameworks used in exploitation, cybersecurity professionals can better defend against real-world threats and protect their digital assets effectively.

Post-Exploitation and Persistence

In the realm of cybersecurity and penetration testing, the post-exploitation phase is a critical step following the successful exploitation of a target system or network. During this phase, ethical hackers and penetration testers aim to establish a persistent presence in the compromised environment and maintain unauthorized access for further reconnaissance and exploitation.

Understanding Post-Exploitation

Post-exploitation involves actions taken after gaining unauthorized access to a system or network. While the initial exploitation phase focuses on vulnerability exploitation, post-exploitation is about maintaining control and gathering valuable information.

The objectives of post-exploitation can vary depending on the goals of the ethical hacker or penetration tester and the nature of the compromised environment. Some common post-exploitation objectives include:

Maintaining Access: One of the primary goals is to maintain unauthorized access to the compromised system or network. This often involves establishing backdoors or persistence mechanisms.

Privilege Escalation: Ethical hackers may seek to escalate their privileges within the compromised environment to gain access to sensitive resources or data.

Data Exfiltration: In some cases, the objective is to extract sensitive data from the compromised systems, which can include intellectual property, user credentials, or other confidential information.

Lateral Movement: Post-exploitation activities may include lateral movement within the network to explore and compromise other systems or segments.

Covering Tracks: Ethical hackers often attempt to cover their tracks by erasing logs, modifying timestamps, or obfuscating their actions to avoid detection.

Persistence Mechanisms

Establishing persistence is a crucial aspect of post-exploitation. Persistence mechanisms are techniques used to maintain access to a compromised system even after a reboot or security measures have been implemented. Some common persistence mechanisms include:

Backdoors: The creation of hidden or remote access points that allow attackers to reconnect to the compromised system at will.

sqlCopy code

Example: Creating a backdoor user account with elevated privileges.

Service Manipulation: Altering system services to execute malicious code upon system startup or at specific intervals.

vbnetCopy code

Example: Modifying a Windows service to execute a custom payload.

Scheduled Tasks: Creating scheduled tasks that run malicious scripts or commands at predefined times.

vbnetCopy code

Example: Scheduling a script to run every hour to maintain access.

Registry Modifications: Making changes to the Windows Registry to execute malicious code during system initialization.

vbnetCopy code

Example: Adding a registry key to run a malicious script at startup.

Malware Deployment: Installing persistent malware that ensures continued access and control over the compromised system.

vbnetCopy code

Example: Deploying a RAT (Remote Access Trojan) that communicates with a command and control server.

Post-Exploitation Frameworks

To facilitate post-exploitation activities, ethical hackers often use post-exploitation frameworks and tools. These frameworks provide a structured environment for conducting post-exploitation tasks. Some popular post-exploitation frameworks include:

Metasploit: Metasploit is not only a powerful exploitation framework but also offers post-exploitation modules and tools for maintaining access and performing various post-exploitation tasks.

PowerShell Empire: PowerShell Empire is a post-exploitation framework that leverages PowerShell to maintain control over compromised systems.

Cobalt Strike: Cobalt Strike is a commercial post-exploitation framework with features for beaconing, privilege escalation, lateral movement, and data exfiltration.

Ethical Considerations

Post-exploitation activities should always be conducted within the boundaries of ethical hacking, with proper authorization and a clear understanding of the rules of engagement. Unauthorized post-exploitation can lead to legal and ethical consequences.

Ethical hackers and penetration testers must prioritize responsible disclosure and act in the best interests of the organization or individual affected by the testing. Data privacy, confidentiality, and security should always be upheld.

Challenges and Risks

Post-exploitation presents its own set of challenges and risks, including:

Detection: Post-exploitation activities may trigger security alerts or intrusion detection systems, leading to detection and potential countermeasures.

Mitigations: Compromised systems may have security mitigations or controls in place that make persistence difficult.

Data Exfiltration: Extracting data without detection can be challenging, particularly when dealing with large volumes of information.

Attribution: Sophisticated attackers may employ techniques to mislead investigators and attribution efforts.

The post-exploitation phase is a critical component of ethical hacking and penetration testing. By establishing persistence and maintaining unauthorized access, ethical hackers can demonstrate the real-world consequences of security weaknesses and help organizations prioritize remediation efforts.

It's essential to conduct post-exploitation activities responsibly, with proper authorization and adherence to ethical and legal standards. Responsible post-exploitation practices aim to improve the security posture of organizations and protect against potential threats.

Chapter 6: Privilege Escalation and Lateral Movement

Gaining Higher Privileges

In the realm of cybersecurity and penetration testing, the ability to escalate privileges is a critical skill that ethical hackers and penetration testers must possess. Privilege escalation refers to the process of obtaining higher-level access rights or permissions than what was originally granted to a user or process. Escalating privileges allows ethical hackers to explore deeper into compromised systems and access sensitive resources that would otherwise be off-limits.

Understanding Privilege Escalation

Privilege escalation can occur at various levels within a computer system, including the operating system, applications, and network services. It can be classified into two main categories:

Vertical Privilege Escalation: In vertical privilege escalation, an attacker or ethical hacker seeks to escalate their privileges within the same user or process, gaining higher-level access rights. This typically involves moving from a standard user account to an administrative or root-level account.

Horizontal Privilege Escalation: Horizontal privilege escalation involves obtaining the same level of privileges but in a different user or process. Attackers aim to gain access to another user's resources or data without necessarily obtaining higher-level permissions.

Common Privilege Escalation Techniques

Privilege escalation techniques vary depending on the target system and the vulnerabilities present. Some common techniques and scenarios include:

Exploiting Vulnerabilities: Identifying and exploiting vulnerabilities, such as buffer overflows or misconfigured permissions, to gain elevated privileges.

sqlCopy code

Example: Exploiting a buffer overflow in a system service to execute arbitrary code with root privileges.

Abusing Misconfigurations: Leveraging misconfigurations in system settings or files that grant excessive permissions.

sqlCopy code

Example: Modifying a system configuration file to grant a standard user administrative privileges.

Executing Arbitrary Code: Running malicious code or scripts that grant higher privileges through code execution.

vbnetCopy code

Example: Crafting a script that executes as a low-privileged user but grants root privileges upon execution.

Password Cracking: Attempting to crack passwords or obtain login credentials for higher-privileged accounts.

vbnetCopy code

Example: Using a password-cracking tool to guess the password of an administrative account.

Exploiting Weak File Permissions: Taking advantage of weak file or directory permissions that allow writing or executing files as another user.

vbnetCopy code

Example: Writing a malicious script to a directory with lax permissions, allowing it to be executed by a privileged user.

Privilege Escalation Vulnerabilities: Identifying and exploiting specific privilege escalation vulnerabilities in software or services.

vbnetCopy code

Example: Exploiting a known vulnerability in a system service that grants unauthorized access to administrative privileges.

Tools and Frameworks

Ethical hackers and penetration testers often use tools and frameworks to aid in privilege escalation. These tools may automate certain steps in the process or provide assistance in identifying vulnerabilities. Some common tools and frameworks include:

PowerSploit: PowerSploit is a collection of PowerShell scripts that can be used to assist in privilege escalation on Windows systems.

Linux Privilege Escalation Check: This script helps identify potential privilege escalation vectors on Linux systems.

Windows-Exploit-Suggester: This tool identifies missing patches and potential vulnerabilities on Windows systems that could lead to privilege escalation.

Ethical Considerations

It's crucial to emphasize that privilege escalation should only be conducted within the boundaries of ethical hacking, with proper authorization and a clear understanding of the rules of engagement. Unauthorized privilege escalation is illegal and unethical and can result in legal consequences.

Ethical hackers and penetration testers must prioritize responsible disclosure when they identify privilege escalation vulnerabilities. These vulnerabilities should be reported to the affected parties or vendors promptly to facilitate remediation.

Challenges and Risks

Privilege escalation carries several challenges and risks, including:

Detection: Privilege escalation activities may trigger security alerts or intrusion detection systems, leading to detection and potentially blocking the attacker.

Mitigations: Some systems may have security mitigations or controls in place that make privilege escalation more difficult.

Credential Requirements: Privilege escalation may require knowledge of valid credentials, which may not always be readily available.

Data Exfiltration: Once higher privileges are obtained, ethical hackers must exercise caution to avoid unauthorized data access or exfiltration.

Privilege escalation is a fundamental skill in ethical hacking and penetration testing. By successfully escalating privileges, ethical hackers can demonstrate the potential risks associated with unpatched vulnerabilities and misconfigurations, helping organizations prioritize their security efforts.

Conducting privilege escalation activities responsibly and ethically, with proper authorization and adherence to responsible disclosure practices, is essential to uphold the principles of ethical hacking and cybersecurity. Ultimately, the goal is to enhance security by identifying and mitigating potential threats before malicious actors can exploit them.

Chapter 7: Web Application Testing and OWASP Top Ten

Web Application Security Fundamentals
In the digital age, web applications have become an integral part of our daily lives, from online shopping and banking to social media and productivity tools. However, this widespread adoption has also made web applications prime targets for cyberattacks, emphasizing the critical importance of web application security. This chapter explores the fundamentals of web application security, the risks involved, and best practices for protecting web applications from potential threats.

Understanding Web Application Security
Web application security refers to the practice of safeguarding web applications and the data they handle from security threats and vulnerabilities. These threats can come in various forms, including hacking attempts, data breaches, and unauthorized access. Web application security is essential to protect sensitive information, maintain user trust, and ensure compliance with data protection regulations.

Common Web Application Threats
Before delving into security practices, it's crucial to understand the common threats that web applications face. Some of the most prevalent threats include:

Cross-Site Scripting (XSS): XSS attacks involve injecting malicious scripts into web pages viewed by other users, potentially compromising their data or actions.

SQL Injection: SQL injection attacks manipulate input fields to execute unauthorized SQL queries on the application's database, often leading to data leakage or modification.

Cross-Site Request Forgery (CSRF): CSRF attacks trick authenticated users into performing unwanted actions on web applications without their consent.

Insecure Authentication and Session Management: Weak authentication mechanisms or poor session management can result in unauthorized access to user accounts.

Security Misconfigurations: Misconfigurations in web application components, servers, or databases can expose vulnerabilities that attackers can exploit.

Web Application Security Best Practices

To mitigate these threats and protect web applications, organizations should implement a robust set of security best practices. Some fundamental practices include:

Input Validation: Validate all user inputs to ensure they adhere to expected formats and prevent malicious inputs from executing code.

sqlCopy code

Example: Implement server-side validation of user-submitted forms to filter out malicious input.

Output Encoding: Encode output data to prevent XSS attacks and ensure that user-generated content is displayed safely.

vbnetCopy code

Example: Use HTML entity encoding to display user-generated content as plain text in web pages.

Authentication and Authorization: Implement strong authentication and authorization mechanisms to control access to sensitive areas and data.

javaCopy code

Example: Use multi-factor authentication (MFA) for user logins and role-based access control (RBAC) to restrict user privileges.

Secure Session Management: Manage user sessions securely, including secure storage of session tokens and their proper expiration.

vbnetCopy code

Example: Store session tokens securely, such as using HTTP-only cookies and secure flags.

Regular Patching and Updates: Keep all components, including web servers, databases, and third-party libraries, up to date with security patches.

vbnetCopy code

Example: Set up automated patching schedules to apply security updates promptly.

Security Headers: Implement security headers, such as Content Security Policy (CSP) and Strict-Transport-Security (HSTS), to mitigate specific vulnerabilities.

vbnetCopy code

Example: Configure a Content Security Policy to restrict the sources of executable scripts on a web page.

Security Testing: Regularly conduct security testing, including vulnerability scanning and penetration testing, to identify and remediate vulnerabilities.

vbnetCopy code

Example: Use automated tools and ethical hackers to assess the security of web applications and infrastructure.

Error Handling and Logging: Implement proper error handling to prevent the leakage of sensitive information and maintain comprehensive logs for auditing and monitoring.

vbnetCopy code

Example: Configure error pages to provide minimal information to users and log errors with relevant details for analysis.

The Importance of Security Training

In addition to technical measures, security awareness and training are essential components of web application security. Educating developers, administrators, and users about security risks and best practices can significantly reduce the likelihood of security breaches.

Security Standards and Frameworks

Various security standards and frameworks provide guidance and best practices for web application security. Some notable ones include:

OWASP Top Ten: The Open Web Application Security Project (OWASP) publishes a list of the top ten most critical web application security risks, helping organizations prioritize their security efforts.

PCI DSS: The Payment Card Industry Data Security Standard (PCI DSS) outlines security requirements for organizations that handle credit card data.

ISO 27001: The ISO/IEC 27001 standard provides a framework for information security management systems, including web application security.

Web application security is a complex and ever-evolving field that demands continuous attention and adaptation. As the digital landscape expands, so do the threats targeting web applications. Organizations must remain vigilant, adopt best practices, and stay informed about emerging security risks to protect their web applications and the sensitive data they handle.

By integrating security measures into the development lifecycle, conducting regular assessments, and fostering a security-conscious culture, organizations can bolster their defenses and reduce the risk of security incidents.

Testing for OWASP Top Ten Vulnerabilities

In the world of web application security, the OWASP Top Ten Project stands as a crucial reference, highlighting the most critical web application security risks. For security professionals, developers, and organizations alike, understanding and testing for these vulnerabilities is paramount to safeguarding web applications from potential threats. This chapter delves into the OWASP Top Ten vulnerabilities, providing insights into testing methodologies and best practices to mitigate these risks effectively.

The OWASP Top Ten Project

The Open Web Application Security Project (OWASP) is a nonprofit organization dedicated to improving web application security. The OWASP Top Ten Project, updated periodically, identifies and ranks the top ten most critical web application security vulnerabilities. These vulnerabilities serve as a guide for organizations to prioritize their security efforts.

1. Injection

The first vulnerability on the OWASP Top Ten list is Injection. Injection flaws occur when untrusted data is included in a command or query and then executed unintentionally. Testing for injection vulnerabilities involves identifying vulnerable entry points and attempting to inject malicious code.

2. Broken Authentication

Broken Authentication ranks second, emphasizing the importance of secure user authentication and session management. Testing for this vulnerability involves assessing the effectiveness of authentication mechanisms, password policies, and session handling.

3. Sensitive Data Exposure

Sensitive Data Exposure is the third vulnerability, highlighting the risk of exposing sensitive information. Testing includes evaluating data encryption, data storage, and secure transmission mechanisms.

4. XML External Entity (XXE)

XXE vulnerabilities are the fourth in the list, involving the processing of XML data that may contain malicious references. Testing for XXE vulnerabilities requires crafting malicious XML payloads and analyzing application responses.

5. Broken Access Control

The fifth vulnerability, Broken Access Control, pertains to improper enforcement of access restrictions. Testing involves attempting unauthorized access to protected resources and evaluating access control mechanisms.

6. Security Misconfiguration

Security Misconfiguration, ranking sixth, refers to insecure default configurations, incomplete security settings, and other configuration-related issues. Testing entails scanning for misconfigured settings and verifying secure configurations.

7. Cross-Site Scripting (XSS)

XSS vulnerabilities, ranked seventh, involve injecting malicious scripts into web applications. Testing for XSS requires identifying input fields vulnerable to script injection and crafting payloads to exploit them.

8. Insecure Deserialization

Insecure Deserialization, at eighth place, revolves around the mishandling of serialized objects. Testing involves manipulating serialized data to execute malicious actions.

9. Using Components with Known Vulnerabilities
The ninth vulnerability on the list underscores the risk of using outdated or vulnerable components. Testing entails identifying and updating components with known vulnerabilities.

10. Insufficient Logging and Monitoring
Insufficient Logging and Monitoring, ranking tenth, highlights the importance of timely detection and response to security incidents. Testing involves assessing logging mechanisms, monitoring capabilities, and incident response procedures.

Testing Methodologies
To effectively test for OWASP Top Ten vulnerabilities, security professionals use various methodologies and tools. Some common approaches include:

Manual Testing: Manual testing involves inspecting web application code, configurations, and functionality to identify vulnerabilities. Security professionals utilize various techniques, such as source code analysis and penetration testing, to find vulnerabilities manually.

Automated Scanning: Automated scanning tools, such as vulnerability scanners and web application security testing (SAST/DAST) tools, help identify vulnerabilities in web applications. These tools can quickly scan and assess web application code and configurations for known vulnerabilities.

Fuzz Testing: Fuzz testing involves sending a large volume of unexpected or malformed data to the application to trigger unexpected behavior. This helps identify vulnerabilities, especially injection and input validation issues.

Security Headers Analysis: Security headers, such as Content Security Policy (CSP) and HTTP Strict Transport Security (HSTS), play a critical role in mitigating specific vulnerabilities. Analyzing and configuring these headers correctly is essential.

Mitigation Strategies

Once vulnerabilities are identified through testing, organizations must take steps to mitigate these risks effectively. Mitigation strategies include:

Patch and Update: Apply security patches and updates promptly to address known vulnerabilities in software components.

Secure Coding Practices: Implement secure coding practices to prevent common vulnerabilities, such as input validation, output encoding, and proper session management.

Access Control: Enforce robust access control mechanisms to limit user access to authorized resources and actions.

Data Encryption: Implement data encryption to protect sensitive data at rest and during transmission.

Monitoring and Incident Response: Establish comprehensive monitoring and incident response procedures to detect and respond to security incidents effectively.

Testing for OWASP Top Ten vulnerabilities is an essential part of web application security. Organizations must regularly assess their web applications to identify and remediate these vulnerabilities to protect against potential threats.

By utilizing a combination of manual testing, automated scanning, and security best practices, organizations can minimize the risk of OWASP Top Ten vulnerabilities. Ultimately, the goal is to create secure web applications that safeguard sensitive data and maintain user trust in an increasingly digital world.

Chapter 8: Wireless Network Hacking and Security

Wireless Network Assessment
Wireless networks have become an integral part of our daily lives, providing us with the convenience of connecting to the internet and other devices without the constraints of physical cables. However, with this convenience comes the potential for security risks and vulnerabilities that need to be addressed through a comprehensive wireless network assessment.

A wireless network assessment is a systematic evaluation of a wireless network's security, performance, and reliability. It involves identifying weaknesses, vulnerabilities, and potential threats to the network's integrity and the data it carries. Next, we will explore the key aspects of conducting a wireless network assessment, including the tools and techniques used, best practices, and common challenges.

Understanding the Scope of Assessment
Before diving into the assessment process, it's essential to define the scope of your evaluation. Consider the following aspects:

Network Size: Determine the size and complexity of the wireless network you will assess. Is it a small home network or a large enterprise network with multiple access points and users?

Goals and Objectives: Clearly define the goals and objectives of the assessment. Are you primarily concerned with security, performance, or both?

Legal and Ethical Considerations: Ensure that your assessment complies with legal and ethical guidelines. Obtain proper authorization and permissions if necessary.

Assessment Tools and Techniques

To perform a wireless network assessment effectively, you'll need a set of tools and techniques tailored to your specific goals. Some essential tools and techniques include:

Wireless Scanners: Use wireless scanners like Airodump-ng (part of the Aircrack-ng suite) to identify nearby wireless networks and their characteristics. These tools can help you discover rogue access points and unauthorized devices.

Packet Capture and Analysis: Tools like Wireshark can capture and analyze wireless traffic, allowing you to inspect packets for anomalies and security issues.

Signal Strength and Coverage Analysis: Assess signal strength and coverage using tools such as NetSpot or Ekahau HeatMapper. This helps identify areas with weak signal coverage or interference.

Authentication and Encryption Analysis: Evaluate the security of wireless networks by examining their authentication methods and encryption protocols. Tools like WPA3-Personal and WPA3-Enterprise enhance security.

Password Cracking Tools: Assess the strength of pre-shared keys (PSKs) by using password cracking tools like Hashcat. This helps identify weak or easily guessable passwords.

Vulnerability Scanners: Tools like Nessus or OpenVAS can be used to scan for known vulnerabilities in network devices and services.

Security Assessment

One of the primary objectives of a wireless network assessment is to identify security vulnerabilities and weaknesses. Here are some security aspects to consider:

Encryption: Evaluate the encryption protocols used for wireless communication. WPA3 is the latest standard and offers strong security.

Authentication: Assess the strength of authentication methods. Strong authentication, such as EAP-TLS, enhances security.

Guest Network Security: If the network includes a guest network, ensure that it is isolated from the internal network and has limited access.

Rogue Access Points: Identify and mitigate rogue access points that can be used to launch attacks or provide unauthorized access.

Password Policies: Review and enforce strong password policies for network access.

Firewall Rules: Inspect and update firewall rules to restrict unauthorized access to the network.

Performance Assessment

In addition to security, assessing the performance of the wireless network is crucial for ensuring optimal functionality. Consider the following performance-related factors:

Signal Strength: Analyze signal strength throughout the coverage area to identify areas with weak or no signal.

Channel Interference: Check for channel interference and congestion that may affect network performance. Adjust channel settings accordingly.

Bandwidth Usage: Monitor bandwidth usage to identify potential bottlenecks and optimize network traffic.

Quality of Service (QoS): Implement QoS policies to prioritize network traffic for critical applications.

Access Point Placement: Ensure that access points are strategically placed to provide even coverage and minimize dead zones.

Documentation and Reporting

A thorough wireless network assessment should be documented, and findings should be reported to stakeholders. Include the following in your documentation and report:

Assessment Goals: Begin with a clear statement of the assessment's goals and objectives.

Methodology: Describe the tools and techniques used in the assessment.

Findings: Present detailed findings related to security vulnerabilities, performance issues, and any other relevant observations.

Recommendations: Provide recommendations for addressing identified vulnerabilities and improving network performance.

Risk Assessment: Assess the level of risk associated with identified vulnerabilities and prioritize remediation efforts.

Action Plan: Outline an action plan for implementing recommended changes and mitigating security risks.

Executive Summary: Summarize key findings and recommendations in an executive summary for non-technical stakeholders.

Challenges and Considerations

During a wireless network assessment, you may encounter various challenges and considerations. These include:

Legal and Ethical Concerns: Ensure compliance with legal and ethical guidelines, obtain proper authorization, and respect privacy.

Wireless Security Updates: Regularly update wireless devices and access points to address known security vulnerabilities.

Wireless Standards: Keep abreast of evolving wireless standards and security best practices to stay ahead of potential threats.

Interference and Noise: Address interference and noise issues that can affect signal quality and network performance.

User Education: Educate network users about security best practices and the importance of strong passwords.

A wireless network assessment is a critical step in ensuring the security and performance of wireless networks. By carefully defining the scope, using appropriate tools and techniques, and documenting findings and recommendations, organizations can proactively address vulnerabilities and maintain a secure and reliable wireless network environment.

Top of Form

Wireless Network Security Measures

Wireless networks have become ubiquitous in our modern world, providing convenient connectivity for a wide range of devices and applications. However, with this convenience comes the critical need for robust security measures to protect sensitive data and prevent unauthorized access.

Securing a wireless network involves a combination of hardware, software, and best practices that collectively create a strong defense against potential threats. Next, we will explore various security measures and strategies to safeguard wireless networks effectively.

Strong Authentication and Encryption

One of the fundamental pillars of wireless network security is strong authentication and encryption. Authentication ensures that only authorized users can access the network, while encryption protects the data transmitted over the wireless connection.

Commands like the following can help configure authentication and encryption settings:

bashCopy code

```
wpa_supplicant -c /etc/wpa_supplicant/wpa_supplicant.conf -i wlan0
```

Wireless networks commonly use the Wi-Fi Protected Access (WPA) or Wi-Fi Protected Access 2 (WPA2) protocols to secure connections. WPA3 is the latest iteration, offering even stronger security.

To implement strong authentication, you can use the Extensible Authentication Protocol (EAP) in combination with WPA3-Enterprise. This allows for secure user authentication using methods like EAP-TLS (Transport Layer Security).

Firewall Configuration

Configuring firewalls on wireless routers and access points is crucial for controlling incoming and outgoing network traffic.

Firewalls can help block unauthorized access attempts and protect against malicious activity.

Commands like the following can be used to configure firewall rules:

cssCopy code

```
iptables -A INPUT -s 192.168.1.0/24 -j DROP
```

Common firewall rules include allowing specific ports for services and blocking all other traffic, as well as filtering traffic based on IP addresses and MAC addresses.

Regular Software Updates

Regularly updating the firmware and software of wireless devices and access points is essential to patch known security vulnerabilities. Outdated software can become a weak link in your network's defenses.

Commands like the following can be used to update software and firmware:

sqlCopy code

```
apt update apt upgrade
```

Many router manufacturers provide automatic update options, ensuring that the latest security patches are applied.

Strong Password Policies

Enforcing strong password policies for Wi-Fi access is a critical security measure. Weak or easily guessable passwords can be exploited by attackers attempting to gain unauthorized access.

Commands like the following can help set password policies:

Copy code

```
passwd
```

Encourage users to create complex passwords that include a mix of uppercase and lowercase letters, numbers, and special characters. Consider implementing a password management system or using passphrase-based authentication for added security.

Network Segmentation

Segmenting your wireless network into different VLANs (Virtual Local Area Networks) can enhance security by isolating different types of traffic. For example, you can separate guest network traffic from internal network traffic.

Commands like the following can help configure VLANs:

bashCopy code

```
ip link add link eth0 name eth0.10 type vlan id 10
```

Segmentation prevents unauthorized users or compromised devices from accessing critical parts of the network.

Disable Unnecessary Services

Disable unnecessary services and features on your wireless router and access points to reduce the attack surface. Commands like the following can help disable services:

bashCopy code

```
systemctl disable sshd
```

For example, if you're not using remote management or a particular service, it's wise to disable them to reduce potential vulnerabilities.

Implementing MAC Address Filtering

MAC address filtering allows you to specify which devices are allowed to connect to the wireless network based on their hardware MAC addresses. Commands like the following can help configure MAC address filtering:

arduinoCopy code

```
iw dev wlan0 set macaddr 00:11:22:33:44:55
```

While this provides an additional layer of security, keep in mind that MAC addresses can be spoofed by determined attackers.

Network Monitoring and Intrusion Detection

Use network monitoring tools and intrusion detection systems to actively monitor your wireless network for suspicious activities and potential threats. Commands like the following can help set up monitoring:

cssCopy code

```
tcpdump -i wlan0 -w capture.pcap
```

These tools can alert you to unusual traffic patterns or unauthorized access attempts in real-time, allowing for immediate action.

Physical Security Measures

Don't overlook physical security. Ensure that your wireless access points and routers are physically protected against tampering or unauthorized access.

Commands like the following can help secure physical access:

scssCopy code

```
rfkill block all
```

Consider placing equipment in locked cabinets or secure areas to prevent physical attacks or tampering.

User Education and Awareness

Educate users about wireless network security best practices. Commands can't protect your network if users share passwords or connect to unsecured networks without caution.

Commands like the following can help educate users:

bashCopy code

```
echo "Protect your Wi-Fi password and avoid public Wi-Fi networks." > wifi_security.txt
```

Regularly remind users to follow security guidelines and report any suspicious activity.

Securing a wireless network requires a multifaceted approach that combines technological solutions, best practices, and user education. By implementing strong authentication and encryption, configuring firewalls, keeping software updated, enforcing password policies, and adopting other security measures, you can create a robust defense against potential threats and ensure the safety of your wireless network.

Chapter 9: Network Sniffing and Packet Analysis

Packet Capture and Analysis Tools
In the world of networking and security, understanding the flow of data packets is paramount. Packet capture and analysis tools play a vital role in dissecting network traffic, diagnosing issues, and uncovering security vulnerabilities. These tools enable network administrators, security professionals, and developers to gain deep insights into how data travels across a network and how devices communicate with each other.

Wireshark is one of the most popular and powerful packet capture and analysis tools available. With a user-friendly interface and extensive protocol support, Wireshark allows users to capture, view, and analyze network packets in real-time. To start capturing packets using Wireshark, you can run the following command:
Copy code

```
wireshark
```

Once the Wireshark application is open, you can choose a network interface to capture packets from and start the capture process.

Tcpdump is a command-line packet capture tool commonly used on Unix-based systems. It provides a quick and efficient way to capture packets and save them to a file for later analysis. To capture packets using Tcpdump, you can run a command like this:
cssCopy code

```
sudo tcpdump -i eth0 -w capture.pcap
```

This command captures packets on the 'eth0' network interface and saves them to a file named 'capture.pcap'.

Tshark, also known as the command-line version of Wireshark, is another useful tool for capturing and analyzing packets. It offers similar functionality to Wireshark but can be controlled via the command line. To capture packets using Tshark, you can use a command like this:
cssCopy code

```
tshark -i eth0 -w capture.pcap
```

This command captures packets on the 'eth0' network interface and saves them to a file.

Ethereal is another name for Wireshark, which is widely used in network analysis. It provides a graphical interface to capture and analyze packets in real-time. To capture packets using Ethereal (Wireshark), you can simply launch the application and select the desired network interface.

Packet capture tools are invaluable for troubleshooting network issues. Whether you're dealing with slow network performance, unexpected downtime, or security incidents, capturing and analyzing packets can help you pinpoint the root causes. By examining packet contents and identifying anomalies, you can diagnose network problems and take appropriate actions.

Intrusion detection and prevention systems (IDPS) often rely on packet capture tools to identify and mitigate security threats. These systems monitor network traffic for suspicious patterns or known attack signatures. When an anomaly is detected, the IDPS can take automated actions to block or alert on potential threats. Packet capture tools are essential for providing the data needed for effective intrusion detection and response.

Analyzing packet captures can also aid in optimizing network performance. By examining traffic patterns and identifying bottlenecks or excessive bandwidth usage, network administrators can make informed decisions to improve overall network efficiency. Packet analysis can reveal opportunities for network optimization, leading to better user experiences and cost savings.

Security professionals frequently use packet captures to investigate security incidents and breaches. When a security event occurs, such as a suspected intrusion or data breach, capturing network packets at the time of the incident can provide crucial evidence for forensic analysis. Analyzing packet captures can help identify the attacker's methods, the extent of the breach, and any data exfiltration that may have occurred.

For those working with application development and troubleshooting, packet captures can be a valuable tool. When dealing with issues related to networked applications, capturing packets can help developers understand how data flows between client and server. By examining the contents of packets and the sequence of communication, developers can pinpoint application-level problems and develop effective solutions.

To effectively analyze captured packets, it's essential to understand various networking protocols. Network packets contain headers and payloads that adhere to specific protocols, such as TCP, UDP, HTTP, or DNS. Analyzing these protocols and their associated fields is critical to gaining insights into packet contents and behaviors.

Packet analysis often involves filtering and sorting packets to focus on specific traffic of interest. Both Wireshark and Tcpdump support powerful filtering capabilities that allow users to extract relevant packets based on criteria like source IP, destination port, or protocol type. These filters help streamline the analysis process and reduce the volume of captured data to a manageable level.

In summary, packet capture and analysis tools are indispensable for various IT and security-related tasks. Whether you're troubleshooting network issues, monitoring for security threats, optimizing network performance, or investigating security incidents, these tools provide the insights needed to make informed decisions. By mastering packet analysis and understanding networking protocols, professionals can leverage these tools effectively to enhance network security and performance.

Analyzing Network Traffic for Vulnerabilities

Analyzing network traffic is a critical task for identifying vulnerabilities in a networked environment. By examining the data packets flowing through a network, you can uncover potential security weaknesses and take steps to address them. Next, we will explore the techniques and tools used for analyzing network traffic for vulnerabilities.

One of the primary objectives of traffic analysis is to detect abnormal or suspicious patterns. Anomalies in network traffic can be indicative of security breaches or potential vulnerabilities. To start analyzing network traffic, you can use tools like Wireshark,

Tcpdump, or Tshark, which we discussed in the previous chapter. By capturing packets and examining their contents, you can gain insights into the normal behavior of your network.

Once you have a baseline understanding of your network's normal traffic patterns, you can begin looking for anomalies. Anomalies may include unexpected spikes in data transfer, unusual port usage, or suspicious communication between devices. To detect these anomalies, you can create custom filters using packet capture tools to highlight specific types of traffic that require further investigation.

Intrusion detection systems (IDS) and intrusion prevention systems (IPS) are essential components of network security. They continuously monitor network traffic and alert administrators to potential threats or vulnerabilities. IDS and IPS solutions can analyze packet headers and payloads, comparing them to known attack signatures or predefined rules. When a match is detected, these systems can take action, such as blocking the malicious traffic or generating alerts.

Analyzing network traffic for vulnerabilities often involves looking for patterns associated with known attack vectors. For example, you may search for patterns that resemble SQL injection attempts, cross-site scripting (XSS) attacks, or malware communication. Packet analysis tools can help you identify these patterns and provide details about the malicious traffic's source and destination.

A critical aspect of network traffic analysis is the identification of unauthorized access or unusual login behavior. By monitoring authentication traffic, you can detect failed login attempts, brute force attacks, or login anomalies. For instance, if a user account suddenly exhibits a significant increase in login attempts, it may indicate a security breach attempt. Analyzing authentication traffic can help you identify and respond to such threats promptly.

Packet capture tools often provide features for exporting captured data to other analysis tools or storage solutions. For long-term storage and analysis, you can export packet capture files (e.g., in PCAP format) to dedicated network analysis platforms. These platforms offer advanced capabilities for deep packet inspection, threat detection, and incident response. Popular network analysis platforms include Suricata, Snort, and Bro.

Another valuable technique in network traffic analysis is the examination of network flows. Network flows represent sequences of packets between a source and destination, usually defined by IP addresses and port numbers. Flow analysis can reveal communication patterns, such as data transfers, connections, and conversations. By tracking network flows, you can gain insights into network behavior and detect potential vulnerabilities or suspicious activities.

Flow-based analysis is particularly useful for identifying distributed denial of service (DDoS) attacks. DDoS attacks involve overwhelming a target server or network with an excessive volume of traffic. Flow analysis can help distinguish legitimate traffic from malicious traffic, allowing you to implement countermeasures to mitigate the attack.

Analyzing network traffic for vulnerabilities also involves scrutinizing protocol-specific issues. Different network protocols have their unique vulnerabilities and security considerations. For example, analyzing HTTP traffic may involve checking for HTTP header manipulation or responses indicating server misconfigurations. Analyzing DNS traffic may reveal signs of DNS amplification attacks or DNS tunneling. Understanding the nuances of various protocols is crucial for effective traffic analysis.

Machine learning and artificial intelligence (AI) are becoming increasingly important in network traffic analysis. These technologies can automatically analyze large volumes of data, detect anomalies, and identify potential threats. Machine learning models can adapt and improve over time, making them valuable tools for detecting novel attack vectors or evolving threats. Integrating machine learning into your network traffic analysis workflow can enhance your ability to identify vulnerabilities and respond to them proactively.

As part of your network traffic analysis process, it's essential to establish a response plan for detected vulnerabilities or security incidents. When a vulnerability is identified, you should prioritize and remediate it promptly. This may involve patching software, reconfiguring network devices, or updating security policies. Having a well-defined incident response plan ensures that you can take swift and appropriate action to mitigate potential risks.

In summary, analyzing network traffic for vulnerabilities is a fundamental aspect of network security. By monitoring and inspecting network packets, you can detect anomalies, identify potential threats, and uncover security weaknesses. Utilizing packet capture tools, intrusion detection systems, and flow analysis techniques, you can enhance your network's resilience against security breaches. As technology continues to evolve, leveraging machine learning and AI in your analysis can provide even greater insights and protection against emerging threats. Remember that effective network traffic analysis is an ongoing process, and staying vigilant is essential to maintaining a secure network environment.

Chapter 10: Reporting and Best Practices in Penetration Testing

Effective Reporting and Documentation

In the realm of cybersecurity and IT operations, reporting and documentation are often overlooked but critical aspects of maintaining a secure and efficient environment. While they may not be as exciting as hacking or configuring network devices, these practices are essential for managing and improving your systems. Next, we will explore the importance of effective reporting and documentation and discuss strategies for implementing them.

Documentation is the foundation of a well-managed IT environment. Without proper documentation, it can be challenging to understand the configurations, systems, and processes in place. Documentation serves as a reference point for administrators, helping them troubleshoot issues, make informed decisions, and onboard new team members. Whether you're managing a small network or a large-scale enterprise environment, maintaining up-to-date documentation is essential.

One fundamental element of documentation is creating an inventory of your assets. This includes hardware devices such as servers, routers, switches, and workstations, as well as software applications, licenses, and configurations. For hardware, it's crucial to record details like make and model, serial numbers, purchase dates, and warranty information. On the software side, keep track of version numbers, licenses, and any dependencies.

Creating an inventory is not a one-time task; it should be an ongoing process. As you acquire or retire assets, update your documentation accordingly. Having an accurate inventory ensures that you can quickly identify and address vulnerabilities, track license compliance, and plan for upgrades or replacements.

Network diagrams are powerful visual tools for documenting your network infrastructure. These diagrams provide a clear representation of your network's layout, including devices, connections, and their relationships. Tools like draw.io, Lucidchart, or even plain pen and paper can be used to create network diagrams. Include details such as IP addresses, subnets, VLANs, and routing information to make the diagrams comprehensive.

Configuration documentation is another critical aspect of maintaining your IT environment. This includes recording the settings and configurations of devices and applications. For network devices, document parameters like IP addressing, routing protocols, firewall rules, and access control lists. In the case of servers and workstations, record operating system versions, installed software, and configuration files.

Configuration backups are essential to ensure that you can quickly restore devices to their working state in case of failures or security incidents. Document your backup procedures, including the frequency of backups, storage locations, and verification methods. Automate backups whenever possible to reduce the risk of human error.

Documentation is also vital for compliance and security audits. Many industry standards and regulations require organizations to maintain detailed records of their IT systems and security practices. By having comprehensive documentation readily available, you can streamline the audit process and demonstrate your commitment to compliance.

In addition to technical documentation, it's essential to document your policies, procedures, and incident response plans. These documents define how your organization approaches security and operational tasks. For example, you should have a clear password policy that outlines password complexity requirements, expiration intervals, and lockout thresholds. Similarly, incident response plans should specify how to detect, analyze, and mitigate security incidents.

Standard operating procedures (SOPs) play a crucial role in ensuring consistency and efficiency in your IT operations. Documenting step-by-step procedures for routine tasks, such as software installations, device provisioning, and system backups, reduces the likelihood of errors and accelerates task execution. SOPs are particularly valuable for tasks that may need to be performed by multiple team members or external contractors.

Reporting is the process of collecting, analyzing, and presenting information in a structured format. Effective reporting enables organizations to make informed decisions, track performance, and identify areas for improvement. Reporting can cover a wide range of topics, including security incidents, system performance, compliance status, and project progress.

Security incident reports are essential for responding to and mitigating security breaches. When a security incident occurs, it's crucial to document the event's details, including the incident's timeline, affected systems, and the response actions taken. This information is valuable for both understanding the incident's impact and for legal and compliance purposes.

Regularly monitoring and reporting on system performance is essential for maintaining the efficiency and stability of your IT environment. Performance reports may include metrics such as CPU utilization, memory usage, network bandwidth, and response times. Analyzing these metrics helps identify bottlenecks, capacity issues, or resource constraints that need attention.

Compliance reports are often required to demonstrate adherence to industry standards and regulations. These reports detail how your organization complies with specific requirements, such as the General Data Protection Regulation (GDPR), the Health Insurance Portability and Accountability Act (HIPAA), or the Payment Card Industry Data Security Standard

(PCI DSS). Maintaining accurate compliance reports is critical to avoiding legal and financial penalties.

Project status reports provide an overview of ongoing projects, including their objectives, timelines, budgets, and progress. These reports help stakeholders stay informed about project developments and ensure that projects are on track to meet their goals. Detailed project documentation, including project charters, scope statements, and risk assessments, supports the creation of effective project status reports.

When creating reports, consider your audience's needs. Tailor the content and format to be understandable and relevant to the intended recipients. For technical reports, include detailed technical data, charts, and graphs. For executive-level reports, provide high-level summaries and key performance indicators (KPIs).

Automating reporting processes can save time and ensure consistency in your reports. Many tools and platforms offer reporting features that allow you to schedule and generate reports automatically. For example, security information and event management (SIEM) systems can automatically generate security incident reports, while network monitoring tools can produce performance reports.

Effective documentation and reporting are ongoing practices that require commitment and discipline. Allocate time and resources to regularly update and maintain your documentation. Review your reporting processes to ensure they remain aligned with your organization's goals and objectives. By prioritizing these practices, you can enhance your IT operations, strengthen security, and streamline compliance efforts.

In summary, documentation and reporting are foundational elements of effective IT management and security. By maintaining comprehensive records of your assets, configurations, and procedures, you can improve operational efficiency and respond more effectively to security incidents.

Reporting provides insights into your network's performance, compliance status, and project progress, enabling informed decision-making. Investing in these practices contributes to the overall health and resilience of your IT environment, ensuring that it meets the needs of your organization and stakeholders.

Best Practices for Ethical Hacking and Penetration Testing
Ethical hacking and penetration testing are essential activities for organizations seeking to identify and remediate security vulnerabilities in their systems and networks. These practices involve simulating attacks on their own infrastructure to uncover weaknesses before malicious hackers can exploit them. However, conducting ethical hacking and penetration testing requires careful planning, adherence to best practices, and a strong commitment to ethics.

The first step in any ethical hacking or penetration testing engagement is obtaining proper authorization. Unauthorized hacking or testing can lead to legal and ethical issues, and it is crucial to have written consent from the organization or system owner. This authorization typically comes in the form of a formal agreement or contract that outlines the scope, objectives, rules of engagement, and legal protections.

Scope definition is a critical aspect of ethical hacking and penetration testing. Defining the scope helps ensure that the testing focuses on the specific systems, applications, and networks that are subject to examination. Excluding unrelated assets reduces the risk of unintended consequences and minimizes disruption to the organization's operations.

Before conducting any testing, it is essential to gather information about the target environment. This information can include network diagrams, system documentation, asset inventories, and details about the organization's security policies and procedures. Understanding the target environment's architecture and configurations is crucial for effective testing.

One of the fundamental principles of ethical hacking and penetration testing is to minimize the impact on the target environment. Testing activities should not disrupt normal operations, degrade system performance, or cause data loss. To achieve this, it is advisable to conduct testing during maintenance windows or off-peak hours, where possible, and to coordinate with the organization's IT and security teams.

When performing ethical hacking and penetration testing, it is essential to use responsible disclosure practices. This means promptly reporting any discovered vulnerabilities or weaknesses to the organization or system owner, providing clear and detailed information about the findings, and assisting in remediation efforts. Responsible disclosure helps ensure that security issues are addressed promptly, reducing the risk of exploitation.

To maintain ethical conduct during testing, it is crucial to avoid any activities that can be perceived as malicious or harmful. This includes refraining from activities such as launching denial-of-service attacks, attempting to access unauthorized information, or causing damage to systems. The goal of ethical hacking and penetration testing is to identify vulnerabilities, not to exploit them.

Documentation plays a significant role in ethical hacking and penetration testing. Thoroughly documenting the testing process, methodologies, tools used, and findings is essential for transparency and accountability. Detailed documentation enables both the testing team and the organization to understand the scope, methods, and results of the engagement.

Maintaining confidentiality is a paramount consideration in ethical hacking and penetration testing. Sensitive information obtained during testing, such as login credentials or proprietary data, must be handled with the utmost care and protected from unauthorized access or disclosure. Testing teams should also respect the privacy of individuals and the organization's data protection policies.

Effective communication is essential throughout the testing process. This includes regular updates to the organization's IT and security teams on testing progress, findings, and any potential impact on operations. Open and transparent communication helps build trust and collaboration between the testing team and the organization.

Continuous learning and skills development are critical for ethical hackers and penetration testers. The field of cybersecurity is ever-evolving, with new threats and vulnerabilities emerging regularly. Staying up-to-date with the latest techniques, tools, and security trends is essential to ensure the effectiveness of testing efforts.

Another best practice is to use a well-defined methodology for ethical hacking and penetration testing. Common methodologies include the Open Web Application Security Project (OWASP) Testing Guide and the Penetration Testing Execution Standard (PTES). These methodologies provide structured approaches to testing that help ensure thorough coverage and consistency.

Before conducting any testing, it is essential to create a clear and detailed test plan. The test plan outlines the objectives, scope, schedule, and methodologies for the engagement. Having a well-defined plan ensures that testing activities are organized and focused on achieving specific goals.

Using a variety of testing tools and techniques is crucial for comprehensive testing. This includes both automated scanning tools and manual testing approaches. Automated tools can help identify known vulnerabilities quickly, while manual testing allows for in-depth analysis and the discovery of unique weaknesses.

Incorporating social engineering testing into ethical hacking engagements is essential. Social engineering involves manipulating individuals into revealing confidential information or performing actions that compromise security. Testing an organization's susceptibility to social engineering attacks helps assess its overall security posture.

To ensure that ethical hacking and penetration testing efforts align with industry best practices, organizations should consider certifications and standards. Certifications such as Certified Ethical Hacker (CEH) and Certified Information Systems Security Professional (CISSP) are valuable credentials for individuals conducting testing. Adhering to standards like ISO 27001 and NIST's Cybersecurity Framework provides a framework for maintaining strong security practices.

In summary, ethical hacking and penetration testing are essential components of a robust cybersecurity strategy. Following best practices, obtaining proper authorization, defining scope, responsible disclosure, documentation, confidentiality, communication, continuous learning, methodology adoption, test planning, tool diversity, social engineering testing, and adhering to certifications and standards are key considerations for successful and ethical testing. By adhering to these principles, organizations can identify and address vulnerabilities, enhance their security posture, and protect their critical assets.

Conclusion

In summary, the "Kali Linux CLI Boss" book bundle, consisting of four comprehensive volumes, takes you on a journey from novice to command line maestro in the world of cybersecurity and penetration testing. Throughout these books, we have delved into the depths of Kali Linux's command line interface, exploring its fundamental concepts, advanced techniques, expert-level scripting, and penetration testing capabilities.

In "Book 1 - Kali Linux CLI Boss: Mastering the Basics," we laid the foundation, providing you with a solid understanding of the essentials needed to navigate Kali Linux's command line. You learned to wield powerful commands, navigate the file system, manage users and permissions, handle packages, troubleshoot issues, and optimize your command line experience for efficiency and productivity.

"Book 2 - Kali Linux CLI Boss: Advanced Techniques and Tricks" elevated your skills by diving into more advanced command line concepts and customization options. You gained proficiency in manipulating files and directories, mastering networking commands, and gained insights into enhancing your shell experience with customizations and shortcuts.

"Book 3 - Kali Linux CLI Boss: Expert-Level Scripting and Automation" unlocked the potential of scripting and automation, showing you how to harness the power of scripting languages like Bash and Python to automate complex tasks. You learned to build advanced automation scripts, tackle network and system tasks, perform web scraping, and enhance security through automation and incident response.

Finally, "Book 4 - Kali Linux CLI Boss: Navigating the Depths of Penetration Testing" took you on a deep dive into the world of penetration testing. You explored the intricacies of setting up a testing environment, gathering critical information through reconnaissance, identifying vulnerabilities, exploiting weaknesses, and securing networks and systems against threats.

As you've progressed through this book bundle, you've developed a formidable skill set, allowing you to confidently wield the Kali Linux command line for various purposes. Whether you're a beginner seeking a solid foundation or an expert striving to master the art of penetration testing, these books have provided you with the knowledge, tools, and techniques needed to excel in the field of cybersecurity.

The journey from novice to command line maestro is ongoing, and this book bundle serves as a valuable resource that you can revisit and reference on your path to becoming a Kali Linux CLI expert. With the skills acquired from these books, you are well-equipped to tackle real-world challenges, secure systems, and contribute to the ever-evolving field of cybersecurity. May your command line adventures continue to lead you to new heights of knowledge and expertise in the world of Kali Linux and ethical hacking.

www.ingramcontent.com/pod-product-compliance
Lightning Source LLC
Chambersburg PA
CBHW071235050326
40690CB00011B/2124